MW00636924

Africa Now

Africa Now is published by Zed Books in assc
respected Nordic Africa Institute. Featuring high-quality, cutting-edge research
from leading academics, the series addresses the big issues confronting Africa
today. Accessible but in-depth, and wide-ranging in its scope, Africa Now
engages with the critical political, economic, sociological and development
debates affecting the continent, shedding new light on pressing concerns.

Nordic Africa Institute

The Nordic Africa Institute (Nordiska Afrikainstitutet) is a centre for research,
documentation and information on modern Africa. Based in Uppsala, Sweden,
the Institute is dedicated to providing timely, critical and alternative research
and analysis of Africa and to co-operation with African researchers. As a hub
and a meeting place for a growing field of research and analysis, the Institute
strives to put knowledge of African issues within reach of scholars, policy
makers, politicians, media, students and the general public. The Institute is
financed jointly by the Nordic countries (Denmark, Finland, Iceland, Norway
and Sweden). www.nai.uu.se

Forthcoming titles

Godwin Murunga, Duncan Okello and Anders Sjögren (eds), *Kenya: The Struggle
for a New Constitutional Order*

Lisa Åkesson and Maria Eriksson Baaz, *Africa's Return Migrants*

Thiven Reddy, *South Africa: Beyond Apartheid and Liberal Democracy*

Anders Themner (ed.), *Warlord Democrats in Africa*

Titles already published

Fantu Cheru and Cyril Obi (eds), *The Rise of China and India in Africa*

Ilda Lindell (ed.), *Africa's Informal Workers*

Iman Hashim and Dorte Thorsen, *Child Migration in Africa*

Prosper B. Matondi, Kjell Havnevik and Atakilte Beyene (eds), *Biofuels, Land
Grabbing and Food Security in Africa*

Cyril Obi and Siri Aas Rustad (eds), *Oil and Insurgency in the Niger Delta*

Mats Utas (ed.), *African Conflicts and Informal Power*

Prosper B. Matondi, *Zimbabwe's Fast Track Land Reform*

Maria Eriksson Baaz and Maria Stern, *Sexual Violence as a Weapon of War?*

Fantu Cheru and Renu Modi (eds), *Agricultural Development and Food Security in
Africa*

Amanda Hammar (ed.), *Displacement Economies in Africa*

Mary Njeri Kinyanjui, *Women and the Informal Economy in Urban Africa*

Liisa Laakso and Petri Hautaniemi (eds), *Diasporas, Development and Peace-
making in the Horn of Africa*

About the author

Margaret C. Lee is associate professor in the Department of African, African American, and Diaspora studies at the University of North Carolina at Chapel Hill. She is the author of *The Political Economy of Regionalism in Southern Africa*; *SADCC: The Political Economy of Development in Southern Africa*; and co-editor of *Unfinished Business: The Land Crisis in Southern Africa* and *The State and Democracy in Africa*. Her current research focuses on Africa's international trade regimes and globalization from above.

Congratulations!
Margaret C. Lee
February 22, 2015

Africa's world trade

Informal economies and globalization
from below

Margaret C. Lee

Nordiska Afrikainstitutet
The Nordic Africa Institute

Zed Books
LONDON

Africa's world trade: Informal economies and globalization from below was first published in association with the Nordic Africa Institute, PO Box 1703, SE-751 47 Uppsala, Sweden in 2014 by Zed Books Ltd, 7 Cynthia Street, London N1 9JF, UK

www.zedbooks.co.uk
www.nai.uu.se

Set in OurType Arnhem, Monotype Gill Sans Heavy by Ewan Smith
Index: ed.emery@thefreeuniversity.net
Cover designed by www.roguefour.co.uk

A catalogue record for this book is available from the British Library
Library of Congress Cataloging in Publication Data available

ISBN 978-1-78032-351-0 hb
ISBN 978-1-78032-350-3 pb
ISBN 978-1-78032-352-7 pdf
ISBN 978-1-78032-353-4 epub
ISBN 978-1-78032-354-1 mobi

Printed and bound by CPI Group (UK) Ltd, Croydon, CR0 4YY

Contents

Acknowledgments

This book has its origins in a year-long conversation between myself and a colleague and friend, Willie J. Jennings (Duke University). The conversation began in the summer of 2009 and ended a year later when we finally agreed that an ethnographic book on trade issues in Africa would make a great contribution to the literature.

When I sent the book proposal to Fantu Cheru, then Research Director at the Nordic Africa Institute (NAI) in Uppsala, Sweden, he immediately commissioned the prospective book as part of the Institute's Africa Now book series. A generous grant was given in 2011 to help defray my traveling expenses. The commissioning of the book by the NAI provided invaluable inspiration to commence working on the project.

I was able to begin writing the book manuscript upon receiving a generous fellowship from the John H. Turner Family. As a Turner Fellow, I had a semester's leave to work on the project. This incredible opportunity was made possible through the University of North Carolina at Chapel Hill's (UNC-CH) premier Institute for the Arts and Humanities (IAH) Fellowship program. All the fellows met Wednesday mornings during the fall of 2011 to discuss each fellow's project and to provide constructive criticism. I want to extend a special thanks to the other IAH fellows for encouraging me to venture into ethnographic work, and for their thought-provoking comments about Chapter 2. They include Ross Barrett, Melissa Bullard, Oswaldo Estrada, George Lensing, Ashley Lucas, Joseph Megel, Sarah Smith, Afroz Taj, and our incredible facilitator, Jane F. Thrailkill.

I discovered that I needed to visit Oshikango, Namibia, the location of a Chinese trading post. With all research funds depleted, John McGowan, who at the time was the director of IAH, provided me with a travel grant. This IAH grant, and a Craver Research Grant from my departmental chair, Eunice Sahle, allowed me to make the journey.

Consistent supporters of my research have been Michael Lambert, a colleague in my department of African, African American, and Diaspora Studies and director of the UNC-CH Center for African Studies, and Barbara Anderson, also a colleague in my department and associate director of the Center for African Studies. In addition to small grants to conduct my field research, in 2011 I received a generous research grant from the Center for the study.

Their support has been invaluable. In addition, the Center was an important outlet for presenting my research findings.

I would like to thank the Institute for African American Research at UNC-CH for a generous research grant in the summer of 2013 that allowed me to make my second trip to China. This grant was accompanied by a research grant from the Center for Global Initiatives.

The chair of my department, Eunice Sahle, provided unwavering commitment and support to the project. And when my research plate was empty of financial funds, she was the first to start searching for resources to fill the plate. I feel exceedingly blessed to have a chair as incredible as Eunice Sahle. I would also like to thank Travis Gore, the department's Administrative Support Associate, for the technological assistance he provided; and Sonia Colon, the department's Business Service Coordinator, for making me financially astute.

The following people read parts, or all, of the manuscript, and provided invaluable insight: Willie Jennings (Duke University); Sharon Fluker (Harvard University); Eunice Sahle (UNC-CH); and Ronald Williams (UNC-CH). A special thanks to Roger Southall (University of the Witwatersrand), who provided an invaluable peer review of the manuscript. I am also grateful to the anonymous peer reviewer. However, I take responsibility for any errors or omissions in the book.

I had the privilege of working with three excellent research assistants: Father Joseph (Uganda); Zulaika (China) and Njeri Jennings (College of Wooster). It would be impossible to acknowledge all the interviewees in China and throughout Africa who granted me interviews for this study. However, without their generosity, honesty, and in some cases bravery, this book would not have been possible.

The Africa Institute of South Africa (AISA) has been my academic home in South Africa since 2000 and thus an outlet for my research. A special thanks is in order to Solani Ngobeni, director of publishing, and Phindile Lukhele-Olorunju, acting CEO, for arranging seminars whenever I am in the country. Also, the Department of Trade and Industry in Pretoria has always provided me with invaluable information. Finally, Julialynne Walker arranged for me to meet the traders interviewed in Johannesburg, South Africa.

The trade union officials who coordinated my research trip to Maseru, Lesotho, were incredible. I would like to extend a special thanks to Shaw Lebakae and his colleagues Elliott Ramochela, Daniel Maraisane, Simon Jonathan, and Martha Mosoang-Ocran. Others I owe a great debt to are Mabaitsi Motsamai, Tsireletso Mojela, and Justice Tsukulu.

In Ghana, my friend and colleague Esther Acolaste (Duke University) arranged for me to meet traders in the market in Accra, and Florence

Hutchful opened her home to me and also arranged for me to meet key individuals related to this study.

Thanks to the individuals who arranged my visit to Oshikango, Namibia. They have requested to remain anonymous. Wilma S. Nchito (University of Zambia) facilitated necessary contacts in Lusaka. In Tanzania and Kenya I owe a debt to those who also facilitated contacts.

Many others gave me support and encouragement as I was working on this project. I would like to thank my friend and confidante Deborah Graves McFarlane for having unwavering confidence in me; Mary Winslow for making sure I remained in my body; Joanne Jennings, who constantly reminded me to take it 'inch by inch'; my daughter Najah Drakes, whose un-selfish love takes my breath away; Barbara Jones Bah, who kept the laughter flowing; and Cousin Tricia (Patricia Williams), who has always been there for me. Finally, the vice-chancellor of the Marcus Garvey Pan-Afrikan University in Mbale, Uganda, B. M. Luutu, continued to shine his light on me.

The book is dedicated to all the women in my life whose wisdom, love, patience, and guidance made me into the woman I am today. Thanks to all my sister-friends who are ever present in my life. For my daughter-friends, I sincerely hope I have inspired you to realize all your dreams.

A special thanks to my South African family – the Mbambelas (Mama Maria, Nonhlanhla, and Sibusiso), who have provided me with a place to call home for twenty-three years in a place called Katlehong Township in the Johannesburg area. The journey to Katlehong, however, has not been the same since Baba Willie made his transition several years ago. We miss him dearly.

In the final analysis I would not have contemplated writing this book without the support of my immediate family; for while I have been traveling the world, they have taken care of our mother. I would like to say a special thanks to my brothers, Charles, Jr, and William Jacob, my sister-in-law Rose and her mother Rita Jacabo. My mother's six grandchildren are the life of her world – Melanie, Charlie, Monique, Wayne, Edward, and William. I would like to acknowledge Jackie Waul and Sheila Tyler for helping to take care of Mama. Finally, I would like to acknowledge my mother for her unwavering love and tireless support for me.

Ken Barlow (Zed Books) deserves an award for patience and persistence. There are no words to thank him for the time he spent reading and editing the manuscript. Ken's keen sense of academic excellence challenged me to be more rigorous and deliberate in my academic endeavors.

Abbreviations and acronyms

AGOA	African Growth and Opportunity Act
ANC	African National Congress
AU	African Union
CMT	cut, make and trim
COMESA	Common Market for Eastern and Southern Africa
DRC	Democratic Republic of the Congo
DTI	(South Africa) Department of Trade and Industry
EAC	East African Community
EPAWA	Enslavement Prevention Alliance West Africa
EPZ	export processing zone
FDI	foreign direct investment
GATT	General Agreement on Tariffs and Trade
GEAR	Growth, Employment and Redistribution
GIS	Ghana Immigration Service
GSP	Generalized System of Preferences
ILO	International Labour Organization
IMF	International Monetary Fund
IOM	International Organization for Migration
ITAC	International Trade Administration Commission
ITEDD	International Trade and Economic Development Division
LDC	less developed country
LECAWU	Lesotho Clothing and Allied Workers Union
LNDC	Lesotho National Development Corporation
MFA	Multifiber Arrangement
MOWAC	Ministry of Women and Children's Affairs
RDP	Reconstruction and Development Program
RECs	regional economic communities
RoO	Rules of Origin
SACTWU	South African Clothing and Textiles Workers' Union
SACU	Southern African Customs Union
SADC	Southern African Development Community
SAPs	structural adjustment programs
SSA	sub-Saharan Africa
Texfed	Textile Federation (South Africa)
TFTA	Tripartite Free Trade Area
WB	World Bank
WTO	World Trade Organization

This book is dedicated to my mother and mother-friends Mama (Carol Lee); Mama Zephyr (Ward); Dr Lois B. Moreland; Mama Maria (Mbambela); and Mattie Stevenson.

My sister-friends.

My daughter-friends.

And to the memory of my great-grandmother Mama Stelle (Estelle Long); my grandmother Mother (Marguerite Ruth Beal); and my mother-friends Georgia Ray Allen, Esi Honono, Helen Brown, Jewel Stripling, and Bobbie Womack.

Introduction

This book, along with a planned forthcoming one provisionally entitled *Africa's International Trade Regimes: Globalization from Above*, introduces the reader to the complexity of sub-Saharan Africa's (SSA) world trade regimes in the second decade of the twenty-first century. In terms of world trade regimes, this book provides ethnographic studies that reveal how traders, mostly working under the radar of official governmental institutions, are involved in very complex financial transactions that inform us about the various networks and components that comprise Africa's world trade at the level of globalization from below. It is at this level that most Africans struggle to make a living amid serious economic challenges. In this volume, the focus is on the individuals involved in the global trade arena. In focusing on traders and their employees, as well as trade unionists, I attempt to humanize Africa's world trade regimes. By careful study and analysis of ordinary individuals involved in trade, we not only gain a deeper understanding of these regimes, they also come alive for us. The traders are no longer inanimate objects at the helm of Africa's trade regimes. They are real people with stories of triumph, defeat, love, and longing to be successful entrepreneurs. These traders are also individuals who pride themselves in their entrepreneurial pursuits and therefore take to the streets in protest against actions that might compromise the integrity of their ability to make a living wage.

The complexity of Africa's involvement in global trade

The rationale behind these two volumes is for students, scholars, policy-makers, government officials, and the general public to begin to understand the complexity of Africa's involvement in the global trade arena. African countries are not only members of the WTO, but their government officials and diplomats participate in myriad negotiations and decision-making processes throughout the world. Similarly, African diplomats and civil servants participate in negotiations with the EU to formulate EU–Africa financial and trade policies. In terms of the US and the African Growth and Opportunity Act (AGOA), African governments are engaged with the US to determine how best to facilitate greater access to the US market for the goods they produce. With respect to China, any attempt to begin to understand China–Africa trade requires deconstructing relationships from the markets in Guangzhou, China, to the capitals of each African country.

Against this backdrop, African governments are involved in negotiating trade deals with individual countries worldwide and on the continent. And they are attempting to integrate their economies through regional economic communities (RECs). Most recently three RECs have joined together to form an even larger trading market on the continent – the Tripartite Free Trade Area (TFTA), which includes twenty-six countries. The three RECs are the Common Market for Eastern and Southern Africa (COMESA), the East African Community (EAC), and the Southern African Development Community (SADC). Many African leaders still have a vision of one day creating a continental-wide regional economic organization that would result in African monetary unity.

Each additional trade agreement or trade regime that an African country negotiates makes the task of realizing African monetary unity more challenging. It also challenges the ability of RECs to achieve their objective – sub-regional integration.

Despite discussions about enhanced regional integration among African countries, it is unlikely given the continent's strong and growing ties to the larger global system. It is very often the RECs that are sidelined in favor of trade regimes that involve what we term in this book 'globalization from above'; the world of the advanced capitalist nations that have formal financial structures and legal economic operations that are considered to be the norm.

With perhaps the exception of South Africa, most countries are deeply integrated into the global economy as developing or least developed countries. Consequently the structural patterns of dependency and underdevelopment growing out of the early European invasions of the continent, the slave trade, the nineteenth-century scramble for Africa, colonial rule, the Cold War, and now the twenty-first-century scramble for Africa, have changed very little. Thus, for the most part, Africa still remains on the periphery of the world economy, which means among the least developed regions of the world.

Although on the periphery, African traders and African trade negotiators do not see themselves as victims of the capitalist-world system. They are making significant strides in changing how the continent engages with the global economy. African traders in Guangzhou, China, for example, are using old and new trading networks to transport goods to the African continent so that Africans can experience the material luxuries that their counterparts in the industrialized world have long had access to, albeit of lower quality. African traders in the markets in Africa are resisting the effort by Chinese traders to dominate the informal economy sector, more appropriately referred to as globalization from below. It is here where Africans are self-employed and operate under the radar of the police or government regulations. Transactions go unrecorded and most agents at this level do not participate in the formal structures of their economies by, for example, paying taxes and putting their money in banks.

African government officials and diplomats are challenging the global North in the WTO and demanding that the trade needs of Africa be addressed before the organization can move forward. African negotiators are rejecting EU efforts to force them to sign economic trade agreements that are not in the best interests of the continent. And finally, trade unionists are unrelenting in their fight for decent wages and better working conditions for people working in US AGOA-designated factories.

Structure of the book

The first chapter of the book, 'Globalization from Above and Globalization from Below', provides the theoretical framework for the study. It presents a framework that is designed to allow us to describe, understand, and make some possible predictions about Africa's world trade regimes. The major research question for this study is the following: How have Africa's trade regimes affected the lives of Africans in this study who are operating at the level of globalization from below?

Chapters 2 and 3 focus on China–Africa relations. In Chapter 2, the reader is taken on a journey to a city in the south of China called Guangzhou, located in Guangdong Province. The specific location is a place in Guangzhou called 'Chocolate City' because of the large number of Africans in the area. For thousands of years Guangzhou has been the gateway to international trade in China and today it is a major gateway for the export of Chinese products to Africa. This city is known today as the 'world's factory.' This chapter attempts to humanize African traders who have migrated to Chocolate City/Guangzhou and created an African trading post by weaving their stories in and out of six major themes: doing business in Chocolate City/Guangzhou; triple illegal/immigrant issues; African men and Chinese women; African criminals in Guangzhou and illicit drug trafficking; Chocolate City at night; and Chinese racism against blacks. The major question explored in this chapter is – How do African traders help us understand what it means to be entrepreneurs in Chocolate City/Guangzhou and what contributions do the traders make towards the enhancement of the living conditions of Africans on the continent?

Chocolate City is indeed the face of globalization from below. Here traders want to make money, believe in capitalism, and largely trade in Chinese counterfeit goods that allow people all over the world, but especially in Africa, to have access to products that they normally would not be able to afford.

In addition to globalization from below, the chapter is guided by three prevailing concepts that attempt to describe and explain the presence of the large number of African traders who have migrated to Chocolate City/Guangzhou. They are the creation of an African trading post; the creation of an African transnational urban space; and the idea that the African immigrant community serves as a bridge between itself and the host community.

3

Chapter 3 takes the reader through a journey to different countries of Africa, including Uganda, Tanzania, Ghana, Zambia, South Africa, Namibia, Angola, and Cameroon. The reader is introduced to African traders in the markets in several African countries that trade in Chinese goods. Some of the traders actually go to China to buy goods for their shops, some import them from surrounding countries, and others buy them wholesale directly from the Chinese in their respective countries. What is perhaps most fascinating about many of these traders is the networks they have for the distribution of their goods – these traders serve as suppliers of Chinese goods to traders who come from surrounding countries to buy in bulk to sell in their respective shops. We learn a great deal in this chapter about Africa's world trade regimes and how globalization from below operates in this part of the world. Again, African traders, through their stories, humanize these regimes for us.

The chapter then focuses on the textile and clothing industry and the challenges that South Africa specifically has faced from Chinese imports as a result of the liberalization of this sector. Similarly, a case study of the challenges posed by the liberalization of the Ghanaian steel sector and the import of cheaper Chinese steel is explored. Here we begin to experience some tension between globalization from above and below. One of the important questions raised in the chapter concerns the relationship between African leaders and state actors at the level of globalization from above. More specifically, are African governments making decisions serving the best interests of their constituents or the elites?

Similar to the African trading post in Chocolate City, the Chinese have created a trading post in Oshikango, the Namibia/Angola border town. An attempt is made in this section to humanize both the Chinese who own the shops in Oshikango and the Africans who work for them. Here we see an even deeper level of tension between globalization from above and below and the elites of Namibia. This is followed by a section on the recent conflict between Ghanaian small-scale gold miners and thousands of Chinese small-scale gold miners who have relocated to Africa in hopes of realizing their economic goals. The final section of the chapter examines the sex trade in Africa as a result of the growing number of Chinese sex workers who have migrated to the continent.

Finally, Chapter 4 turns to US and Africa trade relations. The history of the US African Growth and Opportunity Act is first discussed, followed by a brief overview of US–Africa trade since AGOA, which was first introduced in May 2000 by former president Bill Clinton. The focus of the remainder of the chapter is on the implementation of the special component of the Act – the Textile and Apparel Provision. Here the reader is taken to Lesotho, Swaziland, Uganda, Botswana, Ghana, Tanzania, and Namibia to get an inside view of AGOA factories. Instead of US investors taking advantage of the textile and apparel provision of AGOA, the reader learns that Asian countries were the primary investors in AGOA plants, largely with a view to getting around the Multifiber Arrangement (MFA) that had placed quotas on the number of textiles that Asian countries could export to the US and EU until January 2005. In this regard, many of the AGOA companies, on the eve of the expiration of the MFA, decided to close their African factories without giving notice to the workers. This created a great deal of turmoil in these countries, along with the fact that most of the companies had not abided by, and continue not to abide by, the standards of the International Labour Organization (ILO), a major requirement stipulated in the AGOA. Major violations in these factories have occurred under the watchful eye of the US government. Thus instead of increasing the standard of living of most of the workers (which US politicians claim AGOA has done and continues to do), the chapter reveals that most of the workers are not even making a living wage. The book ends with a chapter that summarizes the book and makes an assessment of the implications for Africa of its trade regimes within the context of globalization from below and Afro-neoliberal capitalism and the elite consensus. It is here that we will offer some final insights into the significance of humanizing Africa's trade regimes.

Methodology

Primary data for this volume was collected from interviews that took place over a period of time between the summer of 2010 and 2013. Many people were interviewed for this study. These include African traders in Guangzhou, China, and various countries in Africa; numerous Chinese traders in Africa; African governmental officials, academics, civil servants, and African trade union officials. Specific interview questions were administered in most cases. Often interviews resulted in extended conversations that continued for hours and in some cases individuals were repeatedly interviewed over a period of weeks. In several cases I had repeated conversations with some individuals since I returned to three countries twice while collecting data for the study. Lasting friendships have been established as a result of the latter. It is estimated that half of the interviewees agreed to use their names. At their request pseudonyms were created for the others. Secondary data was collected from newspapers, academic journal articles, reports, and books.

I refuse to call the people who come alive in these stories 'informants,' a term that is often used in the literature when referring to people who have provided information for a study or research project. To me the use of this term implies that a person is operating as a spy and therefore giving classified data. This is not the case in this study. Persons participated willingly and volunteered to provide information.

Interviews for this volume were conducted in nine countries, China, Ghana, Kenya, Lesotho, Namibia, South Africa, Tanzania, Uganda, and Zambia. In terms of African countries, since most of my field research over the years has been conducted in southern Africa, I decided to expand this study to include East Africa and at least one country in West Africa. With respect to the latter, Ghana, as a major player in the region, seemed to be a logical choice.

As an African American conducting ethnographic research in both China and Africa, I feel that my race had advantages as well as disadvantages. Being Black made it much easier to establish trust among African traders in both China and Africa. In this regard, once trust was established, I was referred to other important traders who would enhance my research. This was especially important in China, where most of the African traders survive under the watchful eye of Chinese security forces. An estimated 95 percent of African traders have overstayed their one-month visa and are living in the country illegally. The importance of my race was really put to the test during my second trip to Guangzhou. On this trip I was part of a larger group whose mission was to assess the health needs of African migrants. When I enquired about bringing one of my colleagues, a Caucasian male, to one of the interviews, I was immediately warned that such an action would compromise my access to information and my credibility. Consequently I had to inform my colleague that he would not be able to travel with me to the interview.

While attempting to get information from Chinese traders both in China and Africa, on most occasions I ran into a brick wall. Most Chinese would declare they didn't speak English, while others would provide only superficial information. As this study reveals, in China the only Chinese person who gave me an interview was a young PhD candidate from Cambridge University. In order to attain the Chinese perspective on their experience working with African traders and as traders in Africa, I had to rely on journalistic articles or peer-reviewed academic publications.

Two theoretical frameworks have been identified for analyzing the data in this study. The first is globalization from below. The second is Afro-neoliberal capitalism and the elite consensus. These frameworks are presented in the next chapter.

1 | Globalization from above and globalization from below

The major theoretical constructs of globalization from above and globalization from below allow us to present a framework for analyzing Africa's integration within the global trade arena. This chapter will provide an in-depth presentation of these two theoretical frameworks with a view to laying the foundation for analyzing the data collected in this study, which focuses on globalization from below. The chapter will begin with a brief historical overview and working definition of globalization, followed by a section on neoliberalism. The third and fourth sections will describe globalization from above and below. The last section of the chapter will present a theoretical framework known as 'Afro-neoliberal capitalism and the elite consensus'. This framework will allow us to debate the decision-making process of African leaders within the context of globalization from above and below. The overarching research question for this study, as outlined in the Introduction, is: How have Africa's trade regimes affected the lives of Africans in this study who are operating at the level of globalization from below?

We start with globalization since it is at the center of the theoretical framework for analysis. Central to understanding globalization from above and below is neoliberalism, which is a relatively new economic doctrine within the context of the long history of globalization. In its current construct, it has been suggested that some neoliberalism advocates have appropriated globalization (see below).

Globalization

According to Nayan Chanda, 'since the first appearance of the term in 1962, "globalization" has gone from jargon to cliché' (Chanda 2002). *The Economist* has suggested that globalization is 'the most abused word of the 21st century' (ibid.). Chanda observes that there has not been a word in recent memory that has resulted in so much emotion and that has simultaneously sparked a plethora of different meanings for so many people. 'Some see it as nirvana – a blessed state of universal peace and prosperity – while others condemn it as a new kind of chaos' (ibid.). Indeed, the literature on globalization is so vast that it is presumptuous for anyone to proclaim to definitively know its origins or definition. In this brief section, an attempt will be made to extract from the literature suggestions about the origin of globalization and to lay the foundation for beginning to understand how it is currently operationalized within the context of globalization from above and below.

According to Yale University's project on globalization,

> it is an historical process that began with the first movement of people out of Africa into other parts of the world. Traveling short, then longer distances, migrants, merchants, and others have always taken their ideas, customs, and products into new lands. The melding, borrowing, and adaptation of outside influences can be found in many areas of human life. (Ibid.)

One fact that seems to permeate a great deal of the literature is that globalization is not a new phenomenon (Held and McGrew 2001: 324–7; Williamson 2002; Stanford Encyclopedia of Philosophy 2002; Duménil and Lévy 2005: 10; Chanda 2002; University of Pennsylvania n.d.). The conceptualization of the different phases of globalization and the myriad definitions of the term will always remain contested territory. The working definition of globalization for this study is that it 'can be conceived of as a process (or set of processes) which embodies a transformation in the spatial organization of social relations and transactions, expressed in transcontinental or interregional flows and networks of activity, interaction and power' (Held and McGrew 2001: 324). Held and McGrew identify four types of changes. The first entails extending the activities of a political, economic and social nature beyond borders (continents, regions and frontiers). The second change is characterized by an increase in the magnitude and interconnectedness of culture, migration, investments, finance and trade. The third involves an increase in the speed of interactions and processes at the global level, and finally, as a result of the latter, the boundaries between global affairs and domestic events become increasingly more fluid (ibid.). In the final analysis, globalization 'can be thought of as the widening, intensifying, speeding up, and growing impact of worldwide interconnectedness' (ibid.).

In the current phase of globalization that began around the early 1980s, some scholars have argued that it has taken on a new form and fundamentally has been appropriated by neoliberalism (Colás 2005: 70; Duménil and Lévy 2005: 9; Saad-Filho and Johnston 2005b: 2; Peet 2010: 3–4).

Neoliberalism

> One of the signal triumphs of neoliberalism as a contemporary ideology has been the appropriation of 'globalization' as a process denoting the universal, boundless, and irreversible spread of market imperatives in the reproduction of states and societies across the world. (Colás 2005: 70)

The most recent transformation of the capitalist world economy has been neoliberalism, which has been the economic orthodoxy of the world since the latter part of the 1970s. Its historical origins leading up to the 1970s are rooted in the problems of the Keynesian welfare state created after World War II. The appropriation of globalization under the guise of neoliberalism has theoretically made it almost impossible to separate the two. For example, within the context of globalization from above and globalization from below, Gordon Mathews and Carlos Alba Vega postulate that 'those who practice globalization from below are in effect "out-neoliberalizing" those who embody globalization from above' (2012: 11).

The Keynesian welfare state and its demise The Keynesian years were characterized in the major industrial countries by significant economic growth rates, ongoing changes in technology, increases in purchasing power, the development of the welfare state, and unemployment rates that were low. This economic situation, however, changed in the 1970s (Duménil and Lévy 2005: 9). For example, various states began to experience fiscal crises, with tax revenue plunging and soaring social expenditures. Keynesian polices, along with other factors, were no longer effective. The situation was worsened by the Nixon administration's decision to no longer support the Bretton Woods institutional framework of allowing fixed exchange rates with the dollar pegged to gold. This was in response to the fact that the US dollar had flooded the world, escaping US controls since they were being deposited in banks throughout Europe (Harvey 2005: 12). Embedded liberalism, which had resulted in high rates of growth, especially in advanced capitalist countries post-1945, was failing to deliver and an alternative was needed in order to avert a crisis (ibid.). The crisis with Keynesian economics, coupled with other issues, gave rise to neoliberalism.

The rise of neoliberalism and the new social order[1] A great deal has been written about neoliberalism and thus the basic tenets of the theory are well known. 'Neoliberalism is in the first instance a theory of political economic practices that proposes that human well-being can best be advanced by liberating individual entrepreneurial freedoms and skills within an institutional framework characterized by strong private rights, free markets, and free trade' (Harvey 2005: 2; see also George 1999).

Other major features commonly known include privatization, deregulation, and the removal of state involvement in most areas of social provision; in essence, the elimination of the welfare state. Most states in the world have adopted some form of neoliberalism, including communist China (Harvey 2005: 3; see also George 1999).

At a more complex level, neoliberalism is said to be 'a particular organization of capitalism which has evolved to protect capital (ism) and to reduce the power of labour' (Saad-Filho and Johnston 2005b: 3; see also Duménil and Lévy 2005: 10). Internal and external forces have been involved in this process. With respect to the former, these have included political, social and economic transformations. External forces include coalitions established between a wide segment of high-powered entities with special interests, including financial (banking), trade, media, landowners, military, increases in mergers and acquisitions, etc. (ibid.). Supporting ideologies of the 'global' center, these relationships have resulted in a huge shift in worldwide power from the majority of people in the world, with significant consequences for countries on the periphery of the global economy (ibid.). With the political spectrum having shifted more towards the 'right,' the influence of finance has become unrivaled, with a significant increase in corporate power (Saad-Filho and Johnston 2005b: 3).

The individuals most closely identified with what was to become the neoliberal orthodoxy were Deng Xiaoping of China, Margaret Thatcher of the United Kingdom, and Paul Volcker and Ronald Reagan of the US (Harvey 2005: 2). As previously noted, the roots of the perceived need for a new economic orthodoxy grew out of the crisis of embedded liberalism which, by the end of the 1960s, had begun to break down worldwide. This was most evident in the crisis of capital accumulation when inflation was increasing, along with unemployment, resulting in global stagflation that continued throughout most of the 1970s (ibid.: 12). With respect to Thatcher and Reagan, Saad-Filho and Johnston argue that they provided a conservatism that was aggressive and populist, which 'became hegemonic worldwide' following a 'coup' spearheaded by Volcker, who at the time (1979) was chairman of the US Federal Reserve System (Saad-Filho and Johnston 2005b: 2; see also Peet 2010: 13).

Human dignity and individual freedoms were fundamental to the thinkers of neoliberalism, especially since they were considered 'the central values of civilization' (Harvey 2005: 5). These values were deemed to be so important that they were threatened by communism, fascism, dictatorship, and any form of state intervention that supported collective judgment over the ability of individuals to choose freely (ibid.: 5). In fact, Margaret Thatcher went to the extreme in announcing that there was 'no such thing as society, only individual men and women,' although as an afterthought she did concede the existence of the family (ibid.: 23).

In 1979 neoliberalism was consolidated as a new economic orthodoxy in the US and Britain (ibid.: 22). Critics of neoliberalism argue that fundamentally it was created to restore the income to the wealthiest people in the world (Mathews 2012: 83–4; Saad-Filho and Johnston 2005b: 1). Not only have the more than three decades of neoliberal freedom given power back to a very select capitalist class, they have also allowed a tremendous concentration of power by corporations to be put in place, which in essence has resulted in a convenient way to expand corporate monopoly power (Harvey 2005: 38).

The model for testing the ability of neoliberalism to truly protect the interest of the elites came with the 1982–84 crisis in Mexico. The Mexico crisis was spearheaded by the country defaulting on its loans. In response, the Reagan administration assembled the power of the US Treasury and the IMF, and developed an agreement that allowed Mexico to roll over all its debt. In return, Mexico had to implement neoliberal reforms. This set the stage for other countries that were in danger of defaulting on their loans to undergo what became known as structural adjustment. Mexico, therefore, became one of the first countries to become part of the 'neo-liberal state apparatuses worldwide' (ibid.: 29).

The Mexico crisis came on the heels of the availability of huge amounts of petro-dollars that had been loaned to developing countries throughout the world by banks in New York following the oil crises of the 1970s. The US government handled the crisis differently from the way it would have been handled under embedded liberalism. While heretofore the lender had to be responsible for bad investments and take the loss, under neoliberalism the opposite became the case; the borrower was forced by international and state powers to take on the cost of the debt, notwithstanding the circumstances of the situation (ibid.: 29). Harvey notes, however, that this is not in keeping with neoliberal theory, but was basically implemented to allow the economic elites to accumulate huge financial returns from throughout the world in the 1980s and 1990s. This resulted in the ability of these power elites in the advanced industrialized countries to receive surpluses that were being taken from poorer countries through structural adjustment programs (SAPs) and international capital flows (ibid.: 29, 31).

The process of neoliberalization, according to Harvey, has fostered a great deal of 'creative destruction.' This has included the destruction of pre-existing institutional frameworks and power, and social relations, as well as divisions of labor; welfare provisions; reproductive activities, land attachments, the challenging of some aspects of state sovereignty (ibid.: 3), and 'debasement of democracy' (Saad-Filho and Johnston 2005b: 1–2). In addition, as previously noted, it created a major shift towards enhanced social inequality and restored economic power to those in the upper class (Harvey 2005: 26; Colás 2005: 70; Duménil and Lévy 2005: 9; see also George 1999; Saad-Filho and Johnston 2005b: 9).

Globalization from above

Although Duménil and Lévy note that many have attributed the misery in the world today to globalization, they warn against this misnomer. While acknowledging that neoliberalism and globalization are related, they are two different sets of mechanism (2005: 9). And, as previously noted, numerous authors have suggested that proponents of neoliberalism have appropriated globalization. Consequently, what is considered to be globalization from above is synonymous with neoliberal globalization (see Peet 2010: 3). These terms will therefore be used interchangeably.

Many of the attributes associated with neoliberalism are also those of globalization from above. First and foremost, the level of analysis of globalization from above is hegemonic. According to Ribeiro, 'the hegemonic world-system has been dominated by the interests of neoliberal capitalist globalization' (Ribeiro 2012: 224–5). Agents in this system thus include states (both developed and developing), multinational corporations, private firms, international organizations, international financial institutions, global governing institutions – in essence, the rich and powerful (ibid.: 223–5, 230; Mathews and Alba Vega 2012: 9; Peet 2010).

Ribeiro further argues that those who operate at the level of globalization from above attempt to project a sense of having 'a monopoly of legality and legitimacy in economic transactions even when they are involved in illegal activities' (2012: 224). Thus agents within the hegemonic world system often attempt to place restrictions on globalization from below with respect to goods that are copied, smuggled and hawked. States and corporations at the hegemonic level are often under pressure from institutions such as the WTO to conform to international agreements, including at the sub-regional level, with a view to defending 'the interests of the capital they wish to attract' (Mathews and Alba Vega 2012: 9). Not surprisingly, economic integration in Europe was a neoliberal hegemonic strategy (Milios 2005: 208).

Even though agents of globalization from above attempt to restrict the 'illegal' activities of agents of globalization from below, the former are not really interested in destroying the non-hegemonic world system given the reality that the hegemonic world often pursues illegal activities vis-à-vis the non-hegemonic world, such as avoiding taxes, laundering money, primitive capital accumulation, and illegal capital flight (Ribeiro 2012: 224).

Richard Peet places the issue of globalization from above within the context of governance institutions (the IMF, World Bank and WTO). He notes that within these 'global governance institutions' there exists one single ideology – neoliberal globalization (2010: 3).

As a final note to this section of the chapter, unlike non-hegemonic globalization, hegemonic globalization can be traced by compiling formal information such as figures from corporate sales, statistics, and other economic indicators (Mathews and Alba Vega 2012: 5).

Globalization from below

'Globalization from below' is globalization as experienced by most of the world's people. It can be defined as the transnational flow of people and goods involving relatively small amounts of capital and informal, often semi-legal or illegal transactions, often associated with 'the developing world' but in fact apparent across the globe. (Mathews and Alba Vega 2012: 1)

Historical and economic context In contrast to what Mathews and Alba Vega term high-end globalization, consisting of transnational corporations with huge budgets and large numbers of lawyers throughout most of the world, what are deemed to be 'low-end globalization' traders are involved in the business of purchasing used or copied products and transporting them either via containers or in pieces of luggage beyond borders and across continents, where they are sold at minimal prices by street vendors. And all over the world this takes place 'under the radar of the law.' There are no lawyers or copyright laws involved in transactions and such transactions take place via personal connections within a cash economy. Given that this is how most people in the world function, the authors warn us that in order to properly understand and study the current world system, one must not only take seriously globalization from above, but also globalization from below (ibid.: 1).

In his seminal article 'Non-hegemonic globalizations: alternative transnational processes and agents' (2009), Ribeiro argues that heretofore globalization from below, or non-hegemonic globalization, has been almost exclusively confined to political movements opposed to neoliberal globalization. Consequently, researchers have not focused on forms of non-hegemonic globalization that are not based on political resistance. Ribeiro thus introduces the concept of grassroots globalization, which he argues is more connected to the economic aspects of globalization, which fundamentally means globalization processes that are non-hegemonic (ibid.: 298).

Further elaborating on the hegemonic versus non-hegemonic aspect of globalization, Fernando Rabossi suggest that if the concept of globalization 'from below' stems from that fact that most constructs of globalization have their origin in a perspective of 'from above,' the real challenge is to alter this reality by proposing different systems or universes (Rabossi 2012: 65; see also Ribeiro 2012: 225).

Non-hegemonic globalization or globalization from below is complex and part of a much larger whole with unique characteristics and dynamics. The complexity of it means that globalization from below has 'complementary and contradictory relations with the powerful agencies and agents of globalization from above' (Mathews and Alba Vega 2012: 6). The two systems therefore are inseparable and thus seem to reinforce each other's existence (Ribeiro 2012: 229–30).

Contrary to what some might think, at a fundamental level globalization from below is not against globalization from above, nor does it seek to destroy it (Mathews and Alba Vega 2012: 7–8; Ribeiro 2009: 325). In fact, in this regard, the agents who participate in globalization from below – traders, international migrants, street hawkers, small entrepreneurs – desire to be just as successful as agents who operate at the level of globalization from above. Given their marginal status within the global economy, however, they must pursue their aspirations and dreams through more informal and at times illegal structures. It is even questionable whether many of these individuals even understand that there is another world that operates at the hegemonic level (Mathews and Alba Vega 2012: 7–8).

Agents and networks At a fundamental level one might be presumptuous and suggest that most, if not all, the activity at the level of globalization from below is illegal and that at the level of globalization from above it is legal. Again, the reality of the capitalist world economy is more complex and dynamic, as briefly suggested in the previous section of the chapter. According to Ribeiro, very often the activities at the level of globalization from below are deemed to be matters for the police to handle (Ribeiro 2009: 314). The reality, however, is that often the capacity to determine what activities are legal or illegal stems from differing power relations between the two systems. In this regard he warns us that not only are the dynamics between what is considered legal and illegal often blurred and complex, but also those operating at either level do not possess the monopoly on morality or honesty (Ribeiro 2012: 221–2).

Many of the activities at the level of globalization from below are indeed illegal. Such activities include the smuggling of humans and organs, drug trafficking, money laundering, corruption, and activities that are Mafia-like. These activities take place at the upper echelons of non-hegemonic globalization. Ribeiro's work (and that of those who have been involved in theory-building around globalization from below) focuses more on the lower echelon of activities – those at the grassroots level of globalization (ibid.). It is here that you find ordinary people who are merely striving to make a living and enjoy some of the material benefits long enjoyed by those who function at the level of globalization from above. Not only are millions afforded employment at this level, but they are also given access to cheap merchandise that would otherwise be elusive. On the one hand Mathews and Alba Vega conclude that non-hegemonic globalization benefits the poor of the world because it provides them with an opportunity to get exposed to the material wealth of the rich and helps hundreds of millions of people from around the globe make a living (2012: 10). On the other, Mathews argues that in the final analysis in some cases these individuals are losers because they 'are like mice nibbling at crumbs fallen from the tables of kings ... the wealth accrued by its merchants and entrepreneurs is only a tiny drop in the bucket' (Mathews 2012: 83) compared to those flourishing at the hegemonic level.

Tax implications for the state One of the major implications for the state from globalization from below is the loss of taxes because transactions usually go untaxed. As a result, governments attempt to alter this reality by encouraging individuals to open bank accounts, formally register businesses and pay taxes (Mathews and Alba Vega 2012: 10). Although this can be a significant problem at the non-hegemonic level, it can also be one at the hegemonic level. While more normal regulations are usually in place, people are able to circumvent the law. And border controls at the hegemonic level are often porous and difficult to manage owing to huge volumes of goods passing through. It is impossible to monitor all such transactions (ibid.: 10). As the world's factory of cheap and fake goods, China is at the center of globalization from below (ibid.: 11). As a state actor, however, China also operates at the level of globalization from above.

The informal economy Seemingly the concept of globalization from below has its origins in the notion of the informal economy, coined by Keith Hart in 1973 (as quoted in ibid.: 2), who noted that the formal economy, which basically involves wage-earning employment, can be distinguished from the informal economy, which usually involves self-employment (ibid.). So are the terms informal economy and globalization from below synonymous? Scholars of the latter would definitely say no and take the position that

> ... it is not fully possible to distinguish between formal and informal sectors of the economies in different societies. Beyond this, the term 'informal economy' is often used in such a way as to implicitly assume separate national economies, each with their own formal and informal sectors. But today, in a world of ever increasing globalization, this is no longer the case. There are no autonomous national economies but a single global economy ... thus we must speak not of 'the informal economy' in this society or that one, but rather of 'globalization from below' encompassing all societies. (Ibid.: 2–3)

Many scholars feel that the term informal economy (sector) remains just as relevant forty years after Hart coined the term. Lindell, for example, argues that today the formal and informal are blurred (2010: 5), which parallels the thinking of globalization from below scholars. In this regard Lindell further argues that even though informal activities are not within the realm of the state regulatory system, this does not mean such activities are not regulated (ibid.: 5). In addition, definitions of informality now reflect the realization that the informal economy in many situations is not just restricted to small-scale activities of the poor, but is also an area in which the non-poor also operate (ibid.: 6).

Reinforcing the importance of the concept of the informal economy, Meagher and Lindell cite an International Labour Organization (ILO) report that indicates 'sub-Saharan Africa is the most informalized region in the world, with 73 percent of the nonagricultural labor force working informally, rising to over 90 percent in parts of West Africa' (2013: 57–8). In further defending the importance of the 'informal economy' and its relevance for today, Meagher and Lindell note that informal economic activity has burgeoned throughout the developing world, especially in Africa, instead of shrinking 'in the face of liberalization and globalization' (ibid.: 58).

Notwithstanding the major theoretical transformations that have been made in conceptualizing the informal economy, for the purposes of this study, the term is used to refer to individuals who are not employed in the formal economy. Globalization from below will be used to analyze data in the study since it is deemed to provide a more rigorous and comprehensive framework for analysis.

What of the future? Is globalization from below a passing phase or will it become an integral part of our analysis of the global economy? Mathews and Alba Vega argue that globalization from below is here to stay, especially if the status quo remains in place, whereby 15 percent of people in the world control most of the wealth and establish the rules. In fact, they predict that globalization from below will outlast globalization from above (Mathews and Alba Vega 2012: 13).

The creation of Afro-neoliberal capitalism and the elite consensus[2]

Neoliberalism and globalization were not simply a matter of certain economic policies giving free rein to capitalist vultures and financial speculators, but, much more, they were an ideological offensive against nationalism and social-ism. The second generation of African leaders, or the so-called 'new breed' leaders, as Western media christened their new African allies, fell in line, adopting neo-liberal policies and the ideological package that went with them. (Shiviji 2009)

Satgar identifies 'three overlapping post-colonial conjunctures' that have resulted in the making of Afro-neoliberal capitalism. The first was the in-ability of African countries to pursue African socialism, Marxist-Leninism, and revolutionary nationalism – all state-led development projects. The second conjuncture was national adjustment and the debt crisis; and the third was the restructuring of the continent to meet the requirements for facilitating transnational capital and the limited implementation of democracy (Satgar 2009: 40–1). All of these identified post-colonial conjunctures (and/or assaults) resulting in internal and external constraints on African development have been thoroughly described, critiqued, and debated in the voluminous literature on the subject.

In the final analysis, as Satgar notes, the combined economic, political, and coercive historical factors have prevented Africa from pursuing an autonomous development path. Instead, the discipline imposed on the continent resulted in the development of Afro-neoliberal capitalism 'that has attempted to legitimize neo-liberal accumulation strategies within ruling class projects of economic and political reform.' Neoliberal accumulation, according to Satgar, has been inserted into the 'common sense' of the majority of Africans through 'various cultural, political and social idioms and practices' (ibid.: 45).

> In this way, Afro-neo-liberal capitalism indigenizes neo-liberalism and restructures African economies, state forms, state–society relations, historical blocs and international relations to harmonize with its goals. At the same time, Afro-neo-liberal capitalism as a concept of control excludes alternative development options for Africa such as delinking, autocentric development and even African capitalism. It is presented by ruling historical blocs as a solution to Africa's organic crisis and embodies the national or general interests of society – an African solution to an African problem. (Ibid.)

As the previous section indicates, neoliberal accumulation strategies are not designed to be developmentally oriented. Instead, policies that call for liberalization, privatization, and so forth reinforce the fact that the market has power over the state and society (ibid.: 46).

The legacy of the last three decades is a shift that has laid the foundation for the emergence of capitalist accumulation within the international economy.

> Global neo-liberal restructuring is establishing a global market civilization and attempting to end the era of national capitalism and autonomous development ... Transnational fractions of Africa's ruling classes have embraced and internationalized neo-liberalism as a new concept of control and ensured that an African version of neo-liberal capitalism is organized. A neo-liberalism with African characteristics has emerged: Afro-neo-liberal capitalism. (Ibid.: 51)

With respect to the above, in order to ensure the functioning of this system, an 'elite consensus' has developed in Africa to guarantee the continuation of neoliberal capital accumulation.

Partially in response to Afro-neoliberal capitalism and the failure of African leaders to deal with growing poverty among the large majority of Africans who live at the level of globalization from below, civil society protest against governmental decisions has increased over the years. In this regard, civil society as a conceptual construct will be used to help in the analysis of data.

Stephen Orvis argues that one of the most heated debates in African politics has been over the definition of civil society. Specifically he notes that whether the person is an optimist or a pessimist, civil society has been defined too narrowly (Orvis 2001: 2). The broad definition of civil society as presented by Orvis is adopted for this study. It includes 'formal or informal collective activity autonomous from the state and family' (ibid.). This means collective activity of trade unions, churches, and professional associations, as well as activities that embrace patronage and ethnic organizations (ibid.: 3).

Conclusion

As is clear, there is a symbiotic relationship between globalization from above and globalization from below. Together they represent all aspects of the capitalist world economy, with agents in both systems converging, collaborating, and engaging in conflicts simultaneously. The pulse of the system is neoliberalism, with agents in both having no desire to destroy either system. As a consequence of this symbiotic relationship, the theoretical framework of globalization from above and below will be woven in and out of the book chapters with a view to analyzing the data presented.

Since African leaders must assume a certain level of responsibility with respect to the impact external and internal forces have on economic dynamics in their respective countries, Afro-neoliberal capitalism and the elite consensus will complement globalization from above and below. Specifically, it will help us to answer our overarching question for this study, which, as previously noted, is the following: How have Africa's trade regimes affected the lives of Africans in this study, who are operating at the level of globalization from below?

2 | Chocolate City (Guangzhou) in China

China would prefer Africans to do business with China without living here, yet 90% of Guangzhou's Africans act as intermediaries between the African continent and Chinese factories. Without them, there would be no business. (Coloma 2010a)

As the above quote indicates, if most Chinese could do business with African traders without Africans being in China, they would be happy. This, however, is not possible because it is the Africans in Chocolate City/Guangzhou who serve as the real conduits for getting Chinese goods to African markets and thus help maintain China's growing economy. A visit to Chocolate City puts to rest any questions as to how the majority of all goods in African markets come from China. With respect to their growing presence in China, many Africans feel that since the Chinese have invaded their continent, they have a right to invade China.

The first African traders to try their luck in Guangzhou did so long before Guangzhou became the place of dreams for many African traders and merchants. Nigerians and Malians were the first to come to Guangzhou in 1992.[1] Most had big shipping companies. Once they got there they felt lonely. The market they were associated with at the time was called Mengfu and the name of the street was Sanyuanli. Igbos from Nigeria use to call it Igbo-Ezaua (all Igbos have come together). There was no work and all clothes sizes were for Chinese. There were language barriers. These few Africans started to mingle with the Chinese and move around. Nigerians advised the Chinese on what they needed in Nigeria and then took them there. Soon, the Chinese were bypassing the Nigerians and sending clothes to other countries in Africa. The Igbos, as serious businessmen, were shocked to discover that the Chinese thought that Africans had little business mentality, and often after complex Nigerian–Chinese business arrangements had been made, the Chinese would eliminate the Nigerians from the deals.[2] The inability of Africans to trust their Chinese counterparts is a theme that not only permeates the personal interviews I conducted, but also the existing literature about Africans in Chocolate City/Guangzhou, as well as African traders in Africa. Most of these earlier traders have made their money and returned home.[3]

This chapter is about the contemporary African traders in the city of Guangzhou, in the southern part of China, where they have established an African trading post. This trading post has become known as 'Chocolate City' by taxi drivers and many of the merchants who trade with them. Chocolate City is an area of Guangzhou where most of the African traders conduct their business. An estimated 130,000 Africans live in Guangzhou (Haugen 2012: 5), the majority of whom are engaged in trade, sending thousands of containers annually to fulfill the demands of African traders on the continent; a demand stemming from the desire of their customers to have both cheap and higher-end quality goods from China.

The two major questions explored in this chapter are: what do African traders, through their oral histories, inform us about being entrepreneurs in Chocolate City/Guangzhou; and what impact are these traders having on the lives of Africans in Africa who primarily live at the level of globalization from below? The ethnographic approach to this subject is designed to humanize African traders and their trade regimes. In humanizing the traders and the regimes they are operating in, we gain a greater understanding of what it is like to work, live, and exist in the complex network of globalization from below in Guangzhou. The traders become more than just 'objects' who facilitate the process of arranging for goods to be transported to Africa and other parts of the world. They are people who daily sit in their stalls or behind desks in offices, located in huge buildings and plazas, and wait for customers to buy their goods so they can make a living. They are people who spend entire days with customers who have traveled to Guangzhou to survey the terrain and then place orders with suppliers to have goods made to be exported out of the country, again mostly to Africa. And finally they are people involved in the freight forwarding business who wait, sometimes for days, for customers to bring their purchased goods for shipment. Each person that we get to know in this ethnographic study helps us to see beyond the material world in which they operate. We get to see them as agents of a very complex and often challenging process, where their daily existence is tenuous, even in cases where immigration papers designate their legal right to be in China.

This is how, at the non-hegemonic level, these traders actively participate in Africa's world markets from China. Each piece of clothing, furniture, set of dishes, etc., that is placed in a cargo container in Guangzhou helps us better understand how African markets operate in the non-hegemonic world. The specified designation on the cargo containers for many of the goods is only the first stop. The final destination of the goods often remains a mystery. For example, some goods arriving at Dar es Salaam port in Tanzania might end up in small towns in the Democratic Republic of the Congo (DRC) or Zambia. Such goods would have been transshipped across borders illegally, evading customs officials, thus depriving governments of much-needed tax revenue. In some cases governments turn a blind eye to these illegal transshipments; in others, attempts are made to bring criminal charges against those involved.

However, it is estimated that only 5 percent of all goods that pass through ports throughout the world are inspected (Mathews and Alba Vega 2012: 10), and at borders, simply because of the volume, 'anything more than cursory surveillance is impossible' (ibid).

The origins of Chocolate City in Guangzhou

Thousands of years ago, merchants and traders in the city that today is known as Guangzhou laid the foundation for African traders and merchants to become part of one of the most important international trade routes of the twenty-first century. Located approximately one hundred miles from the China Sea, this important city is in the 'northern part of the Pearl River Delta, at the confluence of the West, North and East Rivers' (Wang 2007: 534–5). It is less than a two-hour ride by train from Hong Kong.

Guangzhou was first known as Pan Yu (PanYu), which were the names of two hills near by (Garrett 2002: 4). It was over two thousand years ago that ships were sent to Pan Yu by Emperor Qin Shihuangdi,[4] resulting in an important southern sea route being opened (ibid.: 5). Pan Yu later became known as Guangzhou. Westerners eventually began to call Guangzhou Canton, stemming 'from the French, Italian, and Latin terms for a section of territory' (Andrew 2010: 350).

Dong Wang argues that Guangzhou, from its early history, was the center of both domestic and international trade. Such trade was established in silk, marking the beginning of the 'Silk Road on the sea' to Rome as early as 116 CE. In addition to Rome, Guangzhou traded with Arabia, Persia, Ceylon, India, and Syria (Wang 2007: 535–6). The Portuguese were the first colonialists to visit Guangzhou in 1517 (ibid.: 536). The Spaniards were the next colonial invaders (1575), followed by the English in 1636. The English brought with them a new level of colonial penetration of China. From 1715 until the first Opium War (1839–42),[5] the British were Guangzhou's dominant trading partner (ibid.: 536). China's defeat in the war had long-term implications for the Middle Kingdom, and it marked the most turbulent period in the modern history of the country. At war's end, the Treaty of Nanking was signed on 19 August 1842. As part of the treaty, China was forced to abolish its monopolistic system of trade, a number of ports had to be opened to foreign trade, and Hong Kong had to be turned over to Great Britain. For decades Western powers repeatedly launched assaults on China's sovereignty in an effort to gain more economic and political concessions (Lu Aiguo 2000: 16–17). According to Lu Aiguo, it was only after the second Opium War in 1869 that the Qing imperial country really began to come to terms with the consequences of the Western invasions (ibid.: 18). What Paul C. van Dyke calls 'The Great Canton Trade Era' (beginning in the late seventeenth century) collapsed in 1892 (2005: 1).

Today, Guangzhou has reclaimed its greatness as 'one of the most open and fastest growing Chinese cities that supply a large amount of diversified commodities and products for international trade' (Zhang 2008: 384). It has a labor force, according to Wang, that is one of the most efficient in China (2007: 536), and there has been a huge increase in the number of foreigners. Such people from various foreign diasporas are different, according to Zhang, from what the globalization literature articulates. These new arrivals are said by Zhang to be pragmatic about the global economy in that they do not arrive as demand-driven professionals or workers looking for low pay (Zhang 2008: 384). Africans are said to be attracted to Guangzhou's specialized wholesale markets and other stores and shops because they offer goods at reasonable prices for the market back home (ibid.: 389).

While African traders had been coming to Guangzhou since the early 1990s, it was not until the huge influx beginning in the early part of the twenty-first century that an area within a 10-kilometre radius located in Yuexiu District (Xiaobei Lu) and Baiyun District was to become known as Chocolate City (where most of the Africans are).[6]

According to an empirical study of Chocolate City, Nigerians represent the largest group, Malians the second largest, followed by Ghanaians and Guineans. There are traders from the DRC, Senegal, the Gambia, Burundi, Côte d'Ivoire, Kenya, Liberia, Niger, Sierra Leone, South Africa, Tanzania, Uganda, and Zambia. Most traders in Chocolate City are from West Africa (Bodomo 2010: 699–70). There is also a growing number of Angolans in the area. According to Adams Bodomo, 95 percent of Africans identify themselves as 'businessmen' or 'traders' (ibid.: 699). Some of these individuals first came to China as students in the 1980s and later became entrepreneurs (Le Bail 2009: 9).

These thousands of entrepreneurs send annually thousands of containers to Africa. Such activity perhaps reached its peak between 2003 and 2007 when it grew by 294 percent. According to Tristan Coloma, an estimated 90 percent of goods in African markets today come from China, Thailand and Indonesia (2010a).

African trading posts, transnational spaces, and the immigrant community as a bridge to the host community

As is to be expected, the academic community has attempted to make sense out of the growing presence of Africans in China, especially where they are present in large numbers, as in Guangzhou/Chocolate City, where estimates range from 20,000 to 130,000 (Haugen 2012: 5). Some have referred to places like Guangzhou as trading posts, with such posts having been established in other parts of Asia long before China's integration into the world economy. Others have made reference to the creation of transnational spaces and result-ant ethnic enclaves, and finally have proposed that African immigrants serve as bridges to the larger Chinese population. We shall explore these various ideas for their significance for the stories that will be presented.

African trading posts One of the first scholarly attempts to try to understand the dynamics of sub-Saharan African traders migrating to different parts of the world in pursuit of their entrepreneurial objectives is contained in an article entitled 'The emergence of new African "trading posts" in Hong Kong and Guangzhou' by Brigitte Bertoncello and Sylvie Bredeloup (2007). These two authors explore what they call African trading posts established in Hong Kong and Guangzhou in the wake of such posts being created in other places long before China opened its doors and acceded to the World Trade Organization (WTO) in 2001 (ibid.: 100). For Africans, the first stop was Dubai, where it is argued Africans made a major contribution to making it a significant marketplace. As the Asian tigers began to emerge, African trading posts were established in Thailand and Indonesia at the end of the 1980s. Similar posts were established in Japan and Korea by West Africans (ibid.: 99). Bertoncello and Bredeloup draw an analogy between the African trading posts and the Greek trading colony in that both were 'created on the initiative of the foreigner ... that was founded on an understanding between producers and vendors and the functioning of which was closely tied to the hinterland or took place in a foreign enclave' (ibid.: 94).

The longer-established African traders who have shops in Asia have the capacity to 'link the centres of production to the market' (ibid.: 97). In re-drawing the trading routes, they in essence have added to the variety of new products for their African clientele. At the same time they negotiate directly with factories in China, thus taking control of the chain of transport logistics. In addition, because of the system of information they have established at the international level, these African traders are able to maintain contact with their customers and respond to them in a timely fashion. Furthermore, these experienced African traders, who are deemed to have significant power in Asia, were able to become economic operators owing to their experience in interfacing between the African community at large and the local communities. Thus they have made a significant contribution to the creation of African trading posts in Asia (ibid.: 97).

The newer African traders, on the other hand, according to the above authors, while also helping to consolidate African trading posts, have mostly studied other subjects outside their respective countries before making a decision to become international traders, so they are comparatively inexperienced (ibid.: 97).

The clientele of both the older and younger traders, according to Bertoncello and Bredeloup, tend to be mostly African, with one group consisting of merchants who shuttle between Asian trading posts and the markets in their home country, the other consisting of clientele who place their orders from their companies in the United States, Africa, or Europe (ibid.: 98). Two trends on a more global scale can be identified by these African merchants – namely, that whether they hail from another trading post in Southeast Asia or come directly from sub-Saharan Africa, these 'nomads' are 'in increasing numbers incorporating the marketplaces of Hong Kong and Guangzhou in their circuits ...' (ibid.: 100). Of special note is that these African merchants are not only contributing to the economic development of their host country (as employers and taxpayers), they are also helping to transform the districts where they work and live (ibid.: 101).

The disappointments experienced by African traders in China, as noted below, as well as the poor quality of goods that are produced in Guangzhou, according to Bertoncello and Bredeloup, 'explains why the African merchants maintain part of their activity in the other trading and supply posts, playing on the comparative advantages' (ibid.: 100–1).

Transnational space Zhigang Li, Laurence J. C. Ma, and Desheng Xue argue that they have produced 'the first academic study of the country's African migrants.' This is an article entitled 'An African enclave in China: the making of a new transnational urban space' (2009). They have accomplished this through examining the creation of a new African community in Xiaobei, an urban area in the Yuexiu district of Guangzhou. Xiaobei, they argue, is not only a space where transnational business is transacted, but also a place where African migrants try to make a living, even though there is not much local integration or assimilation.

Li et al. refer to Xiaobei as a 'non-state' gateway, where booming economic linkages are being forged between China and Africa, and also a place that provides a new transnational space that is 'challenged by an invisible wall between Africans and local residents due to cultural and social differences' (ibid.: 699). Presumably Xiaobei is referred to as a 'non-state' gateway in light of the authors' contention that it was only recently that at the local level the Chinese state got directly involved in Xiaobei's development as an African migrant transnational space. Heretofore the state at the local level had left the migrants, along with local people and market forces, to create the socio-economic and spatial patterns of Xiaobei as an urban ethnic enclave (ibid.: 714). Li et al. further contend that while most transnational urban spaces or foreign enclaves have not been confronted with any serious problems relating to conflicts with the local population, this has not been the case with the African transnational community under study (ibid.: 703).

The creation of this transnational urban space for African entrepreneurs is placed within the context of three primary significant forces that 'underlie the transformation of Chinese cities, namely market reform, globalization, and migration.' While much is known about the first two issues, the authors argue that not much is known about the latter. Thus the authors use Guangzhou as an example of the emergence of a transnational African community (ibid.: 700).

What has happened in Xiaobei is not considered unusual within the context of globalized cities where international migrants have transformed spaces into enclaves in the process of looking for markets and products (ibid.: 703). In fact, Li et al. argue that the creation of African enclaves in China is merely part of the transformation taking place in China, resulting in the urban part of the country being more heterogeneous and multicultural, both socially and spatially (ibid.: 703).

Notwithstanding the fact that the emergence of Xiaobei as a leading transnational space has been made partially successful by both African traders and Chinese business enterprises, it has failed to result in the integration socially or spatially of the local Xiaobei Chinese community and the transnational African community (ibid.: 713), which is also referred to as an 'ethnic enclave.'[7] This is the case, as Evan Osnos of the *New Yorker* observes, because there exists mutual mistrust between the African migrants and the local Chinese (Osnos, as quoted in Li et al. 2009: 713). Thus, Li et al. note, 'within a largely positive trading environment, the lack of harmonious social relations and cultural understanding on the part of both sides is a serious problem that threatens to disrupt the long-term stability and even sustainability of the transnational urban space for African traders in the enclave of Guangzhou' (ibid.: 713).

Li et al. believe that the distrust between these two communities has only got worse with time owing to the growing numbers of illegal African traders and the steps the legal authorities have taken to control the problem (ibid.: 713). In addition:

> Lack of confidence in trading and difficulties in communicating with the Chinese trading partners have meant that, for many African migrants, their presence in Guangzhou is largely a business necessity, i.e., a way to make a living. Due to the problem discussed above, life in Xiaobei, especially for young African bachelors, is not particularly attractive. With increased immigration control, a worsening trading environment, and declining optimism on the part of the African migrants/traders, the future of Xiaobei as a transnational space is uncertain. (Ibid.: 714)

Notwithstanding the above, Li et al. note that the transnational spaces occupied by Africans in Guangzhou have not resulted in Chinese leaving the area. In fact, the jobs which African firms provide for the local Chinese actually contribute 'to the stability of Xiaobei as a transnational urban space for African migrants' (ibid.: 714).

The African immigrant community as a bridge to the Chinese Adams Bodomo, a Ghanaian scholar at Hong Kong University who writes on Africans in China, is much more optimistic than Li et al. regarding the relationship between the transnational African community in Guangzhou and the local Chinese community. Using the concept of 'bridge' theory, he unequivocally believes that 'Africans resident in Guangzhou, through their activities either intentionally or unintentionally, serve as linguistic, cultural and business links and connections between their Chinese hosts and Africans in their home countries as well as those who arrive newly in China' (Bodomo 2010: 695).

In reality one cannot expect the African community to be fully an enclave and thus isolated from its host community, nor fully integrated into same. But at the same time one can expect, under the right conditions, for the source African community to serve as a bridge between itself and the host community (ibid.: 696).

One of the most important empirical sources of evidence that Bodomo provides to substantiate his bridge theory is the fact that following in-depth discussions with African community leaders in Guangzhou they all agreed that the socio-economic contributions of Africans in the area can be identified as follows: '[B]uilding economic bridges between host and source community; as image builders for Africa; the creation of employment for local Guangzhou people and Chinese from other provinces; and acting as mentors to the young Chinese who work with them' (ibid.: 705).

African traders and the long journey to Chocolate City

Even though China had once again opened its doors to the world in 1978, it was to be over a decade before Africans began to migrate toward Guangzhou, and Chocolate City would eventually emerge during the early twenty-first century. The idea of going to China occurred only after traders and merchants tried realizing their dreams in other parts of Africa, as well as places like Dubai, Thailand, Indonesia, etc. As Osnos notes, the Asian financial crisis around 1998 resulted in huge numbers of African merchants starting to seek new frontiers, leaving places like Bangkok and Kuala Lumpur to venture to China (Osnos 2009). The Chinese government of Hu Jintao became very concerned about the huge immigration to China, and in response to it Chinese authorities announced in 2007 that 'China is not a migration-targeted country' (as quoted in Coloma 2010a) and responded to this general influx of foreigners by unveiling a Chinese green card. Such a card would allow the recipient to remain in China for ten years without a renewal. The ministry made it clear that the new regulations were designed to attract high-level foreign personnel (Osnos 2009). Hao Chiyong, who formally announced the green card, went farther and said, 'There will not be many foreigners applying for the Green Cards' (as quoted in Coloma 2010a). Coloma further noted that it was announced that 'there would be fewer visas for Africans' (ibid.). The clear message was that African traders need not apply, since they did not meet the stated qualifications. In fact, as will be seen below, as more Africans migrated to China, and especially Guangzhou, even more restrictions were placed on their ability to legally remain in the country for an extended period of time.

Of course, the reason for coming to Chocolate City/Guangzhou is to have access to cheap Chinese goods that, in most cases, can be easily packed for transshipment to Africa. Many Africans end up buying their goods directly from the Chinese manufacturer because they know what their clientele back home want (Le Bail 2009: 17). Others who buy directly from the factory often purchase surplus items, at very low prices, left over from previous orders. Even today, some companies contact certain Africans when they have surplus end-of-the-line merchandise (ibid.: 16). In this way, Africans are able to compete with their Chinese counterparts who are sending cheaper goods to Africa. In fact, Yinghong Cheng feels that the Chinese rarely appreciate the 'African migrants' contribution to the Chinese economy – wholesale purchasing and shipping out-of-fashion and "low-end" merchandise to Africa ...' (Cheng 2011: 567). Other African traders, however, have to go through Chinese middlemen (Dyer 2008), which makes the goods more expensive.

With respect to Guangzhou being a center of globalization from below for these African traders, Yang Yang argues that the city represents 'an economic "underworld",' in which transactions are not traceable either by custom officials or economic surveys (2012: 155). The traders, Yang Yang argues, are well aware that the goods they are buying and selling are counterfeit and consequently the agents at the level of globalization from above are being exploited since technology and designs produced at the hegemonic level by huge corporations cost billions of dollars. In addition, African traders in Guangzhou acknowledge that local African manufacturing industries are likely being negatively affected by Chinese products but feel they are doing something good for Africa (ibid.: 167).

> Not many people in my county can afford original products from Europe and America. There is no way we can produce things in Nigeria as cheaply as China can. We come to China because it is cheaper than everywhere else. Because of the goods I take back, African people can buy more variety of things at lower prices. For a long time, we could only get second-hand 'dumped goods' from Europe and we are sick of that. We want something better and I am bringing Africans something better. (Ibid.: 167)

The complicated world of African traders in Chocolate City

Life is very complicated for most African traders in Guangzhou/Chocolate City. Most of the information in this section is based on personal interviews with numerous African traders and is divided into six themes: doing business in Guangzhou/Chocolate City; triple illegal/immigrant issues; African men and Chinese women; African criminals in Guangzhou and illicit drug trafficking; Chocolate City at night; and Chinese racism against blacks.

Doing business in Chocolate City/Guangzhou

Mr Kingsley from Cameroon The taxi ride from my hotel to 514 Bole Trading City in Chocolate City on a busy Sunday morning was very short and I had no forewarning as to what I was about to experience. As we reached the fifth floor of the building my research assistant told me we had arrived at Mr Kingsley's office. Mr Kingsley is a successful Cameroonian trader/businessman. I asked my assistant to please make sure we had the correct office number since we had noticed a number of Chinese staff in the front office. While I had read about African traders having Chinese secretarial staff, this was my first time experiencing it. My assistant assured me we were at the correct place, but as we entered the reception area Mr Kingsley was not to be seen. Instead, there were four Chinese sitting at various desks, one of whom quickly approached us and asked whether she could be of assistance. We informed her that we were here to see Mr Kingsley. She immediately ushered us into an office where Mr Kingsley was sitting behind a huge desk. The consummate successful businessman warmly greeted us and motioned for us to take seats. As I sat down I glanced around the room, which was packed with so many suits that you could not see them all. There were suits that brought back memories from the 1960s to the present.

Mr Kingsley is in the business of making suits and selling them to customers in Cameroon (his home country), Zimbabwe, Angola, Gabon, Ghana, Nigeria, the United States, and France. He was to open my eyes to a totally different dimension of the power and influence of African traders in Chocolate City/ Guangzhou.

Mr Kingsley first came to Hong Kong to visit in 2003. At the time he was working in Cameroon at Starcredit Bank. After one year working for the bank he had a leave period and came to teach English for two years in Shansi Province, in a small town called Yuncheng. At the time he was the only black person in the town. At one point he met a Nigerian who was going to Guangzhou. Kingsley went there and discovered many foreigners. On vacations he would return to Guangzhou and do business. He started sending goods to Cameroon and then he started taking men's suits. He found that the suits from China were much cheaper. For example, an average suit from Italy or France would cost $150 while a suit from China would only cost $40.[8]

While back home he met a gentleman from Morocco who placed an order for 1,000 pieces ('piece' being terminology for a single suit) per month. He then met a person from Douala, and because suits were so expensive there, he also gave him orders. Deciding he could no longer teach, Mr Kingsley returned to China and employed a Canadian to teach in his place. He paid the Canadian from his teaching salary. The only problem was to get his visa extended, which he did. Mr Kingsley met a Chinese making suits and told him he wanted to open a factory. He explained that they would divide the cost of opening

28

the factory. The Chinese would be responsible for taking care of production (workers, ordering the material, overseeing the making of the suits, etc.) and he would take care of the market side (getting the orders, marketing, etc.). This arrangement continued from 2006 to 2008. Then, 'In 2008 I realized my partner was double-crossing me. In reality I found out that we did not own the factory; that my partner had been giving the orders to another factory (the factory was six hours away so I never bothered to go there). In addition, he was not giving me my proper pay for the selling of the suits.'[9]

When questioned as to how he determined the above, Mr Kingsley noted:

> I had received a huge order and wanted to actually see the factory to make sure we had the capacity to fulfill the order. So when I got to the factory I first saw a makeshift sign on the front that had been put there that day saying Kingsley and my partner's name. The chief of staff of the factory knew my partner was seriously intimidated by me, but I had no understanding as to why. When the subject came up of the ownership of the factory I was told that it was not my factory.[10]

So Mr Kingsley fired his so-called partner and hired the chief of staff of the factory he had visited to open and manage a newly created Kingsley factory. He mentored Mr Kingsley between 2008 and 2009. The factory officially opened in 2009. Annually Mr Kingsley gets 100,000 orders for suits and 50,000 for shirts. In May 2011 he was only thirty years old and had moved to China at the age of twenty-three. Mr Kingsley employs 180 workers in his factory; five workers in Bola market; one in Cannon Market; and two in Hong Kong. He also has workers employed at Kingsley Cargo. Owing to Chinese visa rules he is not allowed to hire non-Chinese (including Africans). He designs both suits and shirts. He lives in Guangzhou and has bought a garden apartment, which means it is in a very secure neighborhood with high security. In addition to being married to a Chinese woman, he has a son. 'As long as business is good I'll stay. The issue is my visa. The government won't explain why they won't offer me permanent residency.'[11]

In order to get a residency permit, one has to rent an office, pay taxes, and have Chinese employment (Haugen 2012: 11). Clearly Mr Kingsley meets all of these requirements. Although gaining permanent residency is possible in China (see 'Regulations on Permanent Residence of Aliens in China'), it appears to be a very arduous process that has been elusive for African migrants. Mr Nwoso, who has lived in China for over a decade, posits that the Chinese government gives only one-year residency to African traders. This is because at any moment, even with a legal residency permit, if the government decides that they want you to leave the country, you have no recourse but to leave.[12] Reinforcing Mr Nwoso's assessment, Haugen notes that 'Residence permits provide no guarantee against demands for bribes or forced repatriation' (ibid.: 4) and that 'Informants who held residence permits cited the uncertainty associated with the annual renewal as a major source of distress' (ibid.: 11).

Mr Baron from Nigeria Mr Baron, like Mr Kingsley, owns a factory, which is at least six hours from Guangzhou. Mr Baron, from western Nigeria, studied at Rivers State University of Sciences and Technology, Port Harcourt, Nigeria. He graduated in 2004 with a major in agricultural and environmental engineering. He did his youth service in 2005, then taught from 2006 to 2007. When I interviewed Mr Baron he had been in Guangzhou for only a few years. Like so many African traders, he had come to Guangzhou looking for greener pastures. Back home he was selling mobile phones which were made in China. Then he finally made the journey to Guangzhou with a friend who was dealing with clothing.[13]

> He suggested that I go to the material market. There I met a woman who claimed to be the owner of a factory. Before July 2008 I met and married Betty and then connected to the business. Betty helped me because she knew the language. I started by buying material and having clothes made. My brand became O'Baron. In 2010 I decided to open my own factory making shirts. I have 130 workers at the factory and three workers in my shop. I employ one foreigner – a Nigerian, to do the hiring for the business. My general manager is a Chinese – my wife's uncle. The factory is hours away from Guangzhou. The most important thing is language. If you don't speak the language you can't make progress. We sell to traders in the UK, Canada, South Africa, Nigeria, Mozambique, Botswana, Togo, and the DRC. Annually we sell 300,000 pieces.[14]

Mr Baron continues:

If it takes 1 RMB to make a shirt in China, it takes 20 RMB to make a shirt in Nigeria (as you know, you have serious problems with electricity in Nigeria). We pay our workers 3,500 RMB, which is about US$542, which is a good salary in China. Labor, however, is cheaper in Nigeria, but you have all the other constraints. Why is it cheaper here to have a factory? (1) accommodations are cheaper; (2) feeding is cheaper (I feed my employees); (3) they work six days a week, eight to ten hours per day; and (4) transportation is cheaper. I have a yearly residency permit. My children are foreigners. The best they can do in this country is inherit my business. There are at least one million Chinese in Nigeria. They spoil the market in Nigeria; Nigerians don't disturb them, but they disturb us here.[15]

So who really owns Mr Kingsley's and Mr Baron's factories? Mr Nwoso,[16] one of the most established and successful Nigerian traders in Chocolate City, clarified for me the issue of ownership in China. He first made reference to

China's constitution. He noted that if you examine the section on ownership of property, Article 10 says the following:

Land in the cities is owned by the state. Land in the rural and suburban areas is owned by collectives except for those portions which belong to the state in accordance with the law; house sites and private plots of cropland and hilly land are also owned by collectives. The state may in the public interest take over the land for its use in accordance with the law. No organization or individual may appropriate, buy, sell or lease land, or unlawfully transfer the land in other ways. All organizations and individuals who use land must make rational use of the land. (Chinese Constitution of the People's Republic of China n.d.)

The constitution in Article 18 further notes that:

The People's Republic of China permits foreign enterprises, other foreign economic organizations and individual foreigners to invest in China and to enter into various forms of economic co-operation with Chinese enterprises and other economic organization in accordance with the law of the People's Republic of China. All foreign enterprises and other foreign economic organizations in China, as well as joint ventures with Chinese and foreign investment located in China, shall abide by the law of the People's Republic of China. Their lawful rights and interests are protected by the law of the People's Republic of China. (Ibid.)

With the above laws in place, Mr Nwoso unequivocally notes that there are no Africans with manufacturing plants of their own. If such plants exist, they are owned by their wives.[17]

As will be revealed in the remaining stories, Mr Kingsley and Mr Baron, owing to their marriages to Chinese women and their financial success, are not the 'normal' African traders or merchants in this huge trading enclave of Guangzhou. In fact, most African traders have small stalls, inside large trading centers, and their first encounter is directly with people they hope will buy their goods.

Mr Nwoso from Nigeria Before arriving in Guangzhou in 2000 from eastern Nigeria, Mr Nwoso was trading in garments and fabrics that he imported from Korea and Taiwan (1998–2000). He decided to come to Guangzhou because he could acquire things more easily and because of the weather. Also, importing from both Taiwan and Korea became too expensive. In 2004 he started his own freight forwarding company and was sending goods back to Nigeria. Nigerians, he notes, import the highest number of goods from China. According to official statistics, Nigerians export to Africa from China the second-largest volume of goods. Haugen notes, however, that this information is based on 'official trade statistics' (2012: 12). We know that, at the level of globalization from below, such statistics are not available. In fact, officially the Nigerian government banned the import of foreign textiles in 2002 to curtail foreign competition, according to both Yang Yang (2012: 155) and Mr Nwoso. The reality, however, is that the government ignores its own ban and the goods enter the ports and markets without any problems.[18] Mr Nwoso exports to Nigeria a minimum of thirty containers per month. He employs twenty-three Chinese workers and a few Nigerians illegally, because it is so difficult for foreigners to get a work permit in China. In order to even get to talk with Mr Nwoso, one must be very patient and wait for his availability. He is the busiest trader I interviewed during my two trips to Chocolate City.

Mr Nwoso reports staggering figures for the amount of money that Nigerians bring into Guangzhou each day. He estimates that on every flight coming from Nigeria, people have a minimum of US$2 million in cash. With four flights coming into Guangzhou every day, that means US$8 million per day. 'It is true,' notes Mr Bah from Guinea (see the next section), 'that Nigerians bring in US$8 million a day into Guangzhou.'[19]

Life in Guangzhou, Mr Nwoso says, depends on how you look at it:

It has gotten better since I first arrived. For example, when we first came it was almost impossible to have a shop. Chinese don't like defeat – they want to win, so you have to be smart like them. Most of us operated here illegally in the beginning. We opened a representative office then and officially you could not trade. The only people that could legally trade were trading companies. So we didn't officially have the right to trade. But we did it unofficially. I don't to this day have a license to trade. I pay tax on my representative office. All of us in the freight business give goods to Chinese companies to export to Africa and then we take a cut. All we do is coordinate them and then it goes to a Chinese company. Documentation, everything is done by the Chinese. There is always a Chinese.[20]

'China is like a police country,' remarks Mr Nwoso, because 'they know everything about you.' Further:

They allow Nigerians here because they need the money. When Africans come they have cash; they know the money is helping the lower class in China. They need Africans to stabilize their economy. They really need West Africans. Eighty percent of textiles are from China; ninety percent of all goods in the markets in Africa are from China. Everything they use is from China. The employment in Africa suffers because of this reality.[21]

The police presence in Chocolate City is very daunting. It was very intimidating to me and I always had legal documents permitting me to be in the area. One Nigerian I attempted to interview in June 2013 out in the open with police in front of us insisted that I must follow him to his stall inside the plaza across the road. Once we were safely inside he explained to me that since he was an illegal immigrant, the more visible he was the more he risked being arrested by the police.

So why was he safe in the plaza, but not outside? Mr Nwoso explained that a relatively new policy has been put in place to protect the interests of the Chinese owners of the plaza where Africans conduct their business. A serious raid by the police into these buildings in search of illegal immigrants can easily result in huge numbers of empty stalls. This in turn can result in the Chinese owners of the buildings who rent to Africans going bankrupt if a certain number of stalls are empty following the arrest by the police of the illegal immigrants. Consequently, the police and the Chinese owners have a tacit understanding that amounts to financial remuneration given to the police, and in return they do not enter the buildings in search of illegal African immigrants.[22]

Mr Nanga from Nigeria Mr Nanga is a frustrated man. He travels to Guangzhou once a month to buy goods from his fellow Nigerians in Chocolate City. Mr Nanga has been coming to this part of the world consistently since 2003. He has a shop back home and trades in T-shirts, shirts, and clothes in general. He ships his goods back to Nigeria in a container. According to Mr Nanga, the Chinese are not trustworthy.[23]

> Before I return home I must make sure everything is in the container because they will change the order and put the wrong things in there. I had losses in early years because I did not see the process through to make sure the correct goods were in the container. I am from Lagos and the Chinese don't like Africans. They only need money. Visas are a problem. They only give us thirty days. I come here for two weeks. They should give us one-year visas. Sometimes I can't travel because I don't have a visa. Each time I come here my visa costs $1,300, and my plane ticket costs $1,500. I only continue coming here because Nigerians like Chinese designs and so there is a great demand. So I don't have a choice but to do this. But the Chinese government needs to give me a one-year visa.[24]

Mr Muthui from Kenya Amos Muthui had finished his business and was preparing to return to Kenya when I found him wandering around the Overseas Trading Mall in Guangzhou. Mr Muthui started coming to Guangzhou five years ago to buy goods for his shop back in Kenya. He first started in the shoe business, and after it was no longer profitable he started buying motorbikes and spare parts for the bikes. Before the financial crisis he was coming to Guangzhou monthly and sometimes even twice a month. But now he is able to travel to the area only every three or four months. On this journey in May

2011 he had just bought his normal consignment of motorbikes (the average is between 80 and 120). Mr Muthui says that he makes a very good profit from his trade and the goods enter the Kenyan market duty free. Although he was in a hurry to get back to Kenya, I was able to interview him about his experience as a trader/entrepreneur in Guangzhou. He noted that he can't leave the city until his container is closed and ready to be shipped back to Kenya. Before this happens, however, he must make sure that his order is correct, namely that all the motorbikes are the same (sometimes the Chinese mix the brands of bikes) and he must pay someone to make sure that all the bikes work. In terms of shopping in Guangzhou, he says that the Chinese people are very confusing, dishonest and therefore bad for him. Consequently sometimes he just goes to Dubai to buy his motorbikes.[25]

Mr Emma from Nigeria If there was one person that I had to see upon arriving in Chocolate City, according to Evan Osnos from the *New Yorker*, it was Ojukwu Emma, the leader of the Nigerian community. With Osnos' instructions in my hand I went straight to Cannon Market in Chocolate City and started asking any African I saw whether they knew this man. Osnos had forewarned me that he was so busy that I would likely have to wait hours to talk to him. Luckily, my research assistant called Mr Emma and he was available to see us immediately, presumably because most traders' days don't start until around noon. Mr Emma has basically become an icon in Chocolate City, so I knew he would determine the future direction my access to other traders would take. He started by telling me that:

> Africans come to China just for business. There are no jobs in China. There is a language barrier. Most foreigners are based here. We are having a lot of business difficulties. Things have changed over the last three years. The Chinese have to understand our presence and issues in this country in a different way. We don't have the same visa problems. When you come to Africa the Chinese understand that there are millions of them, for example in Nigeria. So they have had to deal with the immigration problem in this country very differently. The visa issue does create a lot of problems. Once you come to China you come in as one person and then you are forced to leave and return under a totally different identification. This poses a real problem for immigration in this country. Some people commit suicide as a result of this problem. But again we are working with this government on this subject. Once you are forced to leave we discuss with Chinese authorities how you can return.[26]

The Nigerian community in Guangzhou is divided along the lines of the thirty-six states in Nigeria. There are representatives for each state assigned to try to solve the difficulties Nigerians experience in China with respect to business. While Guangzhou is a city where Mr Emma says you can get whatever you need, he is not dismissive of the numerous problems the Nigerian community is confronted with. For example, he notes that:

> Our children are facing a lot of problems. Many black children can't go to school. We are having to send them to international schools which is very expensive and many people can't afford to send their children to such schools. We are now fighting to get our own school for our children. They call our children 'Black Devils.' I don't allow my son, who is of mixed race, to play with Chinese children. Children are supposed to have their own rights. The Chinese train their children to believe that Africans are not human.

Another problem that Mr Emma says Africans and other foreigners are confronted with is the reality that when they run into problems with local Chinese, the police defend the locals, even if they are wrong. This is a problem that Mr Emma feels needs to be resolved. He does feel that the Chinese do respect people if they see they are organized and he doesn't believe they would dare try to kick him out of China.[27]

In May 2011, when I first interviewed Mr Emma, he had been in Guangzhou for thirteen years. He is involved in the import and export business. Upon arriving in Chocolate City/Guangzhou he mainly traded in women's and men's shoes. He discontinued this business, however, because he lost US$1 million as a result of the fact that the Chinese he employed to make the shoes made them with glue that was past its sell-by date. So by the time the shipment arrived in Nigeria all the shoes had fallen apart.[28]

Yang Yang estimates 'that about half of the African traders who come to Guangzhou lose all their money' (2012: 160). Some of this stems from fraudulent exchanges, as in the case of Mr Emma. Knowing this, Mr Muthui from Kenya and Mr Nanga from Nigeria and others must inspect their goods before they leave the port in Guangzhou. This is one of the major hazards of operating at the level of globalization from below. Once transactions are formalized, in most cases there is no recourse through legal means to challenge the illegal exchange of counterfeit goods. At this level transactions take place outside any national calculations and consequently are unreported (ibid.: 57). 'Instead of having institutional guarantees and certificates, these traders may have nothing more than an oral promise or a hand-written receipt that is kept off the books. At the center of the "world's factory," Guangzhou, these African traders use the tools of globalization – fast transnational transportation and extremely convenient communication via mobile phones – to potentially build, with little start-up capital, entrepreneurial enterprises, cutting across continents' (ibid.: 158).

Mr Vianney from Rwanda Mr Nzamwita M. Vianney is a tall, charming man from Rwanda who had one of his secretaries escort us to his plush office. He is clearly not happy being in Guangzhou and immediately let us know that. Born in Uganda, he returned to Rwanda in December 1994, after the genocide of 1994. He went to Dubai with his current company in 2004 and then left there on 27 November 2009, as a result of the recession. Most of his clients, he said, were switching to Guangzhou. Running an export trading company, he exports fifty containers of goods a month from Guangzhou, with 90 percent of the cargo going to Africa. His company is merely an intermediary, which means that people bring goods to them to ship and they find a shipping company. While the business is improving, Mr Vianney hates living in Guangzhou. The only thing the place has to offer is cheap goods. 'There is big racism here and it is open. The Chinese make it clear that the prices you get in the market are higher than the ones given to Chinese.' He gives himself a couple more years in Guangzhou and he definitely plans to leave.

Mr Sengabo from Rwanda Leaving Guangzhou is also at the forefront of the mind of Mr Sengabo, also from Rwanda. Born in Uganda, he left when he was five years old. He went to Rwanda and was there from 1975 to 1992 (he left to go to school in Kenya). He studied in Kenya from 1992 to 1994, thus missing the genocide of 1994. Only one sister survived the genocide. During his stay in Kenya he started having financial problems, so he was not able to complete his studies and thus started trading in Kenya.[29]

Mr Sengabo next went to Saudi Arabia to look for a job and ended up working for Coca-Cola for a year. He then stayed there illegally. He next traveled to Dubai, where he worked in the area of inter-freight from 1995 to 1997. Mr Sengabo started his own company in 1997 and began shipping mostly to East Africa (Rwanda, Kenya, the DRC, Tanzania, and Uganda). Some agents would come personally and place orders, while others placed orders from their respective countries, according to Mr Sengabo. He remained in Dubai until 2005, during which time everything became so expensive that his profits started going down. This same year he came to Guangzhou, but continued shipping to East Africa.[30]

Currently Mr Sengabo has two Chinese workers, but he retains them only for two years. After that, he says, they usually try to start taking over his company. Every month he ships between twenty and twenty-five containers; however, things are not as good now because of the economic crisis.[31]

Like most Africans interviewed, Mr Sengabo turns to the issue of visas.

The Chinese are complicating the process by which Africans get visas. I have to renew my residency permit every year. It's not expensive but they are always coming up with new policies – new documents must be sent to your country to be certified. You have to hope that the person you might send the documents with will take care of business, otherwise you might not get your visa renewed.[32]

Again like most Africans interviewed, Mr Sengabo finds living in China a problem because 'Chinese are always changing policies; Chinese are not honest; they are very complicated; Chinese want to get your business; workers want to take your customers; no security in doing business; they give you counterfeit things and no contracts and you can't go to court; Chinese only like money; their community is very closed.'[33]

> Furthermore, there are no human rights in this country; no justice; all police are corrupt; lawyers are corrupt; many people place orders and request 30 percent upfront and then they change companies and you can't find them. So you lose all the money you have put down on an order. Once they have gotten all the money they need they close shop and then go to another province, so you can't find them. It is really dangerous to do business here.[34] (See also Mathews and Yang 2012: 110 and 113 for similar stories.)

Mr Sengabo wanted to go to the USA. His business is contracts and he wanted to specialize in high-tech machinery, and buy a small factory. He lamented that he couldn't accept orders for electronics from China. He felt he had a market in Africa and the Middle East for electronics and hoped that in 2012 he would be able to leave China.[35]

While most African traders have unfavorable things to say about the Chinese, most Chinese traders in turn are seemingly not impressed with their African counterparts. Since it was impossible to talk to any Chinese traders during my field research trips to Guangzhou,[36] I have to rely on information other scholars have collected.

Lyons et al., in their interviews with Chinese traders, report cultural problems in doing business with Africans, unfair bargaining, fights between merchants and customers, and rudeness (2012a: 883–4). Bodomo reported that the experience of one Chinese woman was that Africans didn't keep their promises. She noted, for example, that

> they would request that the company supply them with the goods within a week, but they would not come to collect their goods on time. Then, after having goods produced for then, they would claim that they did not have the money to pay for them readily available. According to Ms. Li, some Africans who were Christians would profess that these problems were being dealt with 'in the name of God,' implying that there was nothing they could do about these problems. Interacting with African customers was also difficult for Ms. Li because she perceived the African men as being too direct when they met women ... (Bodomo 2012: 54)

Others have complained that some African traders would, for example, place an order for 200 pairs of pants and then only actually buy ten pairs. In such cases the African traders would insist that they still pay the same price per pair as if they were buying all 200 pairs. Chinese traders are annoyed by such unethical business practices. Others complain that when picking up an order, African traders, while leaving their shops, would just grab an item they didn't pay for (Fool's Mountain: Blogging for China, 14 June 2008).

Mr Ali from Uganda Mr Ali from Uganda also hopes his years are numbered in Guangzhou. He came to Guangzhou in 2006 for family business reasons. His uncle is involved in the real estate business and owns a hotel in Kampala. So he is involved in trading – exporting, mainly in building products and finished products for the hotel industry (linen, cutlery, mattresses, etc.). 'Annually we export over one hundred and twenty containers. There are thirty to forty Ugandans in Guangzhou,' Mr Ali notes. In June 2013 (two years after the initial interview) Mr Ali still had no date for returning to Uganda. In fact, he is now talking about one day living half the year in Guangzhou and half the year in Kampala. Like so many African traders, Mr Ali is conflicted. He feels he cannot return home with his family unless he is a very successful businessman who can build a big house and buy a nice car.[37] For now he is stuck in the complex world of globalization from below, seemingly longing for the day when he can return home and be an agent in his uncle's hotel (which he has shares in) and operate within the hegemonic world.

Mr Mutesa from Angola There is no doubt that some Africans are very pleased with their new-found home in Chocolate City/Guangzhou. Mr Mutesa from Angola is one such person. He arrived in Guangzhou from Luanda, Angola, in 2006 to take advantage of trading opportunities. Mr Mutesa established a branch of an Angola shipping company in Guangzhou. He and his colleagues are involved in shipping construction goods back to Angola, including tiles, steel, and furniture. In addition, they buy and ship goods to individual clients in Angola. The company exports many containers a month, depending on demand.[38]

In terms of living in China, Mr Mutesa says that although he finds the Chinese to be closed people, they are not bad and he has a normal life in Chocolate City/Guangzhou. Chinese, he said, like money, but then all people like money. The only problem Mr Mutesa really has is sometimes with the quality of goods that are produced, noting that at times they are fake. He has a residency visa and a working certificate, so he argues that as long as you are here legally, you have no problems. China, he says, is the best market to be in.[39]

Mr Stones from Cameroon Mr Stones, the owner of Mister Stone Shoes, also seems very content being in Chocolate City. Born in Kumba, southwest Cameroon, Mr Stones admits that he was a tearaway growing up, causing his parents considerable challenges. He first came to China in 2005, but didn't really settle in Chocolate City until very recently. In fact, his shop in Bole Market had been opened only one year and two months when I interviewed him in May 2011. Mr Stones has his own brand of shoes that he sells to clients in Venezuela, Nigeria, Ghana, Cameroon, Russia and the United States. He uses two factories to make his shoes and admits that so far the shoe business has not been a profitable endeavor for him. Married to a woman from eastern Europe, Mr Stones is very content in his current environment.[40]

Triple illegal/immigration issues One of the more seasoned traders interviewed for this study was Mr Bah from Guinea. I first met Mr Bah in May 2011 and reunited with him in May/June 2013. A great deal had changed for Mr Bah in two years.

Born in Sierra Leone as a result of the fact that his parents were in political exile, Mr Bah started his business adventures while living in Liberia from 1983 to 1991. He would buy cigarettes from Guinea and sell them in Liberia. He did this for eight years. He left Liberia because of the war and returned to Sierra Leone for six months. Finally able to return to his home country of Guinea in 1991, Mr Bah engaged in the business of selling women's shoes until 1993. He moved on to selling jeans from 1993 to 2001. But things took a turn for the worse after the government destroyed the goods of informal traders, including burning their tables. Mr Bah then traveled to Abidjan (2003), then on to Egypt (2003), and Thailand (2003). Finally, at the end of 2003, he made it to Guangzhou, where he found his brother and sister.[41]

Mr Bah first began to work with his brother, but that arrangement did not produce any financial rewards, so he decided to venture out on his own. From 2004 to 2006 he had a business in which he went from office to office selling sandwiches at lunchtime. The profit from selling sandwiches allowed him to go into the business of selling jeans. The rewards were great and he made lots of money until 2009. Things began to decline when the individuals he entrusted with his business back home (the jeans were being exported to Guinea) decided that Mr Bah must be rich, so they stopped sending money back to him and he lost over US$20,000.[42]

Seemingly things couldn't get any worse but they did. Mr Bah had developed a beautiful line of linen outfits that had an African flare. These designs were outsourced to a Chinese company to be made. One day he looked up in the market and several Chinese merchants had copied his outfits and were selling them at a much lower price which he could not compete with. In addition, several Chinese women who were working for him ended up taking away many of his Guinean clients and starting businesses of their own. He alleged they started sleeping with some of his clients. Mr Bah feels he learned the hard way that some Chinese will take both your ideas and clients away from you.[43]

Life for Mr Bah has not been easy in Guangzhou. First and foremost he is considered, like most Africans, a 'triple illegal person' – an illegal entrant, an illegal resident, and working illegally (Osnos 2009). Mr Bah, again like the majority of African traders in Guangzhou, has overstayed his thirty-day visa and runs the risk of at any moment being arrested and taken to jail. A fine of up to 5,000 RMB (US$750) must be paid for overstaying one's welcome in the area, and then one must have a ticket to return home. Without these two requirements being fulfilled, Mr Bah could be put in jail in Guangzhou indefinitely. In the meantime, each day he waits to hear the banging of the gates in the congested huge indoor market (where he has a shop) warning traders that the police are about to enter the area looking for counterfeit goods. Mr Bah knows that if he gets caught selling them he will incur a huge fine. So he has a strategy to hide such goods as soon as he hears the alarm.

Being both a triple illegal and selling counterfeit goods, Mr Bah is playing with fire. If he were to become legal, Mr Bah would have to pay 5,000 RMB to the police for overstaying his visa, buy a ticket to return to Guinea and apply for a visa to return to China (which he might not get). If he does get it, each year he stays in China he would have to pay US$1,500 to extend his visa in order to remain legal.

When I returned to Guangzhou in May 2013, the first trader I went search-ing for was Mr Bah. I was devastated when I could not locate him. Finally, on my second trip to the market, my research assistant and I found the shop owned by his Chinese wife, so we were able to reunite. Once again, financially life had been very challenging for Mr Bah and so he had moved his shop to a different building. His shop now is an open space next to the elevator on the third floor of the building. There is no security at night for his goods; he just covers everything up and surprisingly no one touches his merchandise. As one of the oldest and most respected traders in the market, who would dare steal from Mr Bah?

Mr Bah's life had changed not only financially, but also personally. He had managed to finally bring his first wife to Guangzhou from Guinea. This woman was the love of his life, but he had never been able to afford a ticket to have her join him in Guangzhou. Thus he had married a Chinese woman and they had two daughters. In 2012 Mr Bah missed his first wife so much that he saved all his money to pay for her plane ticket. The product of this reunion was a beautiful baby girl who was three months old at the time of my visit. One evening, he recounted, his Chinese wife became very angry at him for bringing his first wife to Guangzhou and called the police to have him deported to Guinea. Mr Bah quickly ran out of the house and slept on the street that night. He was frightened because he knew that, had the police found him, he would have been arrested and taken to jail. The police did in fact come to the house looking for him. He is not quite certain why they have not returned, but he knows he is a lucky man.[44] The complications that have resulted from having two wives in Guangzhou will be discussed in the section below on 'African men and Chinese women.' In the meantime, Mr Bah was certain that with the Muslim holy month of Ramadan quickly approaching business would improve tremendously.

Mr Ali from Uganda estimates that it is likely that up to 95 percent of African traders are in Chocolate City/Guangzhou illegally.[45] Generally speaking this is the number that you hear in conversations in Guangzhou. No one knows for sure the number of illegal traders precisely because they are illegal and working under the radar of the police and immigration officials. This is one of the major characteristics of being an agent in the non-hegemonic world system.

The issue of being in Guangzhou illegally is the most pressing problem for the traders, many of whom would like to return home but cannot because of the financial outlay to become legal. And there is also the concern of spending time in jail for violating Chinese immigration laws. Haugen writes that

Undocumented migrants find their mobility severely inhibited; they must carefully assess how, when and with whom they move about in order to avoid police interception. This is a business impediment, as well as a source of personal distress for migrants who engage in trade and the provision of trade-related services. The situation can be described as a 'second state of immobility': the migrants have succeeded in the difficult project of emigration, but find themselves spatially entrapped in new ways in their destination country. (2012: 1)

So what is the origin of this phenomenon? Many trace the problem back to the planning for the 2008 Beijing Olympics.

Africans who first came to Guangzhou in the 1990s and early twenty-first century felt welcome.[46] However, on the eve of the 2008 Beijing Olympics, this changed dramatically. 'We were used to being granted one-year visas allowing multiple entry and unlimited length of stay. In 2008, just before the Beijing Olympics, the authorities decided to tidy up. They stopped renewing visas here. You had to return to your own country to get another work permit' (quoted in Coloma 2010a).

Consequently, as Tristan Coloma notes, 'the constant quest for precious visas can become absurd.' Currently visas given to African traders (unless they have residence status) are valid only for thirty days, which means these traders have to travel outside of mainland China each month in the hope of renewing their visas (ibid.). Even traveling outside every three months to renew your visa with a one-year residency permit can be very dangerous, as I discovered upon returning to Guangzhou in 2013.

Frank, another of my favorite traders, was not to be found. When we enquired about him, we were initially told by one of his Nigerian friends that he had left for Macau to renew his visa and from there was deported back to Nigeria. After several more conversations with Frank's friend, I was finally told the details of his deportation. When Frank first arrived in China he had a Nigerian passport. He overstayed his visa and was forced to leave the country. When Frank re-entered China it was on a passport from Sierra Leone. This, of course, is illegal in any country. So while Frank was waiting for his visa to be renewed so that he could return to Guangzhou in December 2012, the immigration authorizes realized that Frank was not from Sierra Leone and thus deported him back to Nigeria. Fortunately for Frank his wife was from Cameroon, so she was able to salvage some of his assets and then join him in Nigeria.[47] Had Frank been married to a Chinese woman, it is unlikely that she would have joined Frank in Nigeria and therefore Frank would not have been able to salvage any of his goods nor ever have seen his son again. The issue of re-entering China under a different name is a very serious problem in Guangzhou, which will be discussed in more detail in the section on 'African men and Chinese women.'

Returning to the issue of the Beijing Olympics, this major historical event marked a watershed in the history of African traders in Guangzhou, although at the time all foreigners were affected.[48] According to Mr Nwoso, the Chinese government was afraid that foreigners in general might become involved in criminal activities that would disrupt the games, so new immigration measures were put in place to prevent this from happening. The impact of these measures on African traders was devastating.[49]

One day I was waiting for Mr Sam, whom I had asked to compile the history of the first African traders to come to Guangzhou in modern times. He took the task seriously and the day we were scheduled to meet, Mr Sam was very late. I kept calling to find out when I could expect his arrival at Bole Market and he pleaded with me to wait for him. Finally, when he arrived, I asked what took him so long, and thus he began to tell the story of the effort by the Guangzhou government to remove as many African residents of Chocolate City as possible on the eve of the Olympics. I had thought that Mr Sam lived in Chocolate City. Instead, as part of an agreement with the government, he had to move to one of the surrounding cities in order to maintain his status as a trader in Chocolate City, so his journey each day into the city is long and arduous. Mr Sam says the story started in 2008:

A Chinese female agent gave us fake visas. She collected our passports and ran away with them. Then the police rounded us up and forced us to leave Guangzhou. Lots of people therefore no longer live in the city. They broke our doors down and took all our possessions. So all we had were the clothes on our backs.[50]

In 2009, Hélène Le Bail wrote that although illegal immigrants were tolerated for many years, six months prior to the 2008 Olympic Games tougher measures were put in place to arrest illegal residents. Specifically with respect to Nigerians, she notes:

> Last August, it was said that 3000 Nigerians were imprisoned, some of them suffered maltreatment, the number of deaths in the prisons that are covered-up is also preoccupying. What is widely known is that those African [sic] who died trying to escape the police, did so out of fear of being physically abused. (Le Bail 2009: 19)

Noting the problems the African business community faced during the Olympics, journalist Tongkeh Joseph Fowale reported that 'business almost came to a complete halt because of the complete absence of possibilities to obtain or extend visas. Because of this situation, many Africans were left with expired visas and sank underground where many still remain and operate as "overstayers"' (Fowale 2009).

Mr Nwoso, one of the most successful African traders in Chocolate City, shared his story about being deported before the Olympics:

> You have to get a visa for a specific place and that place has to be your place of employment. So because many people went to Beijing to get visas, they checked my visa while I was in Beijing. I had a Beijing visa and my place of employment was Guangzhou, so they sent me home, as they did with a lot of Africans. It was impossible for me to get a visa in Guangzhou. Guangzhou is a 'no-go' area.[51]

He continued:

> In order to get your visa renewed, contacts are extremely important. I currently have a Yiwu visa. So I have to maintain an office in Yiwu as well as a house. I have to have the same here in Guangzhou. So each year, including my visa, it cost me 80,000 RMB to run my business. And this is for a temporary residency visa. If you have the wrong contact, then you will get a fake visa. And the authorities will come after you. You cannot get your papers in order to get a successful visa without an agent. You must hire an agent. So the Chinese are making money off this process. You cannot meet the visa requirements without a Chinese agent. The wrong agent might mean your visa is not extended.[52]

As Yang Yang notes, African traders continued to be targets of the authorities at the time of the Asian Games of 2010, which were held in Guangzhou. The police raids in the African markets and residential areas became so frequent against those with illegal as well as legal visas that people had to determine the quickest way to escape from buildings. The police, she notes, would 'sometimes just arrest anyone with black skin' (2012: 168).

It was a year after the Beijing Olympics, on 15 July 2009, that the now in-famous incident that created a great deal of turmoil in the African community took place in Guangzhou. The situation involved two Nigerians who were running from the police to escape checkpoints for passports. They jumped from a building and one was so seriously injured people thought he was dead. As a result, hundreds of Africans gathered at a local police station to protest against what they deemed to be racial profiling by the police. This incident gained widespread media attention (Cheng 2011: 566; see also Coloma 2010a; Bodomo 2010: 696–9; Pomfret 2009; Schiller 2009).

Following this incident, Abou Kabba noted that 'the raids started again ... My wife opened the door to the police who wanted to see our visas, but I had their papers with me. The policemen started shouting at my children, who were in tears, telling them they'd go to prison – even though my family is registered with the immigration authorities. They knew our papers were in order' (as quoted in Coloma 2010a). There exists a great deal of corruption in the visa industry in China (Rennie 2010: 390–1), as well as a tremendous amount of harassment of Africans, with the police demanding at any time that they produce their passports with a valid visa (Bodomo and Ma 2010).

Then, before the Asian Games in 2010, the authorities forced a lot of Africans to leave, as Mr Bah recounts. 'They just busted down the door of people's apartments and if you didn't have legal papers they would take your stuff and deport you.'[53] According to three Nigerian traders interviewed:

> Traffic police spend their time breaking down doors trying to determine if you are here legally or not. They treat us like we are fools; arresting and beating us like we are fools. They beat us with iron. A lot of Nigerians are in the hospital as a result of these beatings [one gentleman showed how he had been stabbed by the police]. They do it to the women too. The traffic police are members of the Mafia and are thieves. Police break into your residency when you are not there. All these things are happening in many places here.[54]

After hearing these stories I asked the three Nigerians why they were still in China.

> They refuse to issue visas for us to leave and go back home. A lot of people are frustrated – once you've overstayed you must pay a fine. Otherwise you might end up in a cell for one year or more. For overstaying your visa restrictions it is 500 RMB per day. The ultimate charge is 5,000 RMB. Then if you can't pay they put you in jail. Then your family or a friend has to pay the overstay charge along with a ticket back home.[55]

Mr Nwoso suggests that the real reason they are still in Guangzhou is because it's better than being at home.[56]

Mr Ojukwu Emma, head of the Association of the Nigerian Community in Guangzhou, often has to go to the hospital to deal with paperwork relating to Nigerians who have been injured fleeing immigration police. He reported that there have been many cases of people fleeing the police by jumping off balconies and breaking their legs. In addition, in 2009 he estimated that there were two hundred Nigerians in jail waiting to be deported and that the government was sending ten to twenty Nigerians home each week (Osnos 2009; see also Haugen 2012: 9).

In a follow-up interview with Mr Emma in May 2013 he admitted there is no way of knowing how many Africans have been arrested in Guangzhou.

> There is no way to know the numbers of people detained or arrested, or sent back to their countries. It is impossible to talk to immigration. No number can be correct. Even the information forwarded to embassies cannot be correct. Authorities and local police daily arrest overstayers and arrange for their deportation. They will buy a ticket for them if they stay in detention in Guangzhou for two to three months.[57]

African men and Chinese women Mr Bah has many opinions about many things in China, including marriage to Chinese women: 'Chinese women only know money. And if you try and hide it from them, they will call the police and have you deported. I am married to a Chinese woman because she got pregnant (in essence I got "caught"). And they will slap you, these Chinese women, but my wife has learned that it is not a good idea to slap me.'[58]

At least in public Mr Bah, his wife, and their beautiful mixed-race daughter seem to be a happy family. While I had the opportunity to talk to Mr Bah on several occasions, I was always disappointed when I returned to the Overseas Trading Mall located next to the Denfeng Hotel near Xia Tang West Road and his shop was closed. I would often see his daughter in the care of a Chinese woman. When I interviewed Mr Bah in May 2011, he said things were not going too well financially.

The most controversial subject among African traders is marriages/relationships between African men and Chinese women. As I continued to discuss this issue during my trip to Guangzhou in 2013, I realized that consensus was impossible. I was able to gather, however, that there are three overarching opinions on the subject.

The first is that such marriages, specifically between Nigerian men and Chinese women, grow out of romantic love. According to Yu Qui, a PhD candidate at Cambridge University who is writing her dissertation on such relationships:

> Many say African men are more sexy and attractive than Chinese men and much more assertive. The first day they will say I love you and/or I want to marry you. So Chinese women become very curious. Nigerians will be more straightforward. Nigerians are praying every day for God to give him this woman, so the women are impressed.[59]

Is it true, I asked Qui, that Chinese women only want money?

It is true that so many want material things and marry for money. Many of these women are in their twenties and are sexy and beautiful, but don't have money. The second type of woman is one who has everything, sometimes including a husband, but she still wants an African man. There are some serious tragedies out of these situations.[60]

In response to the question about Chinese women beating African men, Qui noted the following: 'Chinese girls beat their husbands and boyfriends. Chinese men accept this. This is part of the culture. It is normal for Chinese women to beat their husbands/boyfriends on the streets. This is because Chinese women want to be number one.'[61]

Such beatings take place over trivial things. This culture of beating men, however, becomes problematic when Chinese women get involved with African men. In fact, Qui identifies several conflicts that arise in marriages/relationships between African men and Chinese women, including education (what kind of school the children should go to), nutrition, language, and the degree of freedom that children should have.[62] Ninety-nine percent of in-laws, according to Qui, are against these marriages.

The children of these mixed marriages/relationships have to go to school and both mother and child experience a great deal of racial discrimination. Most of the discrimination comes from the parents of the children's classmates.[63] Even more problems are created if the marriage is not legal. It is 'only legal when the potential husband's papers are in order. If the husband is not legal, then they can't officially marry.'[64]

A case in point is Mr Bah's marriage. Since Mr Bah is a triple illegal, his marriage to his Chinese wife is not legal. They now have two daughters. With the one-child policy, the first daughter is considered to be legal and has all the rights accorded to a Chinese citizen. The second daughter, however, is not legal because Mr Bah and his wife have not paid the fine to have a second child. According to the Chinese constitution, 'If the fine is not paid, the child has no legal identity.'[65]

As previously noted, in 2012 Mr Bah bought a ticket for his first wife to join him in Guangzhou and they now have a baby girl. So Mr Bah is the father of three girls in Guangzhou. His eldest daughter distinguishes between her younger sisters by calling them the 'white' one and the 'chocolate' one. As per Muslim culture, Mr Bah divides his time equally between his two households. Mr Bah has complicated the non-hegemonic, illegal world he lives in.

There is too much stress having two wives. Three months ago my Chinese wife got mad at me and told me that I give all the money to my African wife. She called the police on me. So I left and slept on the street because of my lack of documentation. The police came that night looking for me, but they never returned. They would have deported me if they had found me in the house the night before. I went home the next day. We are always quarreling. She was mad because I brought my first wife from Africa.[66]

He continues:

My Chinese wife was working in a supermarket and so I brought her into the trading business. Our marriage is not legal. The first child is legal. The second is not legal because of the one-child policy. She can't go to school because she doesn't have proper documentation. They want to fine us 50,000 RMB for having a second child. This would be the case even if the marriage was legal.[67]

Although Mr Bah admits that he really loves his Chinese wife, he says he would never marry a Chinese woman again.

Black women know the meaning of taking care of a husband. They cook for you, wash your clothes. African women are number one. If you want safety, marry a black woman. The Chinese wife only wants money. Every day she shouts and tells me I am a lazy man and I don't work hard. I love her so much, but it's very frustrating. If you have money, my Chinese wife will do everything. If there is money, there is honey. No money, no honey.[68]

Mr Emma, the leader of the Nigerian community, says the problem with these marriages stems from cultural differences, and so one of his missions is to build happy families. In this regard he has established the 'Nigerian–Chinese Family Forum.' He notes that 'many African men are happy with their Chinese wives.' But Chinese women have to be taught about African culture.[69] The most interesting aspect of Emma's Family Forum is that it brings together only the men who are married to Chinese women. The wives are excluded. My efforts to meet with the forum participants were rejected, although such meetings take place every Tuesday evening.

As part of Mr Emma's attempt to create happy families, he is working directly with Chinese officials to get the government to allow the families of mixed-raced couples to be reunited. There is a serious crisis among many of these families, and it usually has its origin in African men who have left Guangzhou and returned under a different name and with a different passport, as in the case of Frank. Again, this is a criminal offense. According to Emma:

Often upon returning they marry and have children. They end up with a Chinese marriage visa. When the authorities find out they have entered under a new passport they deport them. This poses a serious problem to the family structure. Unless resolved, children never see their fathers again. While we have some success in getting some Africans returned, this is not enough. We need to get all fathers returned.[70]

Whether these marriages are out of love or, as Mr Nwoso calls them, 'marriages of convenience,'[71] life for many African traders can become much more complicated as these traders try to realize, as Mr Nwoso says, 'their American dreams in China.'

African criminals in Guangzhou and illicit drug trafficking According to Mr Sam from Nigeria, unfortunately not all the newcomers who came to Guangzhou in the early 1990s were upstanding gentlemen, and some brought with them drugs to add to those ones already in circulation. Mr Sam notes that the majority of men who were buying drugs during this period were from the police and the Chinese mafia. The police would make friends with the Nigerians and allegedly give them drugs to sell. In essence, they would share drugs with the Nigerians.[72] In a 1998 report entitled *Economic and Social Consequences of Drug Abuse and Illicit Trafficking* prepared by the United Nations International Drug Control Programme (UNDCP), it was reported that in 1995 China was a major distributor of heroin to customers in the United States and increasingly African countries were being used for the transshipment of such goods (UNDCP 1998). According to Mr Sam, at that time the Chinese drug dealers were called 'ghosts' and those who brought drugs into China were called 'birds.' These early years partially laid the foundation for the current discontent among Nigerians, and especially with the Chinese police. Many Nigerians in Chocolate City feel that all Chinese think Nigerians are drug dealers and so the price Nigerians must pay, financially, physically, and emotionally, to operate trading posts and remain in this part of the world appears to be excessive.[73]

In response to the many problems Nigerians face in Chocolate City/Guangzhou, Mr Emma 'believes that his people have created their own image problem they need to fix' (as quoted in Osnos 2009). However, with so many Africans jumping off balconies and doing other harmful things to themselves to escape immigration police, in November 2009 Emma was able to sign an 'amnesty agreement.' It was signed with the local government and stipulates that an African who is illegal in Guangzhou and gives himself up to immigration authorities can leave China. This is the case as long as they have the money to buy a plane ticket home. Under these circumstances the traders can return legally to Guangzhou. Those who don't have the money to buy a plane ticket home, however, are likely to be sent to prison and allegedly some are forced to work in state factories. Again, no one apparently knows how many Africans are in prisons in Guangzhou (Coloma 2010a).

Mr Nwoso from Nigeria has his own opinion about the plight of his people in Chocolate City. He notes:

They [the Chinese] study Nigerians well. They keep them on a tight rope so they won't commit crimes. Yes, Nigerians are profiled in Guangzhou. The crime that Nigerians commit is drug trafficking. There are lots of Nigerians in jail in this city for drugs. On the issue of beatings – Nigerians are lousy people. They are out drinking and are very loud. The Communist Police [see below] are called in. If you are caught with an illegal passport you are finished. They will beat you and take you to jail. They will also break into your apartment to determine if you have a legal passport. If you don't, again they will beat you.[74]

In 2009, the Nigerian ambassador to China harshly criticized Nigerians for the crimes they commit in China (Haugen 2012: 11).

On the question of Nigerians being in Guangzhou illegally, Mr Nwoso reinforces what is already known, namely that it is only possible initially to get a visa for thirty days. To extend a Nigerian visa for someone in the city legally would cost US$6,200 per year. Nigerians who don't want any problems go home and return with a passport from another country, such as Ghana. With a passport from Ghana, it costs US$2,800 for the annual renewal. Most Nigerians are in Chocolate City/Guangzhou on illegal passports. When asked about the question of documentation, Mr Nwoso noted that

Since I have been here there has been a group of police known as the 'Communist Police'; they are the first respondents. The government pays their salaries and sees them as legitimate. They give the police information. They report to the real police. They know it's good business, for example, to catch an illegal Nigerian. If you are here illegally the cost of overstaying your visa starts at 500 RMB, with the maximum being 5,000 RMB. So if they catch an illegal Nigerian they will likely bribe him for the 5,000 RMB. This is an alternative to being turned over to the real police. They just stop you on the road and ask for your passport. So the Nigerian will pay the bribe which gives him more time to be here. This might give the illegal Nigerian extra time – from three months to a year. They might not be stopped again for a while.[75]

According to Mr Nwoso, in the old days, if a person was caught by the real police and was illegal, they had to go to jail for a month, but now they just have to pay the fine and leave the country. There is no choice but to leave the country. However, most want to make money before they leave. Many return, however, on another country's passport.[76]

While the production of illegal passports is big business in Africa, the Chinese government has made it more difficult for overstayers to return to China. Specifically, in 2010, the government began installing biometric screening at the airport in Guangzhou. Thus Haugen argues that, depending on how efficient the system becomes, it may be impossible for illegals to re-enter the country under a different passport (ibid.: 11). Again, Frank, who first entered China on a Nigerian passport and later re-entered under a passport from Sierra Leone, is a case in point. Although it took several years for immigration to discover this criminal offense, when it was discovered he was immediately deported back to Nigeria.

Mr Nwoso believes that the major reason for unemployment in Nigeria is China. 'The Chinese saw an opportunity and they seized upon it. They are so fortunate that Africa is not organized. The only industry that Nigeria still has an advantage in is the movie industry. However, because the Chinese are making these illegal DVDs with thirty-two movies in one, gradually the movie industry will collapse.'[77]

'Most Africans have come here as middlemen. It's difficult for an African to invest in China. The only Africans that can invest here are rich Africans,' according to Mr Nwoso. Fundamentally, he sees 'China is a prison without a wall.' And because there is no social life here, African men marry Chinese women. He feels that 'everything is fake; either you are going to cheat someone or someone is going to cheat you.' Again, these are some of the perils of operating in the non-hegemonic world of globalization from below.

The question that is raised here is if the Chinese really are not happy with the African presence in the country, why don't they just give them an exit visa to return home instead of keeping them in the country, especially if they know that 95 percent of them are illegal? The only obvious explanation is that since they make such a tremendous contribution to the economy of the country, including indirectly through guaranteeing employment for many Chinese workers, it is in China's best interests economically to have a strong African presence, especially in places like Guangzhou. Mr Nwoso definitely agrees with this assessment, especially in light of the fact that China is not able to compete with a country like Turkey, which has a better market for textiles and other things. While he feels that China will continue for some time to remain the world's work factory, he notes that African traders have already begun to bypass China to fulfill their entrepreneurial aspirations in places like Turkey, Bangladesh, and Vietnam.[78]

Chocolate City at night Frank, the Nigerian who was deported back to his country from Macau, agreed to show me a bit of night life in Chocolate City in 2011. Most of the Africans have left their families back home, so there is not much to do after a long day of work.[79]

As the sun goes down we take a short walk from Tangqi Market to where the traders relax at the end of the day. Some are traders who actually live and work in the area and some are merchants who have come for their monthly or bimonthly visit to restock their shops back home. We sit down at a designated table and as Frank's friends arrive they crowd around the table and I buy the beers. We are now in the midst of the cheapest accommodation possible in Chocolate City. It is the hub of the place, where you can rent a room for as little as US$10 a night. Though I was not able to see a room, Frank assured me they were clean and habitable.

Unfortunately, it is after several beers that often serious confrontations erupt between Africans and the police. 'One bad move and the police are beating Africans, demanding to see their passports, which is a crime to not have with you at any time in Guangzhou. If the African attempts to defend himself against the police, he will likely find himself in a jail,'[80] Frank informs us.

And there is a dark side to night life in Chocolate City as well – prostitution. There is a syndicate of prostitutes controlled by two women from Uganda. In fact, the situation is so bad that the Ugandan government is currently trying to do something to rectify the problem. Ugandan women are sent to Chocolate City by the ringleaders of the syndicate, thinking there are legal working opportunities in Guangzhou. Once they arrive, they are put to work as prostitutes to pay back the madams who organized their ticket to Guangzhou. Many of these young women get involved with Nigerian men who make many promises to them. Some end up transshipping drugs for these men to other parts of Asia. Some get caught and are prosecuted while others continue their trade in their newly found countries of residence. Why does the Chinese government allow this prostitution to go on? 'Because it's all about money,' argues Mr Ali from Uganda. 'The prostitutes have to stay in hotels and pay taxes.'[81]

Technically prostitution is illegal in China, according to Title 30 of the Regulations of the PRC on Administration Penalties for Public Security (1986). The practice itself is deemed to be a misdemeanor and a person caught usually faces several potential punishments, as long as they don't have a serious venereal disease or a minor under the age of fourteen is not involved, and there is no physical violence or injury. The punishments include a warning; a fine that could be as high as 5,000 yuan; signing a statement of repentance; re-education through labor; or a fifteen-day prison sentence. For the most part, however, owing allegedly to the high unemployment level in China, prostitution is tolerated. It has been estimated that there are at least ten million prostitutes in China and they contribute as much as 5 percent to the country's GDP (Foreign Teachers Guide to Living and Working in China n.d.).

Chinese racism against blacks The issue of racism against Africans is a huge issue in China, and most traders interviewed indicated that they felt the Chinese were very racist. In fact, the issue of Africans being called 'black devils' or 'monkeys' followed me wherever I went in Guangzhou. The racial tension was so overwhelming that I imagined being back in the United States during the Civil Rights era.

Immediately upon arriving at the train station in Guangzhou from Hong Kong, the Chinese were directed to go one way and I another. My luggage was put through the normal security machines at two different places and then finally opened. I found myself hearing the voice of a Chinese woman singing to me, 'Mangoes, mangoes, where are the mangoes?' Shocked, I looked at her and said, 'What mangoes?' To her dismay, no mangoes were to be found in my luggage, so I quickly gathered my things and moved as fast as I could away from what was to become a recurrent nightmare for me – being black in Guangzhou.

My research assistant told me the many stories of being called 'black devil' in Guangzhou and showed me a website that recruits 'white only' English-speaking teachers. Learning English is a serious issue in Guangzhou, made evident by the fact that there is a school in the heart of the city called 'Learning to Speak Wall Street English.' After receiving her first degree from a university in Guangzhou, my research assistant felt she would have no problems getting a job teaching English since she was fluent in Mandarin. On the first day of a two-week assignment, as she entered the class, the students started shouting in Mandarin, 'Help, help, black devil!' At the time of writing, the website that recruits only white teachers was easily accessible and the last line said the following: 'PS: A foreigner whose nationality is from British, Holland or other Europe countries white skin candidate [sic] are willing to work in GZ city is welcome!'

Although there have been periods during which the Chinese government has recruited Africans to teach English, this practice has declined as a result of the worldwide financial crisis. While African teachers were always those hired as a last resort, since the financial crisis more white teachers from around the world have migrated to China to teach. For the Chinese, these are the teachers of preference. To the extent that African teachers are employed they continue to face many obstacles, including racial discrimination and getting visas extended. Many Africans' hopes for a better life have been shattered upon arriving in Guangzhou and not being able to secure teaching jobs (Fowale 2009). Fowale notes that those who are hired to teach often find that children 'block their nostrils to avoid the stench from the black African' (Fowale 2008). In addition schoolkids, upon seeing a black person, hide under their desks. The perception of Africans, which Fowale says is passed down to the children from adults, is that they hail from a jungle without any modern facilities (e.g. infrastructure, modern homes) and that they are black either because the jungle is too hot or because they don't bathe. Chinese, Fowale comments, as a result of the images of Africans they see on TV, have concluded that in Africa there is widespread hunger, unending disasters, and carnage. In terms of African migrants to China, it has basically become a monolithic doctrine that they are 'incompetent and unworthy to take up positions in the four walls of Chinese classrooms' (ibid.).

The idea of foreigners being 'devils' is not new in China. And as Osnos notes, China has a long history of racism with typologies of race being ingrained in traditional Chinese thinking. A fourth-century BC text called the Zuozhuan noted that 'If he is not of our race, he is sure to have a different mind.' Those who were fair skinned reflected beauty and intelligence while the 'black-headed people' were those who toiled in the sun. Chinese writers likened Africa 'to hundun, a folkloric primeval chaos.' Osnos notes that, even at the turn of the twentieth century, scientific racism was promoted enthusiastically, major Chinese philosophers reinforcing the notion that white and yellow people were superior and that the blacks, who were 'monstrously ugly,' should be whitened by diet changes, sterilization, and intermarriage (Osnos 2009).

The nature of the racism against blacks took on a new dimension in December 1988 (Christmas Eve) in what is known as the 'Nanijing' incident. This occurred when two African students were in the process of bringing Chinese girls into their dorms. Enraged by this action, the Chinese gatekeeper entered into a serious dispute with the African men which resulted in a melee with several thousand Chinese students. The government ended up evacuating African students from the campus as well as the city. According to Yinghong Cheng, '[t]he intense racial hatred was reflected in slogans such as "Down with the niggers!", "Niggers go the hell home" and "Niggers! Kill the niggers!"' (Cheng 2011: 562). Twenty-one years later, a similar level of vitriolic language was expressed by some Chinese towards Africans.

'It is a racial invasion!'; 'Public safety is gone!'; 'Are they becoming the 57th ethnic group?' (officially the government identifies 56 ethnic groups in China); 'China is not a camp for refugees; our resources are already scant'; 'Not obeying law and order is their nature, not to mention their body odour!'; 'Go home you African dogs! You are here only to share our businesses and our women!' Comments concerning interracial marriages (extremely rare) between blacks and Chinese revealed the persistence of the discourse of race constructed in the 19th century. They called for 'defending racial stock'. (Ibid.: 567)

In terms of interracial marriages, cyber discussions, according to Cheng, have attacked Chinese women for marrying African men, saying they are bringing shame to China and their ancestors because they are sleeping with smelly and ugly black men (ibid.: 567). They go even farther in saying that

African blacks are an inferior race. Children of Chinese and African blacks should be regarded as mixed but inferior race. If we take no action, this kind of race will blacken China. This has nothing to do with racial discrimination, but simply a matter of eugenics. We should admit that the white is a superior race, the same as us. The children of whites and Chinese are accordingly relatively superior. (Ibid.: 557)

What is most interesting about this debate, which Cheng says is taking place in cyberspace among Chinese who have spent a considerable amount of time in Africa, is that some of the 'netizens' feel 'it is wrong for Africans to create social problems in Chinese cities and impede China's actions in Africa' (ibid.: 561).

African trading posts, transnational spaces, and the immigrant community as a bridge to the host community: a critical analysis

There is no question that the traders in this chapter have created a trading post in Chocolate City/Guangzhou. It consists of longer-established traders who migrated from other trading posts such as Dubai and numerous Asian countries before settling in China (especially Guangzhou), as well as younger/ less experienced traders who migrated directly from sub-Saharan Africa. Most of them seem to have links with merchants who travel from Africa to buy goods as well as clientele from other parts of the world to whom they supply goods. For the most part, such goods are sent to Africa, but others have clientele in the USA, Canada, and Europe. They negotiate deals for merchandise with the locals, either directly from the factories or through an intermediary. As Bertoncello and Bredeloup note, many of the traders have experienced disappointment with the Chinese goods that are produced. It's clear, however, that some African traders export to Africa cheaper Chinese goods, while others have found where the more expensive and better-quality goods are. Fundamentally, they export to Africa what their respective clientele and circulating merchants request. It is very evident that these African traders do make a contribution to the economic development of China by paying taxes, employing local Chinese, and through the transformation of the areas they work and live in.

This being said, a major question to be raised might be how will the 'nomads' (Bertoncello and Bredeloup 2007: 101) make the transition to the next trading post if in fact most are triple illegals and can't pay the fines to leave the country? One of the freedoms that the African trading nomads have had to date is the freedom to leave when greener pastures present themselves. Will China finally reform its immigration policies to let them go to the next trading post, or will they decide to keep them there long after they have achieved their economic aspirations or not realized them at all? The reason that China might want Africans to stay is because in places like Guangzhou they keep the economy going with thousands of containers of goods being shipped to Africa annually. Abou Kabba, who is from Guinea and holds a PhD in organic chemistry, notes that many young Africans see Guangzhou as merely the staging post or stopover on their way to Toyko or Europe. As triple illegals, however, their entrepreneurial desires may not be realized. The integration of China into the world economy has definitely come at a heavy price for African traders/entrepreneurs (Coloma 2010a).

The reasons why Africans have migrated to Chocolate City/Guangzhou are the same that have forced Africans to migrate to other parts of the world. These include economic decline, brutal dictators, lack of human rights in their respective countries of origin, unemployment, lack of educational opportunities, seeking political asylum, and Africa's peripheral status within the world economy. In the final analysis, whatever brought these traders to Chocolate

City/Guangzhou, they have humanized for us what it means to be a trader in this part of the world.

These men are not just invisible objects that for good or bad make sure that items from clothing to furniture to machinery are transported to Africa and other parts of the world. Instead, we can see them as individuals who struggle on a daily basis to make a living in an environment that for the most part is hostile to their existence. These are African traders/entrepreneurs who have migrated to a place that offers opportunities to expand their trading networks, but at the same time prevents them from being free to realize their maximum potential as 'triple illegals' living in a 'prison without walls.' As Bill Schiller notes, the impact the police raids have on these triple illegals is insufferable. 'People are being detained for three, four, six months at a time before they can pay their 5,000 yuan fines. Then if they're released they face the cost of a $2,000 (US) air ticket home. No one can afford that' (Schiller 2009). In addition, as evidenced by these interviews, the psychological trauma is unrelenting.

It is doubtful that when they began the long journey to Guangzhou they could have imagined they would be living a life wondering each day whether they would be arrested, deported, or beaten by the police. The African traders are thus paying a heavy price for the opportunity to be in a place that offers entrepreneurial opportunity but very limited political freedom. As Bertoncello and Bredeloup note:

> People believed that China, it [sic] was going to be easy, that they were going to get everything and then all of a sudden they saw the difficulties ... In December 2006, there was supposed to be a total opening-up: up to now, services like the banks, for example, have been a closed sector for foreigners ... Trading is still very limited for foreigners. It is easier to open a factory than to do business in China ... It is the big African businesspeople who can get the capital that's needed; some Senegalese have a factory for producing real wax in a province next to Shanghai and they have set up their office in Guangzhou, nearby, in another building. (2007: 100)[82]

Is this China's way of colonizing Africa's children by making it very difficult for Africans who want to leave to secure an exit visa? Haugen notes that requiring an exit visa 'distinguishes China from the U.S. and most of Europe,' although it is not unique. The requirement for exit visas can be found in the Middle East, and in Singapore migrants who are undocumented are caned in addition to having to serve prison terms (Haugen 2012: 12–13). Although all overstayers in China must have an exit visa, there is a disproportionate number of Africans who are in Guangzhou illegally with the knowledge of government authorities. Hence the question: why is this allowed to happen? At this juncture one can only speculate that it is because such immigrants contribute so much to Guangzhou's economy, just as the illegal immigrants in the USA contribute to the economy. There is no question that Guangzhou's economy would collapse if all the illegal African traders were sent home.

What of Li et al.'s concept that African traders have created a transnational urban space in the area known as Chocolate City, other areas of Guangzhou and the surrounding cities, where they have been forced to migrate in order to maintain their status in China? Although Li et al.'s article was published in 2009, it seems to still be relevant today, for all evidence points to the reality that the African enclave and the host community continue to experience a great deal of conflict, and continue to live separately, although they often share the same space professionally.

Symbolic of the growing divide between the host country and African migrants was the killing on 19 July 2012 of a Nigerian in police custody in Guangzhou. The problem allegedly stemmed from an argument between the Nigerian and the Chinese owner of a motorcycle over the cost of a fare. Both men were taken to the police station and about four hours later the Nigerian was dead, allegedly beaten to death by the police. Over a hundred Africans protested in the streets of Guangzhou and about three hundred police confronted the protesters (Lin 2012).

There remains much to be desired in terms of greater movement toward socialization between the African enclave in Chocolate City/Guangzhou and the host community, although numerous traders have offices outside the radius of Chocolate City and the more prosperous Africans have moved into garden apartments reserved for the elites of China.

There is no question that the foundation has been laid for the merging of parts of the African ethnic enclave, especially through interracial marriages. We have certainly seen this in the case of several traders, including Mr Kingsley, Mr Bah, Mr Baron, and Mr Emma. Though married to Chinese women, most of these men, like their counterparts who are not married to Chinese women, seem to have reservations about the utility of Bodomo's theory that the African immigrant community can serve as a bridge to their host community. The deep-seated level of Chinese racism against blacks seems to work against Bodomo's theory.

Bodomo, however, remains hopeful that in 100 years there may exist a firmly established African-Chinese ethnic group that will be demanding their full rights as citizens of places like Guangzhou (Bodomo 2010: 694). A century is a long time and a great deal can happen.

In the meantime Lyons et al. suggest that currently the situation in Guangzhou between the host community and the African community resembles an enclave rather than a 'cultural bridge,' stemming both from economic and official pressures. As the situation deteriorates between the two, Guangzhou has become more of an 'outpost' for African traders who increasingly have plans to return home. Thus only if the Chinese government lifts official economic restrictions (e.g. easing foreign currency exchange and restrictions on visa access, lifting barriers to the ability of Africans to import goods into China from Africa) can the relationship between the host community and African traders begin to flourish again (Lyons et al. 2012a: 886).

However, currently Lyons et al. feel that, based on their study of African and Chinese traders in Guangzhou, the growing wedge that exists undermines Bodomo's theory of bridge-building between the two communities (ibid.: 885). Further, 'A strong deterrent against voluntary repatriation is the risk of imprisonment for immigration offenses when one reports to the authorities to pay the fine and apply for an exit visa' (Haugen 2012: 11). This certainly complicates any attempt to establish a bridge between the two countries. Part and parcel of this is the reality that if China continues to make it extremely difficult for members of the African diaspora to obtain residency visas, they will likely become short-term migrants in Guangzhou (Lyons et al. 2012a: 872).

African traders: a concluding assessment

If we return to the two defining questions of this chapter – namely, what do African traders, through their oral histories, inform us about being entrepreneurs in Chocolate City/Guangzhou and what impact are these traders having on the lives of Africans in Africa who primarily live at the level of globalization from below – we have much to ponder. With respect to the first question, we know that for those who have the capital, are not triple illegals, and in some cases are married to Chinese women, Chocolate City/Guangzhou can be a place of business success. Chocolate City/Guangzhou can afford African entrepreneurs the opportunity to realize their full potential, make plenty of money, and live a lifestyle of comfort that is likely not possible in their home countries. And as long as they know and obey the laws of the People's Republic of China, they will be able to escape the raids and arrests suffered by their fellow Africans.

For those who are triple illegals, life in Chocolate City/Guangzhou can be very challenging, ever waiting for the sign that the police are only minutes away from arresting you or imposing fines on the precious counterfeit goods you are trying to sell (purchased from Chinese vendors). Nonetheless, many of these same triple illegals are themselves beating the system and becoming wealthy. There exists a tremendous sense of loyalty among Africans in Guangzhou, and especially among fellow countrymen and women. The traders from Africa who travel to Guangzhou monthly or bimonthly are very loyal to their fellow Africans. They make efforts to buy from them and thus ensure their economic survival. Even though African women are not present in these oral stories for reasons beyond my control,[83] their presence as buyers for the markets back home is very strong, as will be evidenced by their presence in the markets in Guangzhou and their travels to China outlined in the next chapter.

What impact are these traders having on the lives of Africans in Africa who primarily live at the level of globalization from below? The answer is complex. On the one hand we can say the impact is positive. They are exporting to Africa goods that are very much needed if the continent is to continue to develop and grow. The caveat, of course, is that African leaders, if they were committed to development, would long ago have invested the income accumulated from the selling of the continent's natural resources in educating their populations and creating infrastructures that would have allowed them to be competitive with the Chinese. There is no question that the lives of Africans have improved because they can buy cheap generators from China, or cheap cell phones. But the fundamental question for the future is: will Africa be better off in the final analysis by buying from the Chinese, or learning to build their own generators and make their own cell phones? As Mr Nwoso reminds us, the Chinese saw an opportunity in Africa and seized upon it. Imagine if Africans had seen an opportunity in Africa and seized upon it.

On the other hand, as we will see in the next chapter, in some cases the export of Chinese goods has resulted in deindustrialization and the under-mining of formal and informal traders. This is very serious and reflected by the wave of Africans protesting against Chinese traders and the influx of Chinese goods across the continent.

What is the future of globalization from below in Guangzhou?

Yang Yang reminds us that 'China is embarrassed by its involvement and complicity with African migrants in profiting from the production of what is probably the largest amount of fake goods in the world, which undermines its effort to build up the images of its cities as being developed and global' (2012: 168). So does this mean that globalization from below in Guangzhou has a limited future? This is not likely. African and other migrants will continue for some time to travel to Guangzhou in search of their dreams. The non-hegemonic system of operation is deeply embedded in Guangzhou, as evidenced by the very complex and sophisticated underground banking system. Chocolate City/Guangzhou is only one small area where agents from globaliza-tion from below operate. When you enter the shops of Chinese agents and pose the question of whether an item is real or fake, the shopowner replies with no hesitation, 'Fake.'

Some things are changing, however, and will continue to have an impact on African traders. Perhaps the most drastic change is the number of African traders operating in Chocolate City. 'Look around,' Mr Nwoso tells me. 'Do you see how many empty shops are here in this plaza now compared to when you were here two years ago?' Yes, I told him that I had noticed. This is, according to Mr Nwoso, because the middleman is being removed from certain aspects of the trading process, especially in the area of electronics and furniture. So there are no jobs for these people. China has decided to use the internet to advertise these products. So if you want to buy them, you no longer have to come directly to China and work with an African trader (the middleman). Instead you just go on the internet, place your order and send the money to a relatively new system called 'Less Easy Cash' and the money will go directly to the supplying company. The Chinese are taking this process very seriously, so if you commit internet fraud and are caught, you can end up serving up to fifteen years in prison.[84]

A second major change is emerging from competition between the African and Chinese traders. The market has moved from cash to credit owing to the fact that competition has forced the prices down, so that the Chinese are giving credit to buyers. This transition started around 2008. For example, in the case of Nigeria, there are too many suppliers. With prices decreasing and the market reaching its capacity, Nigerians have begun to default on the loans given to them by Chinese traders. Thus tension has developed in Guangzhou at the level of globalization from below among the Chinese and African traders. Mr Nwoso feels that ultimately this system might collapse, especially because there is too much supply in Africa. In fact, the supply in Africa is so huge that it is often cheaper to buy the products in Africa than in Guangzhou.[85] Clearly in some cases it is no longer cost-effective to come to Guangzhou, buy goods for the market in Africa, and then try to make a profit.

A final factor that is changing the dynamics of globalization from below in Guangzhou for African traders is that China is not remaining competitive in the textile industry. In this regard, Mr Nwoso notes that the Chinese government charges huge tariffs on cloth that is imported into China. Such cloth is better than that produced in China and is needed in order to make higher-quality textiles. Turkey, on the other hand, encourages such imports, and exporters of goods receive a rebate. And just as China is no longer competitive in textile production, it is also not competitive with respect to labor. The costs are too high compared to other countries. For African traders, this means that many are now bypassing Guangzhou and moving to Turkey, Vietnam, and Bangladesh to do business.[86]

Given the above, the future for the newer African traders seemingly lies outside of Guangzhou. Perhaps one day in the near future scholars will be writing about African traders establishing trading posts in Turkey, Vietnam, and Bangladesh and assessing the implications for globalization from below.

3 | The non-hegemonic world of Africa–China trade

China is not a bright alternative because there is no free money anywhere in the world. They are aggressive and determined to get it. They are not in love with Africa. For example, if you buy a TV from China you are lucky if it doesn't blast in your face. The government is still stuck with the mortar and brick mentality. It is not like the Chinese are the only ones who know how to build roads, etc. Ghanaian politicians are just eager to show to their people what they've done. Politicians are in bed with the Chinese.[1]

The above statement was made by the Director of Multilateral, Regional and Bilateral Trade, Ministry of Trade and Industry, Accra, Ghana, during an interview on 22 March 2011. Since this statement, a great deal has transpired on the ground, with growing hostility against Chinese traders across the continent. For example, on 21 August 2012, hundreds of African traders from different parts of the city took to the streets of Nairobi, Kenya, in an anti-Chinese protest march. Their grievance was what they deem to be unfair competition from Chinese traders. Reporting for NTV, Mashirima Kapombe noted that 'the traders want the government to stop the Chinese from taking part in business and instead concentrate on construction work' (YouTube n.d.). The traders called for the removal of Chinese businesses from the city. One trader interviewed said that 'My business has gone by over 60 percent since the Chinese came. So we are here to put our foot down as traders and to convince the government that something needs to be done about these people' (ibid.). In addition to accusing the Chinese of unfair trading, they also said they were creating unemployment. As a result of the demonstrations, shops were forced to close to prevent looting. The traders submitted a petition to members of parliament after the prime minister refused to give them an audience (ibid.).

In early July 2012, in Malawi, the Ministry of Industry and Trade sent out a directive indicating that by 31 July all Chinese traders who owned shops in the rural areas of the country had to move their business to cities. This decree was issued because it was determined that Malawian traders could not fairly compete with Chinese retail traders (Malawi News Agency, 5 July 2012). The decree, which is an investment and export promotion bill, allows the Chinese traders to operate only in the four major cities of the country – Blantyre, Lilongwe, Zomba, and Mzuzu. The decree was issued following May meetings with local government authorities and Malawian traders in some rural areas. Protests against the traders took place in twenty-eight districts in Malawi (Ngozo 2012).

One of the traders, Ellen Mwagonba, who has had a grocery store in Karonga since 2003, indicated that her sales started to plummet in 2008 when the Chinese arrived. 'This place is a hive of activity since it is a border area. Business used to be good until the Chinese invaded us, bringing cheap goods and taking away our customers.'

In response to the decree, two civil rights organizations in the country have argued that the government should not victimize foreign traders. 'We are worried about the increasing xenophobic sentiments and attacks on foreign nationals who are doing business across the country,' noted the executive director of the Centre for Human Rights and Rehabilitation (ibid.). Not all the locals in the rural areas are happy with the decree, however, since the Chinese goods are cheaper and they do provide some employment for locals (Malawi News Agency, 5 July 2012).

The opposition to Chinese traders is at both the macro and micro levels. In yet another region of Africa, Senegalese leather slipper makers have refused to sell their pointy-toed slippers to Chinese traders. It took generations for the cobblers in the town of Ngaye Mekhe (referred to as Senegal's shoe capital) to perfect the shoes, which were once a must for local kings and are today considered 'an indispensable fashion accessory for well-dressed Senegalese men' (CallimacHi 2012). But it only took several months for the Chinese to reproduce the shoes using plastic and sell them for one quarter the price of the leather slippers. Since the government of Senegal has refused to stop the flooding of the market with the Chinese replicas, the most prominent makers of the original slippers are fighting back by refusing to sell the slippers to any Chinese. Mactar Gueye, one of the prominent shoemakers, says that when he sees a Chinese person he puts his hand up with his palm open to gesture stop. He says, 'It's not that I'm afraid of them. I just won't sell to them' (ibid.).

But none of that above compares to the 2013 repatriation by the Ghanaian government of thousands of Chinese immigrants who had been involved in illegal gold mining in the country. In the non-hegemonic world of globalization from below, these miners had entered the country illegally, most out of extreme desperation, to fulfill their economic aspirations in Ghana. The rising conflict between Ghanaian miners, who were also attempting to fulfill their economic aspirations, resulted in the Ghanaian government involvement in the crisis. In this particular case we learn a great deal about the perils of operating in the non-hegemonic world (see below).

This chapter, like the previous one, is primarily about globalization from below. In this regard, it seeks to explain and try to understand the impact of the invasion by the Chinese of the informal trading sector of African countries.

Millions of Africans are self-employed in this sector and are under the radar of most governmental regulatory agencies. It is here, at the level of globalization from below, that a lot of unreported financial transactions take place, where there is a great deal of poverty, and where many Africans are earning a living and, in many cases, becoming very wealthy.

The chapter explores the non-hegemonic world of globalization from below and the growing tension between agents in this world – Africans and Chinese. Our major questions to be answered are: (1) is it possible for these two agents (Africans and Chinese) to survive and thrive together at the level of globalization from below; and (2) what are the potential consequences of the growing tension, at times violent, between these two agents at this level of the global economy? By humanizing the agents, again we attempt to humanize Africa's trade regimes and to determine whether the non-hegemonic world has affected the lives of Africans in this study.

Globalization from below and African market traders

In this section we will look at successful African traders/entrepreneurs who are perceived to be very wealthy, as well as those struggling to make a living primarily selling Chinese products. We start our stories in Uganda, and then travel to Tanzania, Ghana, Zambia, and finally South Africa. With respect to South Africa, most of the traders interviewed are not South African. Rather they are traders from various parts of Africa. Asked why the textile and apparel market appears to be controlled by non-South Africans, one trader's response was that it is because most South Africans are focused on going to school and trying to get a more permanent job in South Africa.[2]

Uganda

Auntie Emily By most Ugandan standards, Auntie Emily is a millionaire. She travels once a month to China. Her favorite places to travel to buy goods are Thailand and China. The former produces much better goods than the latter, according to Auntie Emily. In her shop, while most goods are from China, for her high-end customers she has the better-made Thai clothes. Auntie Emily is not your typical African trader/merchant for it was only in the wake of retirement from a good government job that she got into the trading business.[3]

On the eve of retirement, Auntie Emily knew she was not ready to just stay home – she needed an office to go to. So in 1992 she started a small trading business, stocking her shop with goods from the region of the East African Community (EAC), mostly from Kenya. But she realized that she needed to purchase goods that people really wanted. Shortly after, she started traveling to Dubai, Thailand, China, Indonesia, and India. Auntie Emily went to India only twice because she realized the quality of Indian products was not liked by most people.[4]

Auntie Emily buys high-end goods for a middle- and upper-middle-class clientele, mostly in Kampala. So when she goes to China she makes it very clear to her contact person (who is a Chinese woman) that she wants good-quality products. She shops around, decides what she wants, and places an order. It takes three to four weeks for the order to be completed, which is one of her challenges. Then it takes another month for the goods to get to Kampala as they must pass through Mombasa port in Kenya.[5]

Auntie Emily owns two clothing shops, one she manages herself and the other under the management of one of her daughters. I visited the shop under the management of Auntie Emily and it was packed with customers. Even though she had several workers in the shop, Auntie Emily was herself extremely busy. I had her undivided attention until a woman from the DRC entered her shop to pick up an order she had made previously. Since Auntie Emily was one of the first high-end traders that I interviewed, I was surprised to learn of the deep trading connections that exist in this part of Africa. I was later to learn that such connections exist throughout the continent.

Fundamentally, the woman from the DRC could not afford to make the journey to China to buy for her clientele. The word had spread throughout the region that Auntie Emily buys high-end goods. Consequently, traders come from Uganda, Tanzania, Kenya, Rwanda, the DRC, and Burundi to buy from Auntie Emily to sell back home. These are the trading networks that cannot be captured in governmental statistical data because, even if foreign traders/merchants cross borders and declare their goods, how are they entered in trade statistics? Are their goods to be entered as from Uganda or China? Furthermore, if a person comes from Burundi, at what border are the goods declared and, again, where are they from? In addition, very often the officers at the various borders are given a bribe and so lots of merchandise is not even recorded. This is the reality of globalization from below throughout the world.

Not only does Auntie Emily stop the interview with me when the woman from the DRC enters the shop, but I find her talking in Swahili, a common language among East and Central Africans. The DRC trader leaves with three huge bags of high-end clothes to sell back home.

Many people who have studied Africa–China trade tend to believe that most of the goods that are exported to Africa from China are either very cheap or counterfeit. As Auntie Emily's shop indicates, there is a growing middle class in Africa that is demanding high-end quality goods. In fact, according to an article in the *Harvard Business Review* in May 2011, in Africa there is a significant middle class and an expectation that by 2020 the continent will have 'one of the fastest growing consumer markets of this decade' (Chironga et al. 2011: 19). Over the last decade, Africa's real GDP on average grew by 4.7 percent annually. This represents twice the rate of growth in the 1980s and 1990s. As one of the fastest-growing economic regions today, the continent's collective GDP of US$1.6 trillion by 2009 was said to be close to that of Russia's or Brazil's. During the recent global recession, Asia (excluding Japan) and Africa were the only continents that experienced growth. In 2010 Africa's growth rate was 5 percent (ibid.: 118) and remained the same in 2011. The International Monetary Fund (IMF) projected that it would have increased slightly during 2012 (*World Economic and Financial Surveys*, April 2012). So Auntie Emily's high-end clientele should not be a shock to anyone given the increasing expendable income in Africa.

Among Auntie Emily's complaints is that the Ugandan Bureau of Standards (see below) does not function effectively. She asks:

> How can we compete with the Chinese when someone buys a dress from me and takes it to China to have it duplicated? Once it is imported back into this country and washed it loses its color. The Chinese just throw us out of business because their prices are so low. When they go home to buy, they buy from the factories and thus the goods are cheaper. We have to buy from the shops, where the goods are more expensive.[6]

Auntie M. Not far from Auntie Emily's shop is that of Auntie M. Again, by Ugandan standards, Auntie M. is a very successful African trader/entrepreneur. Her clientele is different from Auntie Emily's. Auntie M. admits she imports medium-quality goods from China. She has a small closed-in kiosk in an indoor shopping mall in the Kampala market about one tenth the size of Auntie Emily's. The area around the kiosk is packed with people buying mostly jewelry. How anyone could find anything in the piles of what might be called 'bling-bling' jewelry was a mystery to me. But a great deal of money was changing hands. Auntie M. travels frequently, but to China only every three months. Other places she goes to include Dubai (because it's nearer), Bombay, India, and London. She goes to London specifically to buy little gold earrings for infants. It's the only place she can get them. Like those of Auntie Emily, her goods are imported through Mombasa port. She complains, however, that she has to pay heavy taxes once they enter Uganda. She too has buyers coming from other parts of Africa, including the DRC, Sudan (they buy a lot), Rwanda, and Burundi.[7]

Tanzania Nelson and Josephine Matemu are the owners of Lightness – Ladies, Gents & Children Wear, located in the Karikoo Market, Dar es Salaam, Tanzania. They are doing very well in the market because they import high-end Chinese products. They have clients coming from the DRC, Zimbabwe, Zambia, Malawi, and Mozambique. The Matemus are successful as entrepreneurs because they travel regularly to China to select their own goods. They feel the goods that are brought in by the Chinese are sub-standard. The goods the Matemus import are brought into the Dar es Salaam port in big containers. The only problem is that they pay high duty on imported goods owing to the fact that the Tanzanian revenue authority is effective.[8]

Everywhere one goes in Karikoo Market, one finds mostly Chinese products. But this was not always the case, according to the Matemus and others who have gathered to talk about Tanzania's imports from China. So what happened? In most African countries that once had very vibrant textile and apparel industries, structural adjustment programs (SAPs) imposed on African governments in the 1980s by the IMF and the World Bank resulted in deindustrialization and the subsequent collapse of many industries. As an integral part of the SAPs, which became known as the 'Washington Consensus' (Ha-Joon Chang 2002: 1), among other things, African governments were required to liberalize their trade regimes, allowing for the importation of competitive goods. Such liberalization over a period of years reshaped the terrain of the manufacturing industry, including increasing privatization. No longer able to compete on the international market, most companies collapsed and more efficiently produced and cheaper products replaced the heretofore locally produced textiles and apparel. Huge numbers of people lost their jobs as the industries folded.[9] Imported textiles and apparel became the norm, resulting today in most items coming from China.

In the case of Tanzania, the crowd around the Matemus' shop remembered that, around 1991, most factories closed, leaving huge numbers of people unemployed. At first the vacuum in textiles and clothing was filled by the Indians. But then, in 2005, Chinese goods started coming in to replace Indian goods.[10]

Ghana

Alice Fashion In March 2011, I visited a small, quaint clothing shop in Accra, Ghana, run by two sisters, and owned by one of them. These Ghanaian sisters were accomplished seamstresses, for thirty years sewing clothes for distinguished women. Now they wait for scarce customers to come into their shop. Alice Fashion in Makola Market has fallen on hard times with the decline of the economy. If you went upstairs in the shop, you would find a huge storage area where they have kept orders from years back that were never picked up. When I visited the shop in 2011, it had been about ten years since the sisters put down their sewing tools and started selling Chinese and Thai clothes because they could no longer make a living as seamstresses. The sister of the owner of the shop reminisced about the good old days when she and her sibling excelled at their craft of sewing for Ghanaian women using authentic Ghanaian cloth – some of the best Africa had to offer. Now her sister, she says, travels to China two to three times a year. Clothes in Ghana have become too expensive. So instead of sewing clothes for distinguished Ghanaian women, they sell finished clothes mostly from China. The owner of the shop buys only

65

upscale clothes and sells them to clients in Accra, as well as to traders who come from Nigeria, Côte d'Ivoire, Benin, Kenya, Zambia, and Sierra Leone.[11]

Ironically, shortly before the Ghanaian women stopped collecting their orders from Alice Fashion, in the late 1990s, the textile industries of Ghana began to warn about the potential collapse of the industry due to the influx of huge copies of cheap African prints from China (Axelsson 2012: 246). It is doubtful that at this time the sisters of Alice Fashion knew their fate had been sealed; that the need for their long-honed talent as seamstresses was soon to disappear. One can only imagine how devastating this must have been when they realized what was confronting them. They were aware, however, of what the Ghanaian African print industry meant to the country; namely, it 'allows for the construction of Ghana as a multi-ethnic yet unified nation and an industrializing nation-state on its way up the development ladder' (ibid.: 42), and thus what it symbolized needed to be protected against Chinese African prints (ibid.), especially those that were smuggled into the country, counterfeit, or considered to be morally unjust. In the case of those smuggled in, the Chinese African prints enter the country without the importer paying tariffs, taxes and fees that would give it legal access to the African market (ibid.: 18). Chinese African prints that are counterfeit involve 'the intentional making of copies so that they appear to have the same attributes as the original product' (ibid.: 129); and a Chinese African print regarded as morally unjust 'tries to represent itself as a real African print, when in fact it is not' (ibid.: 171). As Axelsson notes with respect to the issue of a Chinese African print being considered morally unjust, it is tantamount to exploiting the cultural heritage of Ghana (ibid.: 163).

So on behalf of the sisters of Alice Fashion, other Ghanaian traders, the employees of the textile industry, and the nation at large, the government and trade unionists have fought back in an effort to save one of the most important symbols of the nation. In November 2004, the government of Ghana 'launched the National Friday Wear Programme – an initiative that sought to encourage white-collar workers to dress in locally produced textiles, rather than formal dress' (ibid.: 161). This followed a May 2005 announcement by the then minister of trade and industry that African prints could enter only one seaport in Ghana and that all other ports of entry would be closed to such prints (ibid.: 89). On a day in July 2006, an anti-copying team arrested several traders for selling counterfeit Chinese African prints (ibid.: 127). As recently as 2012, those trading in authentic Ghanaian prints were still appealing to the government to enforce previous restrictions that had been placed on the import of African prints (ibid.: 249).

Akua B-Puni Akua B-Puni, a Ghanaian trader in textiles, learned the hard way about buying goods in China. On her very first trip she lost US$16,000 worth of goods because, once the container arrived, the goods she had ordered were not there.[12]

> You pay for quality and they will give you shoddy goods. That's why I don't
> leave now until I see what they put in my container. If there is one thing I want
> people to know it is that the Chinese are crooks. You really have to get to know
> the people well that you are working with. I now have a good Chinese that I am
> working with. It's risky, but sometimes you just have to take the risk. It takes
> years to get to know people that are reliable. If you are going for the first time
> and are not careful, you lose a lot of money. They will cheat you.[13]

Mrs B-Puni travels to China about twice a year and stays about a month. It takes about twenty-one days to produce an order, then watch them load the container.

> Originally I started going to China to buy clothes. Then I started importing
> cloth. I would take cloth from here and have it copied in China. Fabric is really
> a problem in this country. If you buy fabric in China made from African pat-
> terns it is much cheaper. For example, in Ghana you can sell two yards of fabric
> from China for 25 Ghana CDs [cedis], while for that same pattern in Ghana
> you pay 45 CDs. The latter is of better quality and softer, but most people
> can't tell the difference. With the difference in prices, people can afford to
> buy the Chinese fabric. The Ghanaian fabric is too expensive for most people.
> The problem is that one has to pay high duties on these fabrics because it is
> competing with locally produced fabric, so a great deal of smuggling goes on.
> Specifically, a lot of people have their containers shipped to the ports in the
> Ivory Coast or Togo to avoid the heavy tariffs of the government.

She continues:

> They transship the fabric by road. For example, the vehicle with the cloth in
> it might have a lot of food products and the cloth is hidden, so the customs
> official doesn't see it. The major problem with this process is that you take
> a chance on actually getting the cloth because it might be sold to someone
> else before you can actually get it. Chinese cloth is the fastest-selling cloth in
> Ghana.[14]

The details of this transshipment through Lomé, Togo, are elaborated in Axelsson (2012: 89–125).

In terms of the impact on the economy, Mrs B-Puni feels that having access to cheaper Chinese cloth is good because more people are employed as a result of more orders being placed, since people can afford the cheaper cloth. On the other hand, she admits that it has had a negative impact on the textile industry in Ghana and lots of people have lost their jobs. Ghana started importing from China in the 1990s and, though there are three textile companies that still produce, two have closed. The three that still produce are Ghana Textile Company (GTC – P); Alosombo Textiles Limited (ATL); and Printex. The latter, however, primarily produces only uniforms and black and white prints. They can no longer afford to print cloth with color. The two companies that have folded are GMTC and Juapong Textiles. With respect to the survival of the remaining companies, Mrs B-Puni feels 'the government needs to subsidize them, otherwise they will not survive.'[15]

Mrs B-Puni's decision to go into business for herself dates back to when she was in Form 6 at school and her parents separated. She was therefore left to take care of her siblings. She knew she needed to find a job that would allow her to be at home.

> So I became a seamstress and have been for seventeen years. My mother was the one who taught me about trading because she was a trader. I am now married with three children. Once I married I had to move out of the family home, but I had already set up shop there and began hiring workers to sew for me. I still have a business where women sew for me and I teach sewing as well. But I also have a shop in the market where I sell just daily things people need (e.g., candles, air fresheners).[16]

Mr Nana Yaw In Makola Market in Accra, one finds Mr Nana Yaw, who travels to China (Guangzhou) about twice a year to buy personal items. He remains in China for about three weeks and it takes about six weeks for the goods to get to Ghana. Everyone, according to Mr Yaw, gets their goods from China. He feels that the ability to import goods from China is having a positive impact on the economy in Ghana. 'There are a lot of good things imported from China,' according to Mr Yaw. He started going to China in 2004 and makes a good profit. He is able to sell cheaper products and caters to an upscale market. 'Chinese goods are cheaper and are of better quality.' By no means does Mr Yaw feel he is undermining the local industry. In fact, he feels he is contributing to Ghana's economy.[17]

With respect to the current downturn in Ghana's markets, Mr Yaw feels that SAPs caused the beginning of the decline in Ghana's manufacturing sector.

> The problem is clothes: those made in China are less expensive and often are of better quality than those produced in Ghana. At least they are of the same quality. Because of the corruption in this country things will not improve economically. Chocolates produced in Ghana cost more than chocolates imported from China, and that's even after duties are imposed. If not for China, Ghanaians would not have shoes, watches, etc.[18]

Ms Zuweratu One trader, Ms Zuweratu, knows she will not become a millionaire from selling cheap Chinese goods. She has a cart in a well-visited location in the Makola Market and says that foreigners like Ghanaian goods and Ghanaians like Chinese goods. Ms Zuweratu's cart is full of 'bling-bling' Chinese products and one can hardly get a word out of her because she is surrounded by so many buyers. She admits that all the Chinese stuff she sells is nothing but 'junk' and that it's having a negative impact on Ghana's economy. Financially Ms Zuweratu says she does OK but admits that she does not make a large profit from selling Chinese goods.[19]

Mrs LPA I am advised by some previous interviewees to check out a shop that sells women's hair. The shop, they say, is really owned by a Chinese man, but an African woman runs it. As the story goes, the Chinese owner guarantees that the shop is always well stocked, even if sales are not made. So I climb the stairs to the second floor of the outside shopping center to interview the woman in the shop. Mrs LPA agrees to the interview but does not provide much detail. She used to sell food, but the Chinese approached her about selling hair. They knew she could make money in the business, although currently trade is very slow. One of the reasons is that people don't have money. The other is that there is so much competition in this area from other shops. She sells retail and wholesale, the latter to people who have shops. Waiting to see Mrs LPA was a Chinese man whom she just referred to as a friend. He did not enter the shop until I left.[20]

Linn Axelsson and Nina Sylvanus argue that the Chinese have no shops in the Accra Market (2010: 140), which might explain the presence of the Chinese man waiting to see Mrs LPA. It is not uncommon for Chinese to find local entrepreneurs to rent shops on their behalf in countries that don't allow Chinese to have shops, or where the climate is not favorable to such shops.

Zambia A trip to COMESA (Common Market for Eastern and Southern Africa) Market in Lusaka, Zambia, did not reveal any booming millionaires, but definitely some serious traders. A Tanzanian trader who has lived in Lusaka for the last fifteen years says that

> Everything is from China. China has taken over the whole COMESA market. The Chinese are not to be blamed. We are to be blamed because we go to China to buy cheaper things. They reduce the quality of goods. If you buy goods from South Africa but made in China the quality is better than coming from China because South Africans buy better-quality goods. If you want cheaper goods from China you buy from Dar es Salaam. Where we buy from depends on what the market demands.[21]

The Chinese started coming into Zambia around 2003, according to the Tanzanian/Zambian trader. Reinforcing the previous trader's comments, the next trader interviewed in the COMESA Market acknowledged that his goods also come from either South Africa or Dar es Salaam. He has had his shop for four years and has been importing from China for the last three years. Traders come from Mozambique and Zimbabwe to buy goods from his shop. This trader laments that 'we don't have employment in this country because of China.'[22]

A third trader in the COMESA Market goes to China every three months to buy mostly goods for women and children, but admits that he doesn't have the money to stay in China after he places his order. So he has an agent who has an office in Dar (but lives in China) who makes sure the order is correct before it is shipped to him. This trader goes to China, like most we have heard from, because the goods are cheap while they are very expensive in Zambia. He buys middle-quality goods which he imports from the Dar port and most of his customers come from Zimbabwe.[23]

South Africa

Bruma Oriental City Bruma Oriental City is located in Johannesburg across from Bruma Lake, a former flea market where, until recently, one could find traders from most parts of Africa selling their arts and crafts. On the sidewalk across from Bruma Lake, you could find South African women from the Ndebele ethnic group selling their beautifully beaded dolls, jewelry, and place mats, as well as the traditional headdress for Ndebele women to wear on their wedding day. Next to these women you could find immigrants from Zimbabwe selling incredible stone carvings for just enough money to get back home to check on their families before returning to continue trying to make a living. If you crossed the road and slowly passed the vendors in front of Bruma Lake, you could buy beautiful arts and crafts from anywhere in southern or eastern Africa. These vendors, although not able to afford to have a stall inside Bruma Lake, had an advantage over those inside because you had to pass them and take a look at what they had to offer before paying the small sum of two rand to enter the flea market. Once inside the market, you were treated to an incredible assortment of arts and crafts, including some from the DRC. Indian spices were available as well as cheap textiles, clothing and music. At the inside/outside eatery, one could purchase an array of foods from all corners of the world. Finally, if you were a foreigner and needed an extra suitcase to carry home all the new items you had acquired during your day-long adventure at Bruma Lake, you could just walk across the street and buy a piece of luggage from one of the stores inside the mall.

Such an adventure is not possible today. If one takes a journey to Bruma Lake, one will find that the flea market is closed and the traders are gone. The former traders have been given a place not too far from Bruma Lake, but they are no longer outside, so you have to know where to find them. What was the flea market has been bought by a Chinese who is in the process of building a huge complex to extend Bruma Oriental City, which has replaced the mall across from what was the flea market. Oriental City is a huge inside complex with mostly Chinese vendors, selling the same goods. If you look hard enough, or in my case you have someone who has friends with stalls in Oriental City, you can find stalls of African traders who hail from different parts of the continent. On the particular day that I visited Bruma Oriental City, I was able to talk to traders from both Senegal and the DRC.

The trader from Senegal came to South Africa in 1997 for business purposes. He had previously worked in Zambezi Mall in Pretoria and had been at Bruma Oriental Mall for eleven months at the time of our interview. His brother rents the shop from the Chinese and they sell goods from both Thailand and China. He estimates that about 60 percent of their goods are from China, although the goods from Thailand are of better quality. The Senegalese trader faces serious competition from the Chinese. He and his brother get most of their stock from China City in Johannesburg, or directly from China. His brother goes directly to Guangzhou to buy his goods. If business is good he travels to Guangzhou every two to three weeks. But if business is slow, as it was when I was there in March 2012, his brother travels to Guangzhou only once a month. 'Until three months ago people came to buy from the DRC, Angola, Mozambique, Zambia, and Swaziland.'[24] During a trip to the Bruma Lake area in August 2011, I remember seeing the huge buses from the DRC and Mozambique waiting to carry the customers back to their respective countries. But in March 2012, no such buses were to be seen.

Yolande Fariab hails from Lumbashi in the DRC. She came to South Africa six years ago and has been in business in the country since her arrival. Fifty percent of her goods come from South Africa. Ms Fariab travels to China every two months to buy goods and air-freights them back to South Africa. The competition with her Chinese counterparts in Bruma Oriental City is very intense because the Chinese products are cheaper. Her clients come from the DRC, Mozambique, South Africa, Nigeria, Cameroon, and England. Sometimes they buy in bulk and they either fly back home or take the bus.[25]

'Since the ending of the World Cup business has not been that good,' notes Ms Fariab. If the exchange rate of the South African rand to the US dollar is 1 to 7, business is good, she continues. Otherwise, business declines. She is married with two children and the family plans to go back home soon.[26]

China City in Johannesburg With camera in hand I approach this huge shopping complex called China City. Before I can raise my camera to take a picture, a security guard warns me that photography is not allowed inside the mall. So I snap a quick picture outside and proceed (with my designated trader) into the inside mall. Before I enter, however, I notice lots of cars from different parts of South Africa that are packed with goods purchased from China City.

It is almost impossible to find an African who has a shop and is willing to be interviewed, so we exit the internal mall and proceed to the more open part of the complex. We finally find an Ethiopian trader who arrived in Johannesburg in 2010 with the purpose of pursuing his business aspirations. Actually there are at least two Ethiopian shops in the complex, the second one of which is managed by his sister. This young trader had been a student in Ethiopia when he decided to try his luck in business in South Africa. One hundred percent of his goods come from China, he tells me. But unlike many of the other traders, he doesn't travel himself to China. Instead, all of the merchandise in the shop is bought from Chinese wholesalers in Johannesburg. This trader also complains that he has too much competition from the Chinese, who are able to sell at a lower price. The other problem is that they are all selling the same merchandise.[27]

On a more positive note, he does have customers who usually buy in bulk, from Angola, Mozambique, Zambia, and Zimbabwe.[28] In addition, he ships in bulk to Ethiopia via South Africa's Durban port. This story reinforces the point that Africa's trading markets are very complex, with China at the center of most of the activity.

Quebec Central House Determined to find South African traders in the textile and clothing sector, we journeyed to the heart of downtown Johannesburg. Quebec Central House was the destination, and it was there that I found floor after floor of traders from all over Africa. I was able to interview several traders from South Africa who had shops in the building. One of the traders, Ms K., explained that she doesn't buy goods from China because she doesn't want to take the chance that the South African government will destroy them as fake goods. 'Last year at the Durban port they burned a lot of containers. Many people have lost lots of money bringing in fake goods from China,' Ms K. informed me. Instead, this South African trader buys most of her goods from Turkey, Thailand and South Africa; the latter because she supports the government's promotion of 'buy SA.'[29]

A second South African trader, Ms L., told me that she buys all her goods from China, traveling there once or twice a month. She has been a trader since 2005, but business has not been good since the previous year. She buys medium-quality goods from China and caters to a high-end clientele from places like Sandton, a suburb of Johannesburg, which is now the financial capital of the country. Her goods, she says, are better fake brands than those most Chinese sell. Shoes seem to be a priority item in her shop. She used to have a lot of African customers, but that has changed. The competition from the Chinese is tough because they underprice you, she says, but her greatest competitors are traders from Somalia. 'They don't go to China, but buy goods from Chinese wholesalers. Then they sell on the street for much cheaper prices. People in the Quebec market have to pay for rent, so our prices are higher.'[30]

Importing goods from China is clearly a risky business in South Africa. It is for this reason that Mr E. from Mali does not go to China to buy his goods because the government destroys fake stuff that enters the country; rather he buys directly from Chinese wholesalers. He further informs me that many Chinese-owned shops in the area hide their fake goods in the event the police raid their shops looking for such items. Mr E. first came to South Africa from Mali in 2006 to realize his business dreams. He says that 'business is small small.' Back in the old days foreigners used to come and buy from him, but once China City opened, business declined. Mr E. is alone in South Africa and has hired a woman from Zimbabwe to assist him in the shop.[31] He mostly trades in T-shirts, women's wear, and sports items.

Awsane Ngom from Senegal was perhaps the most interesting person I interviewed in Quebec Central House. Mr Ngom came to South Africa in 1996 as a designer and held a job for ten years making traditional African clothes. He left the designing business because people were no longer buying traditional African clothes. So in 2003 he decided to open his own shop selling goods from China. Mr Ngom travels to China once a month and his clients come from all over South Africa. 'I don't have my goods shipped in containers,' he informs me, 'I just bring them in two suitcases because the fashions change so fast that I don't want to have a lot of things that people don't want to buy.' He buys medium- to high-quality goods, and his fake items are designed, like Ms L.'s, to cater to an upscale clientele. The products in Mr Ngom's shop are dominated by clothes and accessories for men. Like all the other traders interviewed, he is affected by competition from the Chinese, although there are no Chinese shops to be found in this part of Johannesburg.[32]

African market traders and the world of globalization from below: an assessment Six themes seem to flow through the stories of African market traders in this section: (1) buying and selling Chinese low-quality and/counterfeit goods; (2) unmanageable Chinese competition; (3) competition among African traders; (4) deindustrialization (see next section); (5) the loss of money in transactions with Chinese; and (6) African trading networks.

Buying and selling Chinese low-quality and/or counterfeit goods Whether talking to Auntie M., Auntie Emily, or any trader in the market in Africa, the conversation is likely to turn to issues concerning the Chinese and how it's very difficult to compete with the allegedly bad-quality goods they import into the country.

Although many African traders complain about cheap, fake, and bad-quality goods from China, this is the reality of globalization from below. Competition is fierce and the goods are not designed for the wealthy, who can buy original high-priced items produced by manufacturers at the level of globalization from above. It is precisely the illegal copying of high-priced items by agents at the non-hegemonic level which many at the hegemonic level would like to destroy, albeit that globalization from above is a reality in the non-hegemonic world as well, given the fact that the two systems both cooperate and compete with each other. The destruction of the non-hegemonic world would put Auntie Emily, Auntie M. and all the other traders in this chapter out of business.

Understanding how globalization from below works, we can view through a different lens the statistics produced by any ministry of trade and industry, whether in the hegemonic or the non-hegemonic world. For as Moisés Naím, in his book *Illicit: How Smugglers, Traffickers, and Copycats are Hijacking the Global Economy*, notes:

> As sovereignty erodes and nations face growing difficulties in controlling their borders, there is every indication that the geopolitical black holes[33] that illicit networks have come to inhabit and cultivate are only going to expand. And unless major changes take place, it is safer to assume that in the future the world will have more, not less of these geopolitical black holes. (2005: 263)

Unmanageable Chinese competition Competition at the non-hegemonic level and the hegemonic level is the same. Prices are reduced to accommodate the demand and theoretically allow the best person/company to accumulate the largest amount of capital. All agents are striving to achieve their economic goals at any cost. The traders in this chapter believe in neoliberalism and consequently free trade. There are always winners and losers in this game. For many of the traders, however, the competition does not stem from Chinese products alone. For years, prior to the Chinese infiltration of the informal trading sector in Africa, African traders went to China to buy cheap goods and sell them for a profit.

The competition that African traders seemingly cannot manage with the Chinese traders is partially a reflection of twenty-first-century dynamics at the level of globalization from below. As we learned in the previous chapter, Africans traveling to Guangzhou to purchase goods to send back home are buying and selling cheap, counterfeit, and fake Chinese goods largely through an intermediary, hence the increased prices for the goods. Under these circumstances, it is not likely that the competition between the African and Chinese traders will diminish. In fact, if Mr Nwoso (Chapter 2) is correct that the African market is so saturated with Chinese goods that is it cheaper to buy them once they arrive in Africa than in Guangzhou, the problem of competition will likely result in some non-hegemonic agents having to find alternative means of employment.

Neoliberal globalization has resulted in the freer flow of people throughout the world. The Chinese 'invasion' of Africa has been no exception. The extent to which the Chinese would penetrate the informal sector in Africa could not have been anticipated. Ironically, the twenty-first century in Africa has resulted in huge numbers of Chinese migrating to the continent in search of economic prosperity. Africa's informal sector for them seems a logical place to settle.

What is problematic about this phenomenon is that this is the sector that has allowed the majority of Africans to survive and thrive. The result of the informal sector being infiltrated by thousands of Chinese has been the civil society protests mentioned at the beginning of the chapter. The level of hostility against Chinese traders continues to increase, with more African governments having to intervene to resolve crises. Paramount to this discussion is: what are the consequences of Chinese taking away jobs in the informal sector that heretofore have been the purview of the indigenous African population? Will the end result be increased poverty and unemployment, resulting in even greater violence against the Chinese?

African leaders, some of whom have allowed huge numbers of Chinese to enter their countries with impunity under the pretense of creating greenfield investments that would result in job creation, have to assume most of the responsibility for the impending continent-wide crisis. Has Afro-neoliberal capitalism once again blindsided African leaders and prevented them dealing with the needs of the vast majority of their populations who live at the level of globalization from below?

Competition among African traders It is most interesting to hear African traders talk of the competition they are experiencing with other African traders for high-end fake Chinese goods. This adds another dimension to competition in the non-hegemonic world, especially in South Africa. As noted in the previous section, there will likely be winners and losers in this game. The trader who has the capital to withstand the competition will be the winner. Again, this kind of competition mirrors that of the hegemonic world.

The loss of money in transactions with Chinese As Mathews and Yang (2012) and Yang (2012) remind us, it is very common for African entrepreneurs to lose money in transactions in China. This is one of the realities of operating within the world of globalization from below. Perhaps Mr Nwoso from Chapter 2 provides the best summary of life in Guangzhou, where most of the traders in this section of the chapter travel to source their goods – 'everything is fake; either you are going to cheat someone or someone is going to cheat you.'

African trading networks Africa's trade regimes, as evidenced by this section of the chapter, are both complex and fascinating. The networks are wide ranging, as we see traders from the DRC, Tanzania, Kenya, Rwanda, Burundi, and Sudan sourcing goods from the markets in Uganda. Traders from Zambia source their goods from South Africa and Tanzania, while traders from Mozambique and Zimbabwe source their goods from Zambia. Finally, traders from the DRC, Angola, Mozambique, Zambia, Swaziland, Nigeria, Cameroon, England, Zimbabwe, and Ethiopia source goods from South Africa. Unraveling these complex networks was one of the most fascinating parts of the journey to these countries. All these goods cross borders, mostly illegally under the radar of government officials, and traders pay no taxes. It is truly a world of globalization from below.

In this regard, not only has neoliberal globalization benefited the agents who create and maintain these networks, but the transshipment of goods allows millions to have access to goods that heretofore have been elusive, many of them fake and of low quality. The traders and the markets are well integrated into the global economy, albeit at the level of globalization from below. The caveat to this integration of Africa's world markets is that the integration we see involves foreign goods and not those produced in Africa. While neoliberal globalization has on the one hand created opportunities for Africans to have access to these goods, primarily from China, on the other neoliberal globalization has also contributed to the inability of Africans to produce their own goods for the world markets. Thus any celebration of Africa's world markets flourishing through the import and transshipment of primarily Chinese goods must be tinged with a great deal of sadness and dismay. Those of us who witnessed Africa's lost decade because of IMF/World Bank SAPs (neoliberal globalization) could not have imagined that in the twenty-first century Africa's world markets at the level of globalization from below would primarily consist of goods transshipped from China. These same agents who are transshipping Chinese goods to the people at the level of globalization from below are also, in Guangzhou, China, doing the same for those who live in Africa at the level of globalization from above.

Textiles and clothing: the special case of South Africa

One of the most consistent areas of the economy challenged by the influx of Chinese products is the textiles, clothing, and footwear sector, which Fanie Herman refers to as the textile industry (2011: 116). Whether these goods are brought in directly by Africa market traders to sell in their shops, exported to Africa by traders from places in China like Chocolate City/Guangzhou, or exported or imported by Chinese traders, the impact of these goods has been devastating to the African market (see Ikhuoria 2010; Schikonye 2008; Baregu 2008; Ogunsanwo 2008; Brooks 2010: 16; Kaplinsky 2008; Meagher 2013: 171). South Africa is no exception to this reality. What is exceptional, however, is its status as a continental economic powerhouse and thus its ability, with its strong labor unions, to take a case of unfair trade practices by a third party before the WTO. Although it could have chosen to take the textiles case before the WTO, it did not. It opted to challenge the Chinese government directly by placing restrictions on the exports of certain textile industry items to South Africa for a period of two years. In this section of the chapter we will examine the background to this unique situation in Africa, report the outcomes, and assess the success or failure of the quota restrictions as they relate to not just the textile industry, but all actors who have a vested interest in this sector.

Of great importance in understanding the textile industry in any African country is the speculation that the viability of its ability to compete internationally was compromised by IMF/World Bank structural adjustment programs (SAPS), as noted previously in this chapter. Fundamentally, countries were forced under SAPS in the 1980s to liberalize their economies, including trade. Most were not able to compete with the cheaper textiles and clothing that entered the market. Many, however, were able to survive, either producing for the local population or for export. The entry into the African market of competitive Asian producers of textiles and clothing, especially from China, marked a major turning point in the history of this sector in Africa. The competition was so fierce that it not only resulted in deindustrialization throughout Africa, but also highlighted the serious weaknesses in most African countries, from poor technology to unskilled labor. Again, South Africa was the only country that fought back.

The story of the South African case against Chinese textiles and clothing began to unfold around the turn of the century, when large quantities of textiles from China gradually made their entrance into South Africa's consumer markets. In response the South African textile industry and labor unions began to accuse China not only of dumping, but also of causing deindustrialization and unemployment (Herman 2011: 116).

Between 2003 and 2006, employment in the South African textile industry reportedly declined from 70,000 jobs to fewer than 50,000. Commencing in 2002 there was a huge surge in imports from China, causing turmoil in the sector (ibid.: 119). In response to this surge of imports from China, the Textile Federation (Texfed), on behalf of its members, filed several anti-dumping applications against China for specific products that were being imported. A number of the cases were successful, resulting in anti-dumping duties being imposed on several Chinese textile products (Brink 2006: 1).

Following Texfed complaints, in 2004 Clotrade, another trade union that represents domestic clothing manufacturers as well as clothing importers, requested that the International Trade and Economic Development Division (ITEDD) of the South African Department of Trade and Industry (DTI) impose safeguards against Chinese imported goods (ibid.: 1). With no response from ITEDD, in June 2005 Clotrade then filed an application with the International

Trade Administration Commission (ITAC), the governmental body that handles trade remedy investigations. The following month the South African Clothing and Textile Workers' Union (SACTWU) also submitted an application to ITAC (ibid.: 1–2).

Clotrade had begun to talk with ITEDD as early as 2002 about the problem. Once ITAC reviewed the Clotrade application it was rejected in September 2006, with ITAC arguing that 'it was not prepared to act outside the parameters of the WTO' (ibid.: 2). Clotrade's safeguard application to ITAC asked that remedial action be taken against the surge in Chinese clothing commencing in 2002. It did not request a WTO remedy. Instead it

> [R]equested that a negotiated position and specifically quotas be imposed; that a significant additional ad valorem duty be imposed on any imports outside the quotas; and that certain minimum values be adopted for customs valida-tion purpose on the basis of Chinese export prices to the European Union and the US. Clotrade requested protection against all imports under Chapter 61 and 62 of the Harmonised Tariff System, covering 263 tariff lines. Clotrade also requested that imports from Hong Kong be covered in the quotas as virtually all clothing imported from Hong Kong in reality originates in China, since very little apparel is manufactured in Hong Kong. (Ibid.: 2)

The SACTWU application to ITAC was slightly different from Clotrade's (ibid.: 3). The issue at hand, however, was why ITAC took no action to safeguard the South African textile industry at this juncture.

Fanie Herman, in an interesting article entitled 'Textile disputes and two-level games: the case of China and South Africa' (2011), notes that initially the South African government didn't want to get involved in the dispute because it feared jeopardizing its trade relationship with China. As for the Chinese, they felt they could dump on the South African market, Herman speculates, because the Chinese traders were not threatened by a reaction from South Africans affected by the dumping and low prices. In addition, since South Africa had given China 'most favored nation status,' supply and demand would determine the prices of goods and services by the free-price system. Finally, the Chinese felt that owing to the low production rates of the textile market in South Africa, it would import additional textiles. In this regard, China could hire hundreds of workers by setting up textile factories in South Africa (Herman 2011: 116).

As the dumping by the Chinese continued into former President Thabo Mbeki's first term, job losses continued to increase. As previously indicated, 20,000 jobs were lost between 2003 and 2006. However, to place the problem of job losses in this sector in perspective, the South African Labour Relations Institute reported that between March 1996 and December 2004, 76,000 jobs in total had been lost (as quoted in Brink 2006: 15).

With growing constituency pressure, both governments began to negotiate a resolution to the problem. An agreement was finally signed on 22 June 2006. The agreement stipulated that quotas would be imposed on thirty-one identified tariff lines. These were classified under the broad categories of clothing and textiles. The quotas were to be in place for two years, commencing in January 2007 and ending in December 2009 (Eeden 2009: 1). '[I]n seven instances the quota will result in reducing the volume of products that may be imported in 2007 by more than 50% vis-à-vis 2005 volumes ... In another eight instances the quotas will reduce total imports by between 25% and 50% and in eleven instances by between 10% and 25%' (Brink 2006: 21). In addition to accepting the quotas, the Chinese government agreed to provide side payments (e.g. direct investments) and to help modernize the South Africa textile industry (Herman 2011: 125). According to Sanusha Naidu, the Chinese government announced that it would provide a US$31.3 million package for development for the textile industry that would include 'technical training under the Skills, Education and Training Authorities (SETs) programme' (2008: 188–9).

The fundamental questions to ask at this point are: what impact did the quotas have on the textile industry and did the South African government use the money allocated by the Chinese for enhancing the capacity of the industry? With respect to the second question, the answer, according to Naidu, is a resounding no! She argues that the government, instead of using the money for capacity-building, used it 'for technical training in agriculture, tourism, defence and foreign affairs' (ibid.: 188–9). While it is also the case that the quotas did not succeed in staunching the bleeding of jobs in the textile industry, the reasons why are a bit more complicated than the simple failure of the South African government to use the money allocated by the Chinese to build capacity in the industry.

In 1994, the post-apartheid government acknowledged the need to invest in building the capacity of the textile industry, given that it was the sixth-largest employer in the manufacturing sector and the eleventh-most important exporting sector of manufactured goods. Therefore, as a priority sector for direct and indirect employment, over US$1 billion was spent on upgrading and modernizing the sector (Wild 2009: 12). Unfortunately, the sector was not prepared for the huge surge of Chinese products that began to flood the market around 2002. By the middle of 2006, 'China's market share of South African global clothing imports was already close to 75%. This, together with the coinciding job losses and an effort to increase stability in the industry prompted Government to restrict clothing and textile imports to 31 items for a two-year period' (ibid.: 13).

Although this decision no doubt made the trade unionists happy, there were many skeptics who, for lack of a better phrase, saw this move as applying a Band Aid to a huge problem. For example, Phi Alves of the South African Institute of International Affairs (SAIIA) argued that the textile industry (clothing, footwear, and textiles) had been in decline for fifteen years and that the fundamental problem was a lack of sufficient investment in capacity, technology, and management in order to ensure that South Africa could be competitive in the international market (Alves 2006b).

Gustav Brink asked the three questions that most critics of the quotas were concerned about: (1) what was the rationale for the quotas; (2) what countries would replace Chinese imports; and (3) if China was not in the equation, would the textile industry be competitive internationally? (2006: 4).

Were the quotas a rational decision? Herman Wild definitely thinks that they were not and South Africa and the textile industry would have been better off taking the case before the WTO 'to seek interim safeguards, rather than pursue them as part of a bilateral agreement' (Wild 2009: 13–14). Others agree that delaying the implementation of the quotas until January 2007 gave importers an opportunity to stockpile goods before the quotas came into effect. Once they did come into effect, because customers continued to want the Chinese products, a great deal of smuggling took place along with under-invoicing (ibid.: 14; Brink 2006: 28).

With respect to the second question of which countries would replace China, the answer is that South Africa began sourcing products for the textile industry from Mauritius, Bangladesh, Malaysia, and Lesotho. Wild laments that 'Perhaps the worst consequence of the imposed quotas is the fact that the supply gap created by the quotas was not filled by the local manufacturing sector' (Wild 2009: 14).

As to the final question, whether the South African textile industry would be competitive internationally if China were taken out of the equation, the answer is evidenced by the fact that the industry had to rely on other countries for needed supplies while the quotas were in place.

Notwithstanding these and other negative critiques of the limited quotas imposed on China as a result of the surge in Chinese imports, at the end of the two-year period the South African government requested that the quotas be extended, which the Chinese government refused (Mataboge 2009).

In light of this experience, it has become obvious that the government can only do so much to protect industries in this globalized world (Wild 2009: 14; Alves 2006a). Brink sadly concludes that 'It is accordingly submitted that the only winner in this case is the Chinese, and that all of South Africa has lost in the process' (Brink 2006: 29).

In 1994, the African National Congress (ANC) of South Africa developed a platform for the first democratic election in the country, the Reconstruction and Development Program (RDP). Embedded in the program document was a pledge to create employment opportunities for the majority population who had been marginalized and left impoverished under white-settler rule and later apartheid. The fundamental promise was to redistribute the wealth of the country, most of which was in the hands of the white minority (ANC 1994). A special position, housed within the president's office, was created for a person to oversee the implementation of the RDP. In 1996, under the leadership of the then deputy president of the country, Thabo Mbeki, a new economic plan was announced for restructuring South Africa's economy. The money allocated for the RDP program was dispersed throughout the relevant ministries (e.g. housing, energy) and the special RDP position within the president's office was abolished.

The RDP was replaced by GEAR (Growth, Employment and Redistribution). GEAR was fundamentally a self-imposed International Monetary Fund/ World Bank (IMF/WB) structural adjustment program. It was thus a neoliberal globalization program that was designed to attract foreign investment into the country. Inherent in GEAR was the notion of free trade, limited governmental intervention in the markets, privatization, and the elimination of the welfare state. According to GEAR, 'Attaining higher growth and significant job creation without undermining macroeconomic stability is recognised as the key challenge facing economic policy. The Government's strategy for rebuilding and restructuring the economy entails:

- A competitive platform for export growth;
- A stable environment for a surge in private investment;
- Restructured public services and government capital expenditure;
- New emphases in industrial and infrastructural development;
- Greater labour market flexibility; and
- Enhanced human resource development.' (Department of Finance 1996)

Among the architects of GEAR were Luiz Pereira da Silva and Richard Ketley from the World Bank (ibid.), one of the premier institutions promoting neoliberal globalization (Peet 2010). With GEAR, Afro-neoliberal capitalism became the foundation of the ruling elite's philosophy regarding South Africa's development. The impoverished masses in South Africa were to be lifted out of abject poverty through the market, and more specifically through foreign investment. Foreign investment would result in job creation and job creation would in turn result in increased capital accumulation and material wealth for the masses. In the meantime, South Africa aggressively began to open its markets to the world, and by January 2000 it had begun to implement a free trade agreement with the European Union.

The elites of the country were well aware of the need to make the textile industry competitive. Under the apartheid regime it was a crucial source of employment, but the industry itself was fragile. Without building up the capacity of the industry to withstand an international onslaught of cheaper and more cost-efficient goods, it was a known fact that the industry would collapse. The ANC-led government, determined not to make the same mistakes as other African countries, was convinced that GEAR was necessary to prevent the need for the imposition of an externally imposed IMF/WB SAP as a last resort to save the economy from collapse.

As predicted, by implementing neoliberal globalization, the textile industry began to bleed and the job loses began to create a crisis. Once the Chinese textiles entered the market, the total collapse of the industry was inevitable. The $1 billion investment by the government in upgrading and modernizing was not enough, especially given the decision to adopt neoliberal globalization as its strategy of economic development and integrate the South African economy into the global economy.

While the offer by the Chinese government to assist in helping to build capacity in the textile sector was a nice gesture, although likely too little too late, the mere fact that the government of South Africa did not invest these funds in the textile industry reflects a lack of commitment not just to those formerly employed in the sector, but to the need to implement welfare policies to help lift the masses out of poverty. As Satgar argues:

> ... Afro-neo-liberal capitalism indigenizes neo-liberalism and restructures African economies, state forms, state–society relations, historical blocs and international relations to harmonise with its goals. At the same time, Africa-neo-liberal capitalism, as a concept of control, excludes alternative options for Africa such as delinking, autocentric development and even African capitalism. It is presented by ruling historical blocs as a solution to Africa's organic crisis and embodies the national or general interests of society – an African solution to an African problem. (Satgar 2009: 45)

In essence, the ANC-led government has no commitment to strategies that challenge the neoliberal orthodoxy and the elite consensus that focuses on self-indulging capital accumulation. With this as an ideological framework for governing, it is extremely difficult for Africa to become further integrated into the global economy, or to experience economic development, with African agents operating at the level of globalization from above or the hegemonic world. This case of the South African textile industry ultimately reflects a clash of interests between globalization from above and from below.

Headline news: we must stop the Chinese onslaught – the special case of the Ghanaian steel industry

Upon my arrival in Accra, Ghana, a friend dragged me to a business office for an appointment she had. While waiting for her, I noticed a newspaper sitting on the counter that had as its headline 'We must stop the Chinese onslaught.' I read the article with great interest and became determined to meet the person being quoted, Mr Kwasi Okoh. As luck would have it, Mr Okoh was the cousin of the person I was staying with in Accra, so after a brief phone call, Mr Okoh agreed to come over for an interview. Mr Okoh is a very charming man on a mission. His mission is to stop the importation of cheap goods from China that will further undermine Ghana's economy. As managing director of Aluworks, Mr Okoh was interviewed by the *Business and Financial Times* (Ghana):

> Aluworks and many other manufacturing concerns have had issues with the dumping of cheap Chinese goods onto the market, which is threatening the very survival of the manufacturing sector ... The textile, the printing, and now the aluminium industries are all threatened and in danger of folding-up and laying-off their workers. Some fast-growing consumer goods companies have also complained about cheap and shoddy goods threatening their livelihoods. In a strongly-worded letter to *B&T*, Mr. Okoh said: 'We can decide to trade. That is what it will amount to, while we watch the manufacturing industry die. If we decide to trade, we will not need any stuff. We will import and deliver direct to customers. We can do it, but we will not be contributing to the economy. The GDP will belong to China and we will introduce increased suffering to Ghana ...'

As a chartered accountant, Mr Okoh spent thirty-two years with Unilever working in East, West, and southern Africa. He was eventually appointed as Unilever Regional Customer Development Manager for Africa and the Middle East. Since retiring from Unilever in 2006, he has been serving as a turnaround manager for different companies in Ghana. As a turnaround manager Mr Okoh picks up a company that is having a hard time and turns it around. The company that he is currently attempting to turn around is Aluworks Ltd in Tema. Aluworks Ltd 'is the only cold rolling mill in Ghana, converting aluminium ingots and/or molten aluminium into flat rolled sheets of various sizes and thicknesses, to be used by downstream customers both in Ghana and abroad, in the main for making roofing sheets, and for making cookware.'[34]

Since 2006, Aluworks has been in crisis, and since 2008 has been under the leadership of Mr Okoh, whose major job is to restore the company to profitability. The current constraint to achieving this objective, as Mr Okoh explains below, is the importation of cheap Chinese aluminum that is posing a challenge to the Ghanaian market. More importantly, as pointed out below, this is transpiring not because Ghanaian aluminum is not competitive or worse than the Chinese aluminum, but because the Chinese government gives rebates to companies in China to export their aluminum at a much cheaper price. It is worth quoting Mr Okoh on this matter at length in order to understand the process of how China is undermining the Ghanaian market because, as he notes, this process is taking place all over Africa. The following information is taken directly from a letter Mr Okoh wrote to the *Business and Financial Times* (Ghana) on 4 March 2011. The letter was published under the heading

'Imports from China killing local Ghanaian industry.' The part that is quoted directly is specifically about the aluminum industry.

Quality versus Price.

Aluworks prides itself with the production of tip top quality goods. In the past, 50% of Aluworks sales were in exports because of the quality. Aluworks is International Standards Organisation (ISO) certified for quality at the highest level (ISO 9001:2008). We are very very certain we can match and surpass the quality of the aluminium products from China. However the Chinese price is so low that people no longer consider quality. If the price were closer, knowing Ghanaians they would opt for quality even for a slightly higher price. But the difference is not slight. It is very very deep. It is an act of war.

Process Costs – China versus Ghana.

The process has various elements, so to allow easy analysis, I have broken it down into sectors as follows.

Markets: There are several commodity markets around the world that regulate sales of aluminium. The major one is the London Metal Exchange (LME), which most of the world uses. The LME cost is what we use in our purchase transactions whether from VALCO [Volta Aluminum Company] or from India or from South Africa, to which is added a premium which covers costs like freight. Chinese industry buys its aluminium from the Shanghai Metal Exchange and the Shanghai Futures Exchange.

Metal Cost: The Shanghai exchange aluminium price is always much higher than the LME. So prima facie we in Aluworks get our aluminium raw material cheaper than any Chinese company. When we buy raw material from around the world we have to incur freight costs and the costs of clearing the raw material through the ports. Currently we no longer import raw material. We are supplied by VALCO which is actually adjacent to us, so there is no freight and no port clearing. Additionally we get most of our supply from VALCO in molten form so we save the cost of having to melt solid metal when it gets to our factory (this saving has allowed us to reduce our prices in 2011).

Conversion Costs: Our visits to China have shown us that our conversion costs are competitive, i.e. the costs of working the raw materials into our finished goods, which we sell to other local companies to make roofing sheets, pots and pans, are good. Indeed we found companies that had higher conversion costs than Aluworks, despite the huge volume advantages that accrue to Chinese companies. Nevertheless we have to admit that in theory Chinese companies should be cheaper because they are larger and should have volume advantages.

Freight Costs: As we buy from VALCO next door we incur no freight. However any product purchased from China has to be shipped across the seas to Ghana and incurs heavy freight to get here.

Clearing Costs: The imported products have to be cleared from the ports adding as much as another 15% at least to the cost. In fact such imports being the equivalent of the product of Aluworks are finished products and ought to attract 20% duty. It is very general knowledge that Ghanaian importers use all sorts of 'ways and means' to pay as little as 5% duty, if any (that is another topic altogether for discussion). So instead of clearing costs of about 30% they end up with about 15% if at all. In any case any import from China will incur some clearing cost.

Profit: None of us works for free so it has to be assumed the Chinese companies that sell the products to Ghanaians for export to Ghana also add their profit before they invoice. Similarly the Ghanaian companies will add their profit.

Effect of the Chinese Export Rebate
I will illustrate the effect using two very simple real live examples.

Example 1 – Ghana:
Cost: On the 22nd of February 2011, the LME was at $2,478 per tonne. For the purpose of this illustration, this is the base price [at which] Aluworks would buy metal supplied by VALCO to Aluworks, on that day (actually we buy on an average cost over a period agreed with the supplier). On the 22nd of February the price on the Shanghai exchange was $2,576 per tonne. So already China metal is slightly more expensive.

Conversion: We convert this into finished coils at about $700 per tonne. Our cost becomes $3,178. We know our conversion cost is favourably comparable to Chinese costs but for the sake of the argument let us say they are more efficient and can achieve $500 per tonne, their cost is now $3,076 per tonne, slightly cheaper than Ghana, but practically at par.

Freight: The coils produced by Aluworks at $3,178 per tonne are in Ghana, there is no need for freight and customers can be supplied immediately. The coils produced for $3,076 per tonne are in China, so the Ghanaian importer must incur freight to bring it to Ghana. That normally costs about $150 per tonne. Ghana is still at $3,086 but the China product now costs $3,226, now higher than in Ghana.

Port Clearance: The Ghana metal is already in Ghana and does not incur any port costs so the cost remains $3,178. China products have to incur duty and have to be cleared. This adds at least 15% i.e. about $485 per tonne, bringing the landed cost in Ghana C&F to $3,711 per tonne. At this stage the China cost is now far far higher than the Ghana cost.

Additions: In Ghana there are some administrative and overhead costs to cover plus having to add profit. When we have done so we should be selling at about $3,400 per tonne. The Chinese cost at C&F should be at $3,711, *before* any administrative and overhead costs and the profit of the importing Ghanaian company (note – this is without having added any profit for the Chinese company!).

Price: Ghana finished product is available for sale at $3,400 per tonne. Chinese companies quote to Ghanaian buyers a C&F price of $2,638 per tonne. HOW POSSIBLE?!? From the analysis so far, their cost is already at a conservative $3,711 per tonne *before* their overheads and profit. HOW POSSIBLE? We know some Ghanaian traders sometimes get it even cheaper. How is that possible?

EXPORT REBATE: The Chinese government wants the aluminium to be sold, so they grant export rebates. The China price of $2,638 is C&F, so it includes the freight, and it includes the suppliers' profit. We know they buy metal at $2,576. It is impossible for all of this to cost only some $60. The difference is the export rebate that has been granted to absorb all the cost (granted to the trading companies by the Chinese Government) allowing them to sell to places like Ghana at such ridiculous prices. It is very deep, as much as $800 per tonne. It is an act of war!

Example 2 – Nigeria:
Our marketing staff visited customers in Nigeria at the beginning of the year. At that time the LME was $2,453 per tonne. Yet Chinese companies were offering to Nigerian customers an FOB price of $2,443 per tonne (i.e. even below LME) and a landed cost of Chinese products C&F at $2,750 per tonne.

Granting for argument's sake that we assume that the Chinese manufacturer has bought his metal at the base LME price (remember the Shanghai price would actually be higher) and converts at $500 per tonne, the Nigerian importer should pay a C&F equivalent of about $3,103 per tonne.

There is no way they could be asked to pay C&F at $2,750 per tonne *after* conversion *and* freight. They are able to do so only because of the Export rebate.

These two examples illustrate the effects of the export rebate which is causing us so much grief. Simple DUMPING!!!!!

Given the above, what can be done to protect the Ghanaian market? The most important step is to impose countervailing measures against the Chinese in this sector, as the USA, Canada, India, and Australia have done. Ghana has recommended countervailing measures which are currently being reviewed by the Tariff Advisory Board established by the Ministry of Trade and Industry. However, Okoh feels it is taking the latter forever to establish a policy, noting that by the time it eventually does the industry in Ghana could be on its knees (ibid.).

The real problem, however, according to Okoh, rests with the government, which he says is 'in bed' with the Chinese since they have built the Ministry of Defense, the National Theatre, and the Accra International Conference Center. In addition, the Chinese are building roads, an oil refinery in Tema, a power plant, and are involved in other industrial projects. Okoh makes it very clear that he is not anti-Chinese and that in fact he buys heavy industrial equipment from China.[35] Nonetheless, he is strongly opposed to the importation of cheap Chinese products that undermine local production in Ghana, thus leaving Ghanaians unemployed and in the end worse off because 'cheap goods end up being more expensive in the long run as they fail frequently necessitating replacement and therefore higher competitive purchase' (Business and Financial Times 2011b).

The debate around Chinese companies infiltrating the various sectors in Africa, very often with devastating consequences, is not often put in perspective. Blinded by the neoliberal orthodoxy, people often assume that African industries are not competitive and therefore cannot withstand the competition from the Chinese or other major trading partners operating from the level of globalization from above.

What Okoh has revealed is that the Ghanaian steel industry, as an example, is not only able to compete with the Chinese steel industry, but also the steel it produces is of a better quality. Clearly the case of Ghanaian steel should be addressed at the hegemonic level. It represents a classic case of a powerful country, in this case China, keeping Africa's world markets marginalized within the global economy by maintaining subsidies on internationally competitive goods. Africa cannot compete with such subsidies and therefore African negotiators are constantly calling for their removal in order to allow African counties to realize their comparative advantage in the international trade arena.

The failure of the Ghanaian government to prevent the import of subsidized and lower quality steel into the country in an effort to protect Ghana's steel industry is partially a reflection of the neoliberal globalization and Afro-neoliberal capitalism that such leaders have institutionalized and kept in place at the risk of the collapse, in this case, of the steel industry and the resultant increased unemployment. The accusation made by Okoh that the government 'is in bed' with the Chinese is a common accusation made throughout the continent (Michel and Beuret 2009; Corkin 2012; Brautigam 2009: 292–7; Corkin 2009; Baregu 2008; De Morais 2011). This resonates with the 'elite consensus' that the objective of many African leaders is the accumulation of capital. This has been sanctioned by the proponents of the neoliberal orthodoxy and deemed to be a normal outcome of everyday life for those who have access to capital. The perception is that in return for allowing the Chinese to have a free hand in African infrastructure development, greater access to Africa's natural resources and its markets, African leaders will be rewarded with economic gifts, what in the literature is referred to as 'rent-seeking.'

It is here that we have a clash 'among' agents operating at the level of globalization from above. Okoh would certainly not deny that he is among the elite of Ghana. But he clearly is not 'in bed' with the Chinese, nor has he opted out of development as a proponent of Afro-neoliberal capitalism. Rather, Mr Okoh is an example of an average Ghanaian whose prime interest lies with the commitment to ensure that Ghana realizes its developmental potential and its comparative advantage within the international trade regime.

We destroy counterfeit Chinese goods

During my research trip to Guangzhou, China, one of the traders, Mr Ali, noted that the Chinese government is very concerned about the reputation the country has gained for producing shoddy and counterfeit goods and is in the process of trying to correct this image.[36] Perhaps this is why, in Chapter 2, Mr Bah was concerned about the market being raided by the police in Guangzhou to collect counterfeit goods the traders were selling.[37]

The issue of Chinese counterfeit goods in African markets is always a point of conversation among traders, buyers of the goods, and African governments. In an interview, Dr Terry Kahuma, former director of Uganda's National Bureau of Standards, who was responsible for overseeing the destruction of counterfeit goods that enter the market, lamented that the impact of counterfeit Chinese goods on Uganda's economy is negative. Not only do they waste people's money, but they are also dangerous. For example, the electrical cables are thinner and cause fires. Then there are counterfeit Chinese circuit breakers. 'Now if you have a Chinese fire extinguisher, then you have a huge problem.'[38]

In 2010, Dr Kahuma estimated there were between 10,000 and 20,000 Chinese in the country and they were continuing to come. He makes it very clear that his bureau is not responsible for bringing them to Uganda. Rather, he says, it is the government, once again pointing to the fact that the Chinese have built the State House and the National Bureau of Statistics, as well as the Ministry of Foreign Affairs.[39]

Dr Kahuma does admit that the bureau doesn't have standards for lots of items imported into the country by the Chinese. However, with those they do have standards for, they destroy those that are counterfeit. Some of the items that are earmarked for destruction include tiles, because wall tiles are substituted for floor tiles; and although Ugandans make toothbrushes, the Chinese make the same toothbrushes and import them as 'made in Uganda.' The toys they import into Uganda 'are hopeless. If the toys have wheels they fall off. They look good in the shop, but once the kids play with them they fall apart. There is no Chinese product in this town that works!'[40] Dr Kahuma's deputy, Mr Mackay Aomu, indicated during the interview that he had bought what he thought was a Panasonic radio for his mother and it didn't work.[41]

In addition to the issue of Chinese counterfeit goods being imported into Uganda, Dr Kahuma has other related concerns. He feels, for example, that the Chinese have taken over the import business and undermined Uganda's industries; they have killed local industries, including textiles, food and beverages, electrical appliances, furniture, and shoes. With respect to the textiles that are imported, Dr Kahuma feels they 'are so horrible! The fiber that they use is not of good quality – it has fewer threads, and they starch the shirts to make them look good. But once you wash it that's the end of that shirt or suit.'[42] Jane S. Nalunga of SEATINI in Kampala says that 'While a Chinese pair of shoes will carry you to church, you have to carry them back home.'[43] Another issue of concern for Dr Kahuma stems from the herbal medicine and medical techniques brought in from China. Many of them, he argues, are fake.[44]

In terms of genuine Chinese investment in the country (there are a few factories that have been built), there is not a problem, according to Dr Kahuma. The problem, however, arises when Chinese come in saying they are investors, register a company, and in reality all they import are goods for their shops from China.[45] During a visit to the market in Kampala, I was able to get only one Chinese trader to talk to me. The trader, a female, informed me that the blankets she was selling were manufactured in Uganda. Unable to speak Buganda, I asked my research assistant to enquire whether this was the case. He had a conversation with one of the workers in her shop and he assured my research assistant that the blankets had been imported directly from China.[46]

Another issue of concern for Dr Kahuma is the transport of goods.

> We have a problem with the transport of goods. For example, ten containers of goods are supposed to go to the Congo. The papers say they have gone through our border, but only two containers actually go to the Congo. We can't trace where the other eight have gone ... Goods for Uganda are stopped in Kenya.[47]

As a result of the above, 'UNBS [Uganda National Bureau of Standards] has to do night watches to try to see where the containers are going. Most are from China.'[48]

On a final note, Dr Kahuma introduces us to the fact there is not one homogeneous Chinese population. According to Kahuma:

> Chinese compete among themselves. They fight bitterly against themselves. One was making suitcases in Uganda and complained about another Chinese who was bringing in sub-standard suitcases from China. So I went to see his suitcases in the market. I picked up one and the handle came off. Now we have to examine the quality of his goods.[49]

During a visit to Uganda in March 2012, I was informed that Dr Kahuma had been removed from his position. Rumor had it that it was because the Ugandan government was not pleased with the aggressive way in which he was preventing Chinese counterfeit goods from entering the market.[50]

The destruction of counterfeit Chinese goods is not unique to Uganda. A conversation with a member of Tanzania's Fair Trade Commission reveals that the government has destroyed a lot of counterfeit goods, including motorcycle spare parts, DVDs, generators, electrical goods, and radios.[51] 'There are two options for those caught with counterfeit goods: (1) they have to pay a fine of $2 million shillings and destruction cost; or (2) they have to go to court and pay for court cost of $10 million shillings. They also have to do time in jail. We therefore prefer the former to the latter.'[52]

According to the Commission, although 86 percent of all goods pass through the Dar es Salaam port, there are only five agents who monitor all goods coming into all the ports in Tanzania. Consequently, the Commission was in the process of hiring more people to strengthen the division. The Commission also often raids businesses in the market when people come and tell us about the selling of counterfeit goods.[53]

Even though the law was passed to curtail counterfeit goods entering the country as early as 1963, it did not come into force until 2005. Perhaps more alarming is the fact that the first chief inspector was not appointed until 2007. The problem of counterfeit goods entering the Tanzanian market commenced with the introduction of trade liberalization in 1985.[54] In an interview, Mr Clement F. A. Nyaaba, Director of Multilateral, Regional and Bilateral Trade in the Ministry of Trade and Industry, Accra, Ghana, also indicated they destroy all counterfeit goods that enter the country, including Chinese goods.[55]

As noted above, the South African government has a very aggressive policy regarding the destruction of Chinese counterfeit products, to the point that some traders refuse to import them into the country themselves, although they might sell them in their shops. The Nigerian government has also been involved in the destruction of Chinese counterfeit products (Ikhuoria 2010: 136; Whitby 2010). In June 2012, Angolan customs officials discovered 1.4 million packets of a counterfeit malaria drug called Coartem, imported in a shipment of loudspeakers from Guangzhou, China. The non-counterfeit drug is made by Novartis, a Swiss pharmaceutical giant. The medicine was enough to treat over half the annual malaria cases in Angola (Faucon et al. 2013). 'The counterfeits seized in Luanda contained none of the active ingredient in real Coartem. Instead, they were made of calcium phosphates, fatty acids and yellow pigment, according to a copy of a Novartis analysis of the tablets.' Novartis is collaborating with various government entities in Luanda to fight against the shipment of counterfeit Coartem and has added new security features to the packaging of the drug in hopes of making it more difficult for copies to be produced (ibid.).

It is obvious that some of the fake and counterfeit goods exported to Africa from China are counterproductive to enhancing the lives of those operating at the level of globalization from below. Attempting to stop the most dangerous Chinese counterfeit and fake goods in this study are the governments of Uganda, Ghana, South Africa, Nigeria, and Angola. Electronic goods that can potentially maim or kill people and fake medicines are the most egregiously harmful exports. It is here that one can understand the desire by hegemonic agents to prevent the illegal activities of non-hegemonic agents. In this regard, globalization from below undermines any effort to increase Africa's integration into the global economy and foster economic development. The consequences of such activities are detrimental to the very survival of the individuals that globalization from below is designed to help.

It is here that one can imagine the majority of agents in the non-hegemonic world joining forces with those in the hegemonic world to protest against those in the non-hegemonic world who are threatening the lives of agents from below. One can perhaps call this a checks-and-balance system, since those selling dangerous commodities must be isolated from their fellow residents in the non-hegemonic world.

Globalization from below and Chinese market traders

This section examines two places where there exist large concentrations of Chinese involved in trade. The first is a Chinese trading post in Oshikango, Namibia, and the other is in Ghana, where thousands of Chinese have migrated and become involved in illegal mining. They both inform us about interesting dynamics that transpire between themselves and the local population as well as government officials in the non-hegemonic world of globalization from below. The situation of Chinese gold miners in Ghana demonstrates how illegal activities on the part of an immigrant community can go terribly wrong and result in consequences of unimaginable proportion. This case is an anomaly in Africa and perhaps in the entire non-hegemonic world.

The case of the Oshikango trading post If there is a Chinese 'trading post' in Africa that comes close to replicating the African 'trading post' in Chocolate City/Guangzhou, it might be located in the Namibian border town of Oshikango. It is here that you will find, according to Gregor Dobler, an estimated one hundred Chinese shops that sell goods to Angolan traders (2009: 707). Not only have they created a Chinese trading post in Oshikango, but also, one could argue, a transnational urban entrepreneurial space and an ethnic enclave in the area (see Chapter 2). George Lo, director of the First National Bank of East Asia, refers to the area that includes the town of Oshikango and its border with Angola as a Chinese–African trading hub. This hub, Lo argues, is an example 'of a trend to boost ties in a post-crisis scenario' (Macauhub 2010). What is even more important is what Lo refers to as the trading corridor that 'stretches from the copper production area in Zambia as far as the town of Oshikango on the Namibia side of the border with Angola which "is becoming a regional trading hub as more Chinese wholesalers supply Angola with goods through there"' (ibid.). Lo further notes that 'The trading corridor between China and Africa is seen by many as the most exciting chapter in the global economic shift' (ibid.).

Like the African traders in Chocolate City/Guangzhou, Chinese traders on Namibia's border migrate to Oshikango strictly for business purposes. They have selected Oshikango because it represents the most attractive market in the area. Their modus operandi is to bring goods from China into Namibia for a much cheaper price than their Namibian counterparts, which means they are in competition with the latter (Dobler 2009: 709–10). Those in this enclave of Chinese entrepreneurs, like other minority entrepreneurs, are deemed to be strangers in the area (ibid.: 710). Nonetheless, the Chinese form alliances for protection with segments of their host country. These political and economic alliances that are established by Chinese with well-connected Namibian individuals '[create] an additional rent income for some Namibians without changing their economic behavior, and it prevents economic development in the country rather than fostering it' (ibid.: 710). Fundamentally, according to Dobler, these privileged Chinese businessmen are able to consolidate their status in what is deemed an increasingly hostile environment against Chinese migrants. They are further able to position themselves as middlemen between themselves and new Chinese arrivals, thus resulting in 'an increasing stratification of the emerging migrant community' (ibid.: 708–9).

Much has changed in Oshikango since Dobler did his field research in the area. A 2012 visit to the area still reveals a Chinese trading post, albeit perhaps not as large as it was before the financial crisis hit the area between 2009 and 2010. According to a Chinese trader interviewed in March 2012, many of the traders had either returned to China or moved on to other places, such as Angola or the Caprivi Strip near Zambia.[56] Nonetheless, many have remained in the area, although no one seems to have any idea about the present number. One Chinese trader interviewed estimated the number to be 200 to 400,[57] while another estimated it to be as high as 3,000 to 4,000.[58] Establishing the exact number of Chinese in the area is made more difficult by the fact that many Chinese are not at the border post. For example, one Chinese trader indicated that because there was no space for him in Oshikango to open a shop, he decided to go to a town called Eenhana to do business.[59] Attempts to get accurate figures for the number of Chinese in the area proved to be a challenging experience (see below).

The origin of Oshikango as a boom border town dates back to around 1996, when a fragile peace followed years of war in Angola. Fundamentally it was easier to access goods from the southern border with Namibia than in the war-torn capital city of Luanda (Dobler 2009: 711–12). Prior to the establish-ment of a Chinese trading post, there were earlier traders in the area from Pakistan, Lebanon, and Portugal. The first Chinese-owned shops were opened in 1999 (ibid.: 712).

Most of the Chinese shops are family-run and the owners have no connec-tions with other Chinese-owned shops prior to arriving in Oshikango. Many come to the area because they have heard about business opportunities from relatives or friends, and through official Chinese governmental publications. Thus Chinese shopowners, hailing from different places in China, come to Oshikango as competitors (ibid.: 716).

These traders come to Namibia on their own in search of better lives. Nonetheless, they do serve as an important asset for the Chinese government because they are expanding China's export industry. In a similar vein, they provide an important avenue for Africans to get goods at a relatively cheap price to which they might not otherwise have access (ibid.: 717).

> By providing Chinese goods to Angolan wholesalers, Chinese shops in Oshi-kango are linking two different trade networks. Here, Chinese networks and Angolan networks begin. Retail trade of Chinese goods in Angola takes place outside of Chinese shops; goods are sold alongside many other commodities in the mainstream retail trade and the end users often do not know that they are buying Chinese commodities. (Ibid.: 714)

According to Dobler, 'All in all, Chinese shops in Oshikango are doing well' (ibid.: 715), and 'profit rates vary between 10 and 25 percent (after transport costs, but before taxes and costs), very occasionally reaching 50 percent. All goods are sold for cash' (ibid.). 'Most dealers do the bulk of their business with textiles, shoes, mattresses and electronics; additionally, they sell com-modities ranging from motorcycles to ... cooking equipment, or wall clocks ...' (ibid.: 713). The majority of Chinese I interviewed indicated that business was good, although several lamented that things were much better prior to 2009.

Chinese traders in this Namibia–Angola trading post experience some of the same problems that Africans experience in their trading post in Chocolate City/ Guangzhou, as outlined in Chapter 2. One of the striking similarities, albeit not at the level that Africans experience in Chocolate City/Guangzhou, is growing hostility against the Chinese. Many Namibians complain that Chinese goods are cheap and are designed to cheat them out of their limited, hard-earned money; and the Namibian construction industry complains about Chinese competition. The end result is growing 'xenophobia and resentment against Chinese in general and Chinese shop owners in particular. Even though, un-like in neighboring Zambia, Zimbabwe or Lesotho, this resentment has not yet found its outlet in violence against Chinese shops, it still creates serious business problems for Chinese minority entrepreneurs' (ibid.: 718).

Dobler identifies three ways in which the xenophobia towards or resentment of Chinese shopowners plays out in the way trade business is facilitated. Again, what is most glaring about the examples relates to the dynamics between the older and more well-connected Chinese shopowners and the more recent Chinese migrants.

The first case focuses on the relationship between Namibian customs officials and Chinese shopowners. With customs officials having a great deal of power over the importation of Chinese goods, they 'have a lot of leeway to differentiate between businesspeople they like and those they do not. This makes officials' goodwill essential for successful business and opens up a space for patronage' (ibid.: 718).

The relationship between Namibian customs officials and established English-speaking Chinese traders, according to Dobler, remains good, while newly arrived Chinese traders have more difficulties in creating good relationships with customs officials. This disparity reinforces the stratification between these growing sets of Chinese migrants. In addition, as a result of the growing anti-Chinese sentiment in Namibia, it has become increasingly difficult for both the police and customs officials to ignore the obvious illegal business practices of Chinese traders, including 'overpricing and currency regulation contraventions linked to it' (ibid.: 720).

With respect to overpricing, most of the Chinese goods that reach Namibia are tremendously underpriced in terms of their declared value at customs, allowing the Chinese to make huge profits on the goods. Even though this under-invoicing technically 'does not directly cheat the Namibian state out of import duties and taxes as the goods are traded offshore, it allows the traders to under-invoice their Angolan counterparts as well, and minimize import duties or bribes in Angola' (ibid.: 720). In the final analysis the Chinese traders are able to accumulate huge amounts of untaxed and unregistered, mostly US, currency. This currency is then either smuggled to China or sold to local Chinese from South Africa, who in turn are able to earn huge sums of money from big currency transactions (ibid.: 720).

Under-invoicing poses a problem regarding the actual amount of goods that are being imported and exported between African countries as well as to and from China. As a result, it is speculated that for most African countries, including Namibia, the amount of goods imported from China is at least twice the book value (ibid.: 721, n16).

Commencing in 2007, the growing anti-Chinese sentiment in Namibia resulted in a change in governmental policy with regard to the illegal personal transport of foreign currency out of the country. A Chinese trader was arrested at Windhoek's airport for having more than US$500,000 in his suitcase. Other similar arrests followed (ibid.: 720–1).

The second way in which xenophobia toward and/or resentment of Chinese shopowners plays out in Namibia centers on the ability of Chinese migrants to gain work permits. This, according to Dobler, is 'the most important channel through which growing resentment is being felt' (ibid.: 721). Prior to 2005, it was relatively easy for Chinese businesspeople to get work permits to open shops. In response to growing anti-Chinese sentiment, this changed, however, and it became extremely difficult for potential shopowners to gain entrance. Most now have to look to brokers for assistance. One type of broker is an established Chinese businessman in Namibia who also works as an immigration person. This person might charge up to 12,000 euros for his service. In this case, the Chinese broker will provide both a workplace and housing for the new arrival as well as appropriate documents (ibid.). The alternative is to just buy a work permit from a Chinese businessman for approximately 2,500 euros. In both cases it is alleged that a percentage of the money goes to senior persons in the Department of Home Affairs (ibid.: 721).

A major means for established Chinese businesspersons to gain access to work permits is through setting up manufacturing enterprises in keeping with the Namibian government's development goals (ibid.: 722). Investing in Namibia is highly encouraged, although, according to Dobler, it has not resulted in any significant development (ibid.: 726). This is because the government continues to encourage foreign direct investment (FDI). Consequently, most established Chinese shopowners have a so-called manufacturing plant in Oshikango. On the 'official books' such plants hire local Namibians and they might assemble motorbikes, or produce blankets, or mineral water, or print windscreen stickers (ibid.: 722). In reality, according to Dobler, none of the manufacturing plants is functioning. 'There is not one functional Chinese-owned manufacturing plant in Oshikango. "You know, it's easy," one trader told me. "You just import some machinery from China. It need not even work. It costs you N$50,000 to get it here. Then, you can get 20 work permits and sell each of them for N$20,000. That's good business"' (ibid.: 722). It is thus very obvious that the Namibian government's new and more restrictive immigration policy is a failure. Chinese in Oshikango call these 'plants for paper.' Everyone knows that manufacturing is a necessary smokescreen, while the real money lies in wholesale trade (ibid.: 722). The resultant failure of the immigration policy has, like the previous governmental policy to impose more stringent rules on Chinese immigration, led to greater stratification among Chinese shopowners and a greater bond between some Namibian authorities and a select number of established traders. The amount of corruption stemming from these practices is unknown (ibid.: 722). These policies have also led to an increase in the sale of Namibian land.

In 2012, there was still no evidence of Chinese investment in industrial development in Oshikango. Since Dobler did his field research, however, the Chinese have constructed a hotel – Sun Square Hotel – which has a fishing pond where you can find Chinese with fishing rods in the evening attempting to catch fish.

The question of Chinese work permits was a subject of concern, so I went to talk to the head of immigration on the Namibian side of the border post to determine whether in fact there was corruption in the allocation of such permits. It was also at this meeting that I enquired about the number of Chinese in the area. Needless to say, the immigration official informed me that I would have to return to Windhoek, the capital of Namibia, and get permission from the Ministry of Home Affairs before he could answer any questions. Angered by my questioning, the official proceeded to ask my research assistant in their local language where he had 'got me from.' We were immediately escorted out of his office and this visit, unbeknown to me at the time, began an arduous and somewhat frightening experience in Oshikango.

The day after my visit to the immigration office, my research assistant received a call on his cell phone (he has no clue how the official got the number) ordering him to return to the immigration office immediately or else they would come and get him. Upon arriving, he had to assure the official that I had only a writing pad and no camera or computer. After his release we headed to the official government office in the area for a series of scheduled interviews. Upon arrival we were told that the CEO had received a call from the mayor of Oshikango telling him not to allow me to talk to anyone in the office. Shortly after, my research assistant received another call from the immigration official, instructing him to pass on the message that he would be paying me a visit at the motel where I was staying. Upon arrival, the immigration official demanded to see my passport and proceeded to have the official information on my passport and entry visa copied. Fortunately, upon arrival at Windhoek airport, I had been given a business visa, which was required in order to conduct research in Namibia. Without a business visa, I could have been arrested and taken to jail.

What was glaring about this series of events was that the Namibian government is very embarrassed by the Chinese trading post in Oshikango and does not want the world to know what is really happening. The Chinese clearly control the place and have not provided any of the much-needed industrial development in the area. They have built only the hotel and Chinese complexes, including Man Dan, Namchi Park, Commercial Park, Freedom Square, Dragon City, China Village and Oshikango China Plaza. On a visit to Commercial Park I interviewed a Chinese trader who told me that his boss had got his work permit; that he did not have to apply for a visa or permit.[60] This is no doubt the type of information that the immigration official did not want me to discover.

In addition to the above, the government of Namibia is no doubt embarrassed by the fact that a major source of employment in Oshikango is in Chinese shops. Among the Namibians who work in Chinese shops who were interviewed, the consensus was that the Chinese are horrible employers. A large percentage of the workers make only N$350 per month ($US48), and have no benefits. Most are required to work all day, from 8.30 to 5.30 without a lunch break, although in some cases they are given N$5 a day for lunch, but they can't leave the shop premises. Therefore someone has to come by to sell them food. There was, however, one group of employees who did get an hour off for lunch. Some were required to work seven days a week and were not given holidays, or were not paid additional money for holidays. Most, however, were required to work six days a week.[61]

Although some workers were pleased with the way they were treated by their Chinese employer, most said they were disrespected (e.g. called niggers, monkeys, lazy). The only reason they came to work was because they didn't want to just stay at home. As one person noted, what can you expect from workers if you pay them so little? Several workers said that although the Lebanese also treat their workers poorly, that at least they pay them well, so they would prefer to work for them.[62]

Ironically, every Chinese shopowner I interviewed had positive feelings about the people of Oshikango. They all commented that they liked living in Oshikango, the people were friendly, and they did not plan to leave. One specifically commented that he liked the money.[63] Conversely, it was very difficult to find any Namibian who spoke positively about the Chinese, and in fact most felt that it would be great if they were to leave the area. The one government official I did get to interview explained this dichotomy by saying that in general Namibians are seen as generous people. But if they had better choices they would not work for the Chinese, but for other people. I was further told that it's not that Namibians hate the Chinese as a people, rather that they hate the way they are treated. In addition, a lot of complaints are from people who can't compete with the Chinese.[64] In this regard, the non-Chinese shopowners did all complain that they were having a difficult time competing with the Chinese. The one change that has occurred recently in terms of the Chinese traders is that some have begun to put their money in Namibian banks as a result of being robbed.[65]

Through transformation of landownership polices in Oshikango beginning in 2004, Chinese businesspeople were able to buy up a large percentage of land in the area, including prime land closest to the Angolan border (see Dobler 2009: 722–4). Buying such land was a prerequisite for investing in the country. The outcome of this massive sale of land to the Chinese has been the creation of shops close to the border. Again, for the well-established Chinese businessperson such investments have resulted in a closer relationship with local businessmen and politicians. For newer Chinese immigrants who have rented shops primarily from more established Chinese businesspeople, many envisage moving on to greener pastures elsewhere. The latter have not been able to establish closer relationships between themselves and their host community (ibid.: 742–5).

Paulina Haimbodi has a shop in Namchi Park and thus rents from the Chinese. She is the only Namibian I saw with a shop at the border. Ms Haimbodi says this is because most Namibians can't afford to have a shop close to the border as the rent the Chinese charge is so high. Instead, most Namibians have their shops outside Oshikango. There is a row of shops at the border that I was told are owned by Namibians but all are rented to Chinese traders.

Ms Haimbodi is both a hair stylist and sells fake hair from China that she purchases from a vendor in South Africa. She complains bitterly about the situation she finds herself in. First of all, she argues that the quality of the building she rents from the Chinese is bad. Secondly, and perhaps most significantly, she feels angry about not having her own property at the border post. She says, 'The town council sold out to the Chinese. I bought a plot in June 2011; they wouldn't let me build – I can't get a permit and I refuse to pay a bribe in order to get a permit.'[66] She laments that although she stayed in Oshikango during the war there is not a bright future for the town. 'The Chinese will be here forever controlling Oshikango.'[67]

The case of the Chinese gold miners in Ghana

> When the Chinese miners are preparing to depart to sell their gold in [the] Ashanti regional capital, Kumasi, they fire their weapons into the air to ward off potential highway robbers ... (Bax 2012)

The story begins in the 1990s in Shanglin county, located in China's southern Guangxi province, with the depletion of gold. Shanglin had been a gold-mining area for generations, so when there was no more gold to be mined, the residents of the county began to migrate in search of other gold-mining opportunities. They first migrated to other areas of China, mainly Heilongjiang province in the far northern part of China, where they continued prospecting for and mining gold (He 2013).

Ghana, the second-largest producer of gold in Africa, seemed likely to fulfill the hopes of many of the gold miners. The first wave of Chinese gold miners came to Ghana in the 1990s. At this time there were very few Chinese in the country (Jiao 2013). According to a spokesperson for the Shanglin government, in 2006 the 'gold rush' started and to date an estimated 12,000 Shanglin natives have been involved in gold mining in Ghana (Xinhua, 13 June 2013). In 2010, large numbers of Chinese miners arrived in Ghana as the price of gold was soaring. Most came from Shanglin country, while others came from Fujian, Heliongjiang, Henan, and Hunan provinces (Jiao 2013).

Lured to Ghana by dreams of becoming rich, between 20,000 and 50,000 illegal Chinese miners were in the country on 14 May 2013, when Ghana's president, John Mahama, announced the beginning of a crackdown on what were deemed to be illegal Chinese in the country prospecting for gold (Jiang 2013). Ghanaian law (Ghana Minerals and Mining Act 2006) prohibits foreigners 'from small-scale gold mining on plots under 25 acres.' Before coming to Ghana, the Chinese miners usually raise up to $500,000 from family savings and bank loans in an effort to start a small gold-mining company (Jiao 2013).

There are many stories of families borrowing money to send someone to Ghana in the hope of becoming wealthy. Shen Aiguan, a mother in Shanglin who was waiting to hear whether her son had survived the governmental crackdown, lamented that 'My son might be killed in Ghana, but if he comes back he's dead anyway.' This is because Shen's family had borrowed US$489,000 for her son to build a mining operation in Ghana (Levin 2013). For all families who have borrowed money, it will take more than a lifetime to pay off creditors and family members.

This issue of Chinese being illegal in Ghana and mining for gold in some respect parallels that of the thousands of illegal market traders in Guangzhou, China, discussed in Chapter 2. Having access to proper visas is a problem for these illegal miners, who usually work with Ghanaian visa brokers to obtain the documentation to enter the country. Most of such activity is illegal and involves paying high sums of money to such brokers, gold-mining bosses, and Ghanaian immigration officers. Many miners first arrive in Togo and are then brought across the border to Ghana. They are usually given on-arrival tourist visas instead of work permits, and to the extent that they *can* obtain a work permit it is not legal (Jiao 2013). Official government corruption and complicity in the illegal activities of the Chinese miners have allegedly been widespread (He 2013; Nkwanta 2013; Jiao 2013; South China Morning Post 2013).

The crackdown was implemented for several reasons. One had to do with the environmental degradation resulting from the heavy machines the illegal miners import into the mining areas (Bax 2012; Jiao 2013; Dong 2013). Also problematic was the violence, on the part of both Chinese miners against locals and locals against the illegal miners. In response to safety concerns, some of the illegal Chinese had bought guns to protect themselves (He 2013; Nkwanta 2013). Immediately after the crackdown many illegal Chinese miners went into hiding out of fear for their lives (Nossiter and Sun 2013; Wang 2013).

The real reason for the crackdown, however, was the fact that the illegal Chinese mining encroached on the economic lifestyle of local Ghanaian mining prospectors. As noted earlier, only Ghanaians can acquire licenses to operate small-scale mining operations. Foreigners, however, 'can provide technical support and equipment.' In this regard, some Ghanaians who own small-scale mining operations have invited illegal Chinese to assist with equipment and funding. Wang suggests that these Chinese miners entered the mining business in Ghana without a proper understanding of the issues relating to having a license to operate (Wang 2013). Thus many Chinese assumed they had a legal partnership with landowning Ghanaians, although simultaneously admitting they did not have valid documentation (Jiang 2013).

The importation of heavy mining equipment in small-scale mining communities became problematic because 30 percent (an estimated one million) of Ghanaians prospecting for gold use shovels and picks, noted the Chamber of Mines. Their estimated output was 3.9 million ounces in 2013 (Bax 2012). The lives of these miners have been drastically affected by the partnership arrangements between some Ghanaian small-scale miners and their Chinese partners. With respect to the larger operations stemming from Chinese investments, locals complain that the Chinese primarily hire Chinese relatives and friends, and even other illegal immigrants instead of local Ghanaians. When the latter are hired, they receive lower wages than their Chinese counterparts (He 2013).

In addition to the above, local Ghanaians are resentful of the way some Chinese display their conspicuous wealth from gold mining. 'The people have targeted the Chinese ... for the wealth they exhibit. They drive very expensive cars,' Adu Yeboah, a youth activist, notes. Nkwanta reports that there are activists who 'feel compelled to take the law into their own hands' (Nkwanta 2013). As previously noted, some Ghanaians have responded violently to the illegal Chinese migrants as a way of displaying their resentment (ibid.).

The situation had got out of control – the government had no choice but to take action against the illegal Chinese gold miners. Again, this conflict appears to be unique in the literature on globalization from below.

Chinese market traders and the world of globalization from below: an assessment There are more differences than similarities in these two cases of Chinese traders in Africa. Perhaps the similarities lie in the complicity in illegal activities on the part of the Chinese and local governmental authorities, and the general opposition in both countries to the Chinese. Around this opposition there are issues of perceived unfair employment and competition. Finally, the Chinese in both cases have migrated to Africa in search of employment opportunities that would remain elusive in China. They have made the long journey to Africa in the hope of getting wealthy. In the case of Oshikango most Chinese traders have realized their economic aspirations in the non-hegemonic world and most are likely to remain indefinitely. The difference between the two cases is glaring.

The Chinese in Namibia have the support of the Namibian government, which is on the one hand embarrassed by their economic dominance, but on the other is committed to protecting their longevity in Oshikango. Although Chinese, they form an integral part of Africa's world markets at this important border post.

In addition to humanizing the Chinese traders, we have also humanized some of the locals who work for them. With the exception of a few, the workers are not happy with their jobs and feel sorely mistreated by the Chinese. The government of Namibia does not seem to be concerned about this treatment and, in fact, one can surmise that those complicit in allowing the Chinese to dominate this important area of Namibia have bought into Afro-neoliberal capitalism and the elite consensus.

The Chinese market traders, although agents of globalization from below, do not have to operate below the radar of government officials. None of their activities is deemed illegal and the Namibian government seems to be complacent about the fact that they do not collect any taxes on goods imported into the area.

In the case of Ghana, while some Chinese have realized their financial objectives, the majority have been repatriated back to China or have gone into hiding, fearful of the backlash from both locals and governmental figures. Their presence in the country is tenuous, as is the presence of most African traders in Guangzhou, China, because they are illegal migrants. Every aspect of their existence in Ghana seems to be illegal and at the level of globalization from below.

The case of the gold miners from China informs us about the level of desperation some people living at the level of globalization from below experience daily and the extent to which they will go in an effort to become rich. These migrants begin their journey in the country as illegals, in some cases acquire land illegally, and then feel it is within their right to protect themselves with guns against local Ghanaians who challenge their legality. They encroach upon the locals, whether it is by destroying their land with huge machinery to prospect for gold, or getting involved in the archaic local gold-prospecting practice of using shovels and picks.

The hostility that exists towards the illegal Chinese miners, which has resulted in violent conflict and the repatriation of thousands back to China, seems to be an anomaly within theory-building at the level of globalization from below. Ghanaian governmental intervention on behalf of the local gold miners reflects a commitment on the part of the government to ensure a level of employment for those who live in the non-hegemonic world. More specifically, however, the government response seems to be more a reflection of the power of civil society in Ghana. Clearly the Ghanaian government knew that thousands of illegal Chinese were working in the country. It was only when ad hoc civil society groups began to protest about the illegal Chinese miners that President John Mahama announced they would be repatriated. Earlier conflicts in 2012 had not resulted in any governmental action being taken against the illegal Chinese miners.

However, through this conflict we humanize the workers and the gold market in Ghana. Ghana's world gold market is controlled at the hegemonic level not just by transnationals such as AngloGold Ashanti, but also by thousands operating at the non-hegemonic level who are enhancing their development by selling their gold as a means to make a living wage. In the final analysis, these two case studies indicate that Africa's trade regimes are affecting the lives of Africans in this study in a negative way.

The sex trade: prostitutes as commodities to trade in the world of globalization from below

One of the most controversial issues in the world today is the question of human trafficking. Unfortunately, as great migrations occur around the world, unscrupulous individuals take advantage of the political and economic vulnerability of some human beings and turn them into human slaves. These individuals have certainly taken advantage of Chinese women in this regard. That being said, there are women who, largely for economic reasons, volunteer their bodies to be used for economic purposes. In the stories below, we will encounter both types of Chinese sex workers.

As trial judge Mrs Elizabeth Ankomah read out her verdict on Monday, 22 June 2009, eight Chinese women who had been forced into prostitution in Accra, Ghana, shouted at the top of their lungs in celebration, and wanted only to know when they would be able to return home. They had been lured to Ghana for the sole purpose of providing for the sexual needs of the Chinese expatriate community. Award-winning journalist Anas Aremeyaw had undertaken six months of intensive undercover investigation to reveal one of the most horrendous Chinese sex trade operations in West Africa (including Ghana, Nigeria, Togo, and Kenya). At the helm of the Chinese sex trafficking mafia was King James Xu Jin, his wife, Chou Xiou Ying, and her younger brother, James Sam Shan Zifran. They were all sentenced to hard labor in Ghana. James received seventeen years, his wife and brother-in-law twelve years each (Anas 2009a, 2009b).

The sex trade in Chinese women was busted on 14 February 2009 at Blossom Palace, a very expensive casino in Labadi, Accra. Following the six-month undercover investigation, the Ghanaian CID staged a raid on the casino. According to the well-respected publication *The Crusading Guide*, Anas noted that the women, some as young as nineteen, were sold for US$6,000 each and were lured to the region with the promise of good jobs.

> They are lured here with promises of honest, well-paid jobs, only to have their passports and return tickets confiscated. The travel documents may be recovered, but only after one had paid off the cost – invariably inflated – of the trip to Accra. They are beaten and threatened with a high debt to be repaid only through the sale of their bodies. They are thrown into debt bondage and forced to sell their innocence and human dignity for their master's gain in nightclubs and casinos. (Anas 2009b)

Among the entities the women appealed to for help to gain their freedom were the Chinese government, the Ministry of Women and Children's Affairs (MOWAC), the International Organization for Migration (IOM), UNICEF, and Enslavement Prevention Alliance West Africa (EPAWA). They were all returned home to China safely (Anas 2009a).

In 2011, it appeared that Ghana was revisiting this nightmare with new reports by the Ghana Immigration Service (GIS) that prostitutes were again being trafficked. A plea was made to individuals as well as non-governmental organizations (NGOs) having evidence about this new trafficking to come forward (Citifmonline 2011).

The sex trade of Chinese women in Angola took the form of the abductions of nineteen Chinese nationals who were then forced into prostitution. They were rescued by Chinese and Angolan police on 25 October 2011. Eleven suspects were arrested in Luanda and an additional five people were arrested in China for involvement in the Angola abductions. The nineteen female victims are safely back in China (Yan 2011).

The traffickers had lured women who were impoverished in China to allegedly lucrative jobs in Angola. Once in Angola they were forced into prostitution to pay back the money they received in advance for their plane ticket. The women who were rescued hailed from Jilin, Henan, Sichuan, and Anhui provinces, along with Guangxi Zhuang autonomous region. Three of the women were found when the police raided a club and sixteen more were discovered in a dark room that was approximately seven meters underground. The sex trade racket was run by two brothers – Sun Yinghao and Sun Hongbao. They had invested a significant amount of money to rent an international entertainment club called Zhong, located in the Benfica district in the capital of Angola, Luanda.

While there are other cases of sex trading in Africa by unscrupulous Chinese (see, for example, Xinhua 2010), the most scholarly account to date of the subject of non-coerced Chinese prostitution appears to have been undertaken by Basile Ndjio in an article entitled '"Shanghai beauties" and African desires: migration, trade and Chinese prostitution in Cameroon' (2009). The case Ndjio describes is reminiscent of the competition between Chinese and Africa traders in a typical African market.

At the core of the problem is the reality that the Chinese prostitutes often sell their services at a much cheaper price than the African prostitutes. For example, according to Serge Michel and Michel Beuret, 'There are roughly three hundred prostitutes in Doula, who congregate in the more down-at-heel areas like the Quartier Village or Carrefour Elf Aéroport Village. Chinese prostitutes will turn tricks for as little as 2,000 CFA ($4.25), whereas the locals, the famous Wolowoss, won't get in bed for less than 5,000' (2009: 116).

Ndjio begins his article by telling the story of how a newspaper reported (in

July 2006) that some local Douala (the economic capital of Cameroon) prostitutes had pledged to make life difficult for young Chinese prostitutes if they had enough nerve to move into 'their territory' (Ndjio 2009: 606). Reportedly this local group of prostitutes had established 'a vigilante group to protect their zone of operation that was under the threat of a "Chinese invasion"' (ibid.: 606). Ndjio notes:

> The seemingly xenophobic demeanour of these local prostitutes echoes the aggressive attitude of many market women and petty retailers from Nkoulouloum market in Douala town towards Chinese traders who are often portrayed as 'invaders' or 'unscrupulous profiteers' who allegedly live off poor Africans to whom they sell low-quality products. (Ibid.: 606)

This only serves to remind us how complex Africa–China trade is. It transcends the visible marketplace to invade the invisible bedroom space. Rather than the dehumanizing sex trade of Chinese workers in West Africa and Angola, it is a fight for trading space in the sex industry between local and Chinese prostitutes in Doula.

One of the most interesting aspects of the sex trade in Doula is that it transcends race, whereas the literature so far indicates that in West Africa and Angola the clients of the Chinese prostitutes seem to be all Chinese nationals. In Cameroon, the space for prostitutes is highly contested with Chinese prostitutes serving both Chinese nationals and working-class Cameroonians (ibid.: 609).

Ndjio suggests that the Chinese prostitutes represent another example of the depreciated and cheap commodities that China exports not only to Cameroon but the rest of Africa as well. The commodities are exported through organized Chinese trade networks. 'As such, the ambivalent representation of these Asian sex workers by the local populations only reflects the general perception that commodities exported to Sub-Saharan Africa by China are generally "cheap junk", though they are widely available and accessible to poor Africans' (ibid.: 608).

Suffice to say, it is not the objective here to detail the history of the relationship between local prostitutes and their Chinese counterparts in Cameroon. What is most relevant for this study is the notion that the space contested by these women has caused such despair and fierce competition that parallels can be drawn with the traders in a typical African market as they fight for a piece of the scanty economic pie (ibid.: 607).

This area of study, namely Chinese prostitution in Africa, according to Ndjio, 'is one of those issues that has been ignored either because "we can find no information," or because they "have not yet manifested themselves clearly"' (ibid.: 607). As Chinese migration to the continent continues, the sex trade and the resultant competition between locals and Chinese prostitutes will no doubt play a greater role in the debate around sex as both a traded commodity and the illegal trafficking of human beings. However it is defined or redefined, it will no longer be off limits to those of us studying the selling of commodities because one way to problematize the debate is to see the competition between local prostitutes and Chinese prostitutes as a struggle for contested space in which to sell their commodities (bodies).

The sex trade in the world of globalization from below represents the most unethical, illegal, and unforgiving aspect of the non-hegemonic world. Although it is also part of the hegemonic world, at the level of globalization from below it is often the poorest of the poor who engage in such activities to survive and feed their families. As we have seen in this section, most of the women discussed were lured into being prostitutes with promises of jobs that would help them realize their dreams of a better life. The trade in bodies as commodities should be considered a crime against humanity.

The non-hegemonic world of Africa–China trade: implications for globalization from below and Africa's trade regimes

China's footprint on the African continent in the twenty-first century has had unanticipated consequences in general, and more specifically in the area of trade at the non-hegemonic level. Perhaps the most significant consequence is the invasion of the informal sector. This is most significant because, as we have begun to witness, informal traders are either becoming unemployed because they cannot compete with cheaper Chinese products, or in some cases are finding it severely challenging to stay in business as a result of same. This phenomenon is a reflection of several realities of neoliberal globalization. The first is the ability of migrants to move more freely throughout the world in search of economic opportunities that are not available in their home countries. Heretofore most economic migrants attempted to become financially secure by gaining access to more advanced capitalist countries such as the USA and the states within the EU. Since 11 September 2001, the possibility of migrating to these countries has all but vanished. Hence, in the case of Africans in Guangzhou, China (Chapter 2), the joke is that they are living their American dream in China. Similarly, some Chinese economic migrants can be said to be living their European and/or out-of-China dream in Africa.

In this chapter we have humanized the market traders, from both Africa and China. Clearly there are Africans and Chinese who are benefiting from the trade as well as the trade networks and thus have become very wealthy. On one hand, they have increased the living standards of large numbers of Africans at the level of globalization from below and provided them with access to goods that heretofore have remained elusive.

On the other, we have witnessed major protests against the Chinese traders and, in the case of Ghana, the massive repatriation of illegal Chinese gold miners.

Civil society protests against the Chinese and their involvement in the 'informal' sector of Africa date back to at least May 2005, when the Kampala City Traders' Association (KACITA) sent a document to the Ugandan government entitled 'The issue of aliens in Uganda, as affecting the economy: where does Uganda gain? And where does it lose?' Among the issues the document raises is 'why the Ugandan government allows the Chinese to undercut local Ugandans out of business and allows Chinese capital repatriation to be almost 100 percent?' (Lee et al. 2007: 34). The concerns raised by African traders and the protests that have taken place throughout the continent against Chinese infiltration of the 'informal' economy might negate some of the gains stemming from Africa's increased integration into the global economy in terms of its trade regimes.

It seems that while some have benefited from this integration, others have not, and in fact may now be worse off than prior to the Chinese invasions of the 'informal' sector. If globalization from below is here to stay, the question becomes what steps should African leaders take to ensure that the continent does not implode in the wake of growing numbers of Chinese at the non-hegemonic level who continue to migrate to Africa. These migrants are not moving to the continent with the support of the Chinese government. As in the case of Ghana, many have raised money from their families and through financial institutions to facilitate their mobility.

Although the Chinese are not the first foreigners to invade Africa's informal sector, they have seemingly penetrated farther than previous invaders. As the ILO study mentioned in Chapter 1 indicates, an estimated 73 percent of Africans in the non-agricultural sector work in the informal sector. The Chinese invasion of this important sector is having a negative impact on informal wage employment in Africa. Perhaps the situation would be different if, as in the case of the USA, many migrant workers were doing jobs that natives are not willing to do. In the case of Africa, however, the Chinese traders are actually exacerbating problems of unemployment and poverty. Is this the price to be paid for newly constructed roads and governmental buildings in Africa?

Critics have long argued that while the Chinese have a strategy for Africa, Africa does not have a strategy for China. Hence, Chinese negotiate with African leaders on a bilateral level and in fact create problems of divide and rule, with African leaders requesting the same privileges given to their neighbors. If African leaders were to develop a Chinese agenda through, for example, regional economic organizations, they would be in command of what happens in Africa, including the non-hegemonic world of globalization from below.

Finally, is it possible to say that, through the circuitous networks discussed in this chapter, Africa's trade regimes have been further integrated into the global economy? Although the answer is yes, the irony, as noted previously, is that such integration has primarily taken place with Chinese goods and not African goods.

4 | Humanizing the US African Growth and Opportunity Act (AGOA): inside apparel and textile factories

This final chapter deviates from the approach of the previous two chapters regarding the issue of Africa's trade regimes and traders facilitating same. Here we examine an official trade regime established by the US government with the objective of enhancing Africa's access to the US market, especially for apparel and textiles – the US African Growth and Opportunity Act (AGOA). The agents who are at the helm of facilitating these transactions operate at the hegemonic level, or that of globalization from above, including US government officials and transnational corporations that invest in the apparel and textile sector. The workers who actually prepare the apparel and textile garments for export to the USA live in the non-hegemonic world, or that of globalization from below. Therefore, in this chapter we see the symbiotic relationship between these two systems and understand how they operate as one global entity. Of special note is the power welded by agents in the hegemonic world in relation to those in the non-hegemonic world.

The chapter begins with a brief overview of US–Africa trade relations. The remainder of the chapter will place AGOA in historical and contextual perspective; examine the special Textile and Apparel Provision; look at case studies stemming from this provision; examine whether AGOA workers have been able to build prosperity and the inherent contradictions in the Act and its implementation; critique AGOA's possible future; and assess the symbiotic relationship between globalization from above and globalization from below.

A brief overview of US–Africa relations

Formal US trade relations with Africa commenced only in May 2000 when former US president William Jefferson Clinton signed into law the US African Growth and Opportunity Act (AGOA). With AGOA, the US government not only planned to give African countries greater access to the US market, but eventually to establish free trade areas (FTAs) with specific African regional economic organizations. The first attempt to create an FTA with the Southern African Customs Union (SACU) was a dismal failure. With the prospective US–SA FTA, the USA, according to Peter Draper and Nkululeo Khumalo,

> ... sought to use the FTA to, among other things, eliminate barriers to its goods and services exported to the SACU market; strengthen intellectual rights, build

alliances for the World Trade Organisation (WTO) negotiations; and level the playing field vis-à-vis the EU. (2007: 1)

Since AGOA is the first official trade program established between the USA and sub-Saharan Africa (SSA), it is fundamentally impossible for the USA to compete with the EU because EU–Africa trade relations officially date back to the Treaty of Rome and the creation of the European Economic Community (EEC) in 1957. Basically, AGOA, as a unilateral trade program, does not have formal bilateral consultation processes that can result in dispute settlements. Thus changes to the legislation can be made by US policymakers. This results in long-term uncertainty and thus risks to investment in export capacity. However, Eckart Naumann notes that '[t]he legislation is unique in that it provided the impetus for a significant paradigm shift and interest towards Africa, but also in the sense that it garnered uniquely strong bi-partisan support in its original and subsequent legislative passage' (2010: 4).

Over the last few years, the USA, like the EU, has begun to come to terms with the changing dynamics of the global economy; namely, that there was a movement from North–South trade, investment and development to South–South and South–East trade, investment and development. Thus, in a 2012 interview, the US ambassador to the African Union (AU), Michael Battle, acknowledged that 'If we don't invest on the African continent now, we will find that China and India have absorbed its resources without us, and we will wake up and wonder what happened to our golden opportunity of investment' (Hickel 2012). It is interesting that it has taken the emerging powers of China, India, Brazil, and Turkey for the Western powers to see Africa as more than a conflict-ridden basket case, full of corrupt leaders and impoverished people who need to be saved by the West.

AGOA in historical and contextual perspective

AGOA was embodied in the US Trade Development Act of 2000 (US Congress 2000). The major objective of AGOA was to increase SSA countries' access to the US market and vice versa. Section 103 of the Act states that: Congress supports:

1 Encouraging increased trade and investment between the United States and sub-Saharan Africa;
2 Reducing tariff and non-tariff barriers and other obstacles to sub-Saharan African and United States trade;
3 Expanding United States assistance to sub-Saharan Africa's regional integration efforts;
4 Negotiating reciprocal and mutually beneficial trade agreements, including the possibility of establishing free trade areas that serve the interests of both the United States and the countries of sub-Saharan Africa. (Ibid.: 3)

Countries have to meet certain conditions, however, in order to be considered AGOA-eligible countries. They include:

1 [a] market-based economy that protects private property rights, incorporates an open rules-based trading system, and minimizes government interference in the economy through measures such as price controls, subsidies, and government ownership of economic assets;
2 the rule of law, political pluralism, and the right to due process, a fair trial, and equal protection under the law;
3 the elimination of barriers to United States trade and investment ...
4 economic policies to reduce poverty, increase the availability of health care and educational opportunities, expand physical infrastructure, promote the development of private enterprise, and encourage the formation of capital markets through micro-credit or other programs;
5 a system to combat corruption and bribery ...
6 protection of internationally recognized worker rights, including the right of association, the right to organize and bargain collectively, a prohibition on the use of any form of forced or compulsory labor, a minimum age for the employment of children, and acceptable conditions of work with respect to minimum wages, hours of work, and occupational safety and health; ... does not engage in gross violations of internationally recognized human rights. (Ibid.: 4)

If the president of the United States determines that an eligible SSA country does not comply with these conditions, they are removed from the eligibility list. Currently, there are forty AGOA-eligible sub-Saharan African countries. Beyond the conditionality imposed on these countries being reminiscent of those imposed by the International Monetary Fund (IMF) and the World Bank under structural adjustment programs (the neoliberal orthodoxy), it is interesting to evaluate whether or not these AGOA exporting companies are in compliance with the provisions relating to the treatment of workers outlined in the Act.

Prior to AGOA, SSA countries exported to the USA under the Generalized System of Preferences (GSP), which listed 4,650 products that could enter the US market duty free. With AGOA, an additional 1,835 products were added to the list for duty-free entry into the USA from beneficiary countries. The caveat was that these new items could be imported as long as they did not compete with those of US domestic producers. Nonetheless, there were numerous items of great importance to some African countries that were eliminated from the AGOA list in the textiles and footwear sections. Such items are therefore subjected to high tariffs (Lee 2004: 5).

In addition to the above, many traders have complained of serious difficulties in gaining access to the US market. As one African summarized the

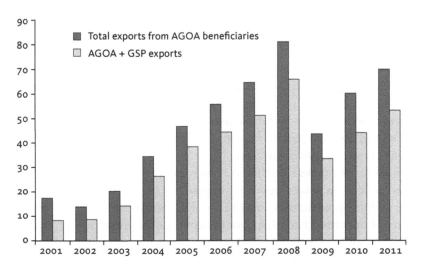

4.1 Total exports from AGOA beneficiaries (US$ billions) (*source*: Schneidman and Lewis 2012: 6)

situation, for African countries to be AGOA-eligible, the requirements are not merely minimum economic deregulation, but basically the total destruction of all tariff protection and the opening of African markets to a flood of goods from America that undermine local industry. Further to the point, with what he terms the imposition of draconian policies comparable to the IMF/World Bank structural adjustment programs (SAPs), African countries really don't have a choice but to become AGOA beneficiary countries, because otherwise they lose access to the US market (Hickel 2012). Given this reality, it should be no surprise that the balance of trade is in favor of the USA.

Specifically, only a select group of countries have been the major beneficiaries of the Act. The primary beneficiaries have been oil-producing countries, including Nigeria, Angola, the Republic of the Congo, Equatorial Guinea, Chad, and Gabon. South Africa, a non-oil-exporting country, has been a major beneficiary as a result of its ferroalloys and cars exported to the USA (Diamond 2009). As Figure 4.1 indicates, between 2001 and 2008 there was a significant increase in African exports to the USA, which began to decline in 2009, but have since increased again. Since 89 percent of these exports are petroleum products, Schneidman and Lewis acknowledge that they would have entered the US market duty free under the US GSP, without AGOA having been enacted (Schneidman and Lewis 2012: 7). This reinforces a major problem with AGOA statistics, namely that the government figures are disingenuous since they give credit to AGOA when credit is not warranted. Fundamentally, 11 percent or less of goods exported to the USA from Africa actually enter under AGOA. The African textile and apparel sector provides the majority of exports to the USA, while a smaller percentage comes from a few other sectors.

In fact, in a March 2011 study undertaken by Condon and Stern, the authors concluded that the only product group in which stimulation of exports has occurred under AGOA is apparel. In this regard, less developed countries' (LDCs') exports under the AGOA trade regime are dominated by apparel, predominantly from Lesotho, Madagascar, and Malawi. Beyond apparel, there are no other significant exports from LDCs. In addition, even though AGOA has been instrumental in enhancing apparel exports to the USA for the very small number of SSA LDC countries, the larger economic impact has been very modest. In this regard, there has been minimal transfer of skills or capital and 'linkages with the local economy have been weak.' In addition, the Asian investors have been the primary economic beneficiaries along with US importers. Beyond the apparel sector, 'the marginal preferences are low and AGOA has consequently had little or no impact on exports' (Condon and Stern 2011: 5–7).

The AGOA Textile and Apparel Provision

The original Textile and Apparel Provision of the Act is very complex, and therefore I refer readers to the original document for in-depth details. Here a summary will be provided of the most significant details, including the various amendments.

Section 112 of the Act provides for the 'Treatment of Certain Textiles and Apparel.' The apparel articles that are allowed to enter the US market must not only be assembled in an AGOA beneficiary country, but also the country itself has to have a visa to export to the USA. There are twenty-seven countries that currently have visas. The Act stipulates very stringent requirements for obtaining a visa (US Congress 2000).

Textile and apparel articles that have preferential (duty-free, quota-free) access to the US market must be assembled in one or more beneficiary SSA country. These include (1) articles that are cut from fabrics or yarns wholly formed in the USA; or (2) apparel articles wholly assembled and formed in one or more beneficiary country from yarns that originate in the USA or one or more beneficiary SSA country. This provision was to be operative for seven years beginning 1 October 2000, and the apparel imports were not to 'exceed the percentage of the aggregate square meter equivalent of all apparel articles imported into the United States in the preceding 12-month period for which data are available' (US Congress 2000: 9).

For the less developed countries (defined as having a per capita income of less than $1,500 per year in 1998 based on World Bank figures) treatment would be extended through 30 September 2004 for apparel assembled wholly in one or more less developed countries regardless of the country of origin of the fabric used (ibid.: 9–10). This is known as the third-country fabric provision. The caveat to the Act is that if the imported items damage or pose a threat to the domestic industry of the USA as a result of a surge, then the

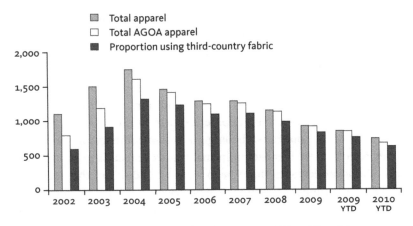

4.2 African clothing exports to the USA, 2002–10 (US$ millions) (*source*: www.AGOA. info)

president could suspend the duty-free access of such articles at the request of the affected parties (ibid.: 10).

AGOA has been amended by Congress five times since 2000. The amendments in this part of the chapter will refer specifically to those relating to the Textile and Apparel Provision (see Appendices A–D).

One of the most serious problems with AGOA is that it is not a permanent provision of the US government and therefore African countries are always concerned about the possible expiration of AGOA. This fact makes it very difficult to have continuity in investment and employment. To this end, the third-country fabric provision,[1] under which 95 percent of AGOA apparels enter the US market (Schneidman and Lewis 2012: 4), was scheduled to expire on 30 September 2012. It was only on 3 August 2012 that Congress extended this provision until 2015. The consequence of this last-minute extension was that many people lost their jobs owing to the fact that the US clothing industry places its orders months in advance for the upcoming new season. Specifically, an estimated 35 percent of such orders were lost as American companies decided to source their textiles and apparel goods from non-African producers (ibid.: 28). Leading American companies that have sourced apparel from AGOA companies in Africa for making T-shirts, jeans, and shirts include Land's End, Target, Calvin Klein, Vanity Fair, Victoria's Secret, Old Navy, the Gap, Wal-Mart, and Levi's (ibid.: 9).

Again, currently there are twenty-seven countries eligible for this provision. Figure 4.2 indicates Africa's clothing exports to the United States between 2002 and 2010, while Figure 4.3 indicates the countries that benefited the most from the AGOA Textile and Apparel Provision between 2000 and 2010. As Figure 4.3 indicates, the major beneficiaries have been Lesotho, Madagascar, Kenya, Mauritius, Swaziland, and South Africa.

Between 2001 and 2004, AGOA beneficiary countries' exports (clothing) to

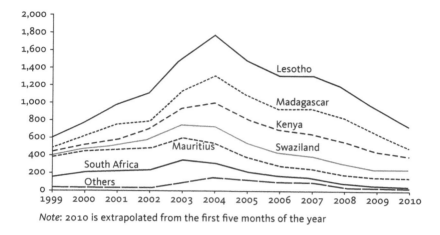

Note: 2010 is extrapolated from the first five months of the year

4.3 US textile and apparel imports from top AGOA exporters (US$ millions) (*source*: Elliott 2010)

the USA experienced a huge increase, culminating in a total of $1.75 billion. This included $1.6 billion under duty-free AGOA provisions. The majority of these exports were shipped under the third-country fabric provision. This was to change drastically, however, between 2005 and 2009, with AGOA clothing exports declining by 44 percent (Naumann 2010: 21–2). In 2011, an estimated US$850 million was exported to the US. The majority of the investors in textiles and manufacturing are from Singapore, Hong Kong, and Taiwan. Other investors are from South Africa, the USA, France, India, Bahrain, and Israel (Thompson 2010: 469).

Many companies, primarily Asian, but also some from South Africa and the USA, decided to invest in the textile and apparel industry in Africa. For many Asian companies it was a means to circumvent the restrictions placed on them as a result of the Multifiber Arrangement (MFA), initially implemented under the General Agreement on Tariffs and Trade (GATT) and later extended under the World Trade Organization in 1995 as the Agreement on Textiles and Clothing (ATC). The former was in place from 1974 to 1994, or the end of the Uruguay Round of trade negotiations in the GATT. Under the MFA, quotas for textile and clothing were governed by the MFA and negotiated bilaterally, thus allowing for specific quantitative restrictions to be placed on textile and clothing when increases in imports were thought to or did cause a threat or serious damage to a country importing the goods. When the GATT was replaced by the World Trade Organization (WTO) in 1995, the MFA was replaced by the Agreement on Textiles and Clothing (ATC), which put in place a transition phase for ten years for the removal of tariffs. The ending of clothing and textile quotas is usually simply referred to as the ending of the MFA. As will be seen below, this had a devastating impact on the textile and apparel industry in numerous AGOA-designated countries. Many Asian textile and apparel companies resorted to investing in the industry in African countries in order to bypass the MFA. Consequently, many of these same companies pulled out their investments on the eve of the ending of the MFA. And as noted in a report on AGOA, 'The looming phase-out of the MFA was publicly ignored by policy makers from both the United States and Africa when the AGOA came into effect in 2000, and even in 2005 when the consequences of the phase-out became clear' (De Hann and Stichele 2007: 12).

In a 2012 paper, Lorenzo Rotunno, Pierre-Louis Vézina and Zheng Wang challenge the origin of some of the AGOA textile and apparel exports to the USA. Specifically, they argue that a large percentage of such exports actually originated from China and were transshipped through AGOA-eligible countries (Rotunno et al. 2012: 2).

The major thesis of Rotunno et al. is that as a result of the strict quotas placed on Chinese apparel entering the USA during the final years of the MFA, 'quota-hopping Chinese assembly firms' took advantage of the fact that the AGOA Textile and Apparel Provision had no rules of origin (RoO) for countries that were eligible for the third-country fabric provision and used them to temporarily transship apparel to the USA. Fundamentally, the RoO loophole in the AGOA Textile and Apparel Provision gave Chinese exporters the opportunity to use what they call 'screwdriver plants' (factories that only assemble products from parts produced elsewhere) to transship their goods, thus avoiding the MFA quotas (ibid.).

Quasi-finished products that required minimal assembly work were exported from China to these 'screwdriver plants' and then exported to the USA as if they were actually made in specific AGOA countries. According to Rotunno et al., this accounts for the boom in AGOA exports to the USA commencing in 2001 (ibid.: 1–2). Similarly, the ending of the MFA in 2005 accounts for the rapid decline in AGOA exports and the departure of footloose factories (ibid.: 2). While others have heretofore had anecdotal evidence of this taking place (see Naumann 2008; Fernandez-Stark et al. 2011; Lall 2005), Rotunno et al. actually empirically traced the transshipment beginning in China to the AGOA factories, and then on to the USA (ibid.: 4).

Chinese assembly firms were encouraged both by AGOA's lack of RoO and the MFA quotas. Rotunno et al. thus conclude that if you combine these two incentives then direct transshipment accounts for an estimated half of apparel exports to the USA under AGOA during the boom period. If this is broken down by specific countries, the authors estimate that these polices 'may account for as much as 64% of Botswana's apparel exports; 45% of Kenya's, 35% of Madagascar's, and 23% of Lesotho's' (ibid.: 14). Such exports from AGOA 'screwdriver plants' were mainly sweaters, T-shirts, and basic trousers, which were items that under the MFA were quota-restrained products (ibid.: 3).

AGOA factories: the workers are human beings

This part of the chapter will examine two AGOA textile and apparel bene-ficiary countries – Lesotho and Swaziland – and two companies that were in-volved in exporting apparels under the AGOA provision – Tri-Star and Ramatex.

Lesotho In 2003, the Baneng factory began operating in Lesotho, and by December 2005 it was closed. The 730 workers returned after the Christmas break to find the building abandoned, which meant they did not receive any job termination benefits. Lieketseng Lephallo worked for the Baneng factory from 2003 to 2005. She did sewing and was considered multi-skilled on the machine. Her job consisted entirely of stitching on one machine making T-shirts, specifically hemming the sleeves and bottoms of the shirts. Since Lephallo was a multi-skilled worker, she was paid R750 per month as opposed to R650 per month for a non-multi-skilled worker. When asked how she was treated, Lephallo said:

> there was lots of stress, tough times; if you missed the target you were sent to
> the office to sign a warning ... If you made your target from Monday to Wednes-
> day, but not Thursday to Friday, they would tell you to go home and think
> about it and you wouldn't get paid. If you continued to get these warnings, the
> final one you would be dismissed. If you are sick and the doctor would give you
> a sick leave, you might be dismissed.[2]

Lephallo, like all the workers in this chapter, became an AGOA worker because she was living in the non-hegemonic world of abject poverty. She originally traveled to Maseru, the capital of Lesotho, from Qacha'sneck (300 kilometers from Maseru) to be a nanny for her sister's new baby. After the child grew up she went to work for Baneng Company. In the factory Lephallo was never called by her name, only 'hey you.' Her working hours were from 7 a.m. to 5 p.m. She and her colleagues were forced to work extra hours without pay. They were not paid for their overtime because the monitors were not working overtime.[3]

'If you were sewing and made a mistake, they would throw the fabric you were working on in your face.' Lephallo explained it was the local supervisor who would insult the workers and charge them for making a mistake. 'You would always have a local supervisor because of the language gap and then the Chinese supervisor. The former was always trying to please the latter.'[4]

> You could only go to the toilet twice a day and while you had provision of
> drinking water, you would be reprimanded if you drank too much. If you drank
> too much water, you might find a Basoto supervisor sitting in your chair when
> you returned which could result in dismissal that day. To prevent this from
> happening, one might ask your supervisor to bring you the water, but they

would usually refuse saying that you would end up going to the toilet too many times.[5]

Lephallo has no idea how many workers actually worked in the factory because there were so many different divisions. She was involved in one strike. The owner fled at the end of the month in 2005. It took the government seven months to pay their wages. 'The payment of the wages was announced over the radio saying that we should come and get our pay ... My tenure in the company ended when the owner fled.'[6]

Again because of poverty, Lephallo decided to work for another AGOA company called Tai Yuam from 2005 to 2009. 'It was worse than the first company. For example, you only received R3[7] per day versus R50 per day extra for meeting your target.'[7]

> In this company the local Basoto supervisor pinched you after you came back from getting water and if you were late to work you were instructed to go back home. You also got hit with your garment if you made a mistake. In terms of production requirement, you were on a line and basically required to produce 1,500 shirts a day. The official working hours were the same as Baneng Company, but if you hadn't met your target by 5 p.m. you would have to work until 7 p.m. and even then you would not have been considered as having met your target because you had to work overtime. If people behind you were slow, you would be penalized for that.[8]

Lephallo left the company in 2009 because she was ill owing to her feet getting cold. Then she got TB. She says that while she has been unemployed since 2009, she would never work for an AGOA company again. 'It's useless because what I earn is for commuting. There is no purpose in that.'[9]

Workers with Hong Kong International Knitters were a bit luckier than those from the Baneng factory (the first factory Lephallo worked for). The former opened in 2000 and closed in March 2004. However, the 1,049 workers were given terminal benefits (De Hann and Stichele 2007: 14). As will be seen below, this is an exceptional case. In fact, another factory, TW Garments, closed in December 2004 but none of the terminal payments was forthcoming to its 1,600 former employees (ibid.).

Thabo Thamae also worked for an AGOA factory. It was originally known as Old Rivers Textiles, but it was one of the factories that left the country in 2004 and moved to Vietnam prior to the end of the MFA. The factory was bought by another company and was called Santinkon when Thamae was an employee. His job at Santinkon was in the packing department.

> I would take finished materials and take [them] to the packing department. I was moving in different departments where there were hazards and I was not provided with a face mask. The smell was suffocating for me. Sometimes I had

to walk through the water room. Electrical equipment was hanging all over the place. No one was wearing helmets.[10]

According to Thamae, there was tremendous pressure and he didn't feel safe. Once you made a mistake you were expelled from the company. His wages were only M650 but his monthly expenses were at least M1,500.[11]

There were about 150 men working in the factory and they were mostly involved in cutting the cloth, while the women were responsible for the laying of the cloth. 'Women, especially pregnant women, were not given tender care and all workers were under pressure, with employers all the time telling them that there were plenty of unemployed people who were in line for their jobs.' Sick leave was not acceptable, according to Thamae, and so they were told that 'if they wanted to rest they should rest forever.'[12] Working hours were from 7 a.m. to 5 p.m., and, reinforcing Lephallo's experience, overtime hours were not clocked on their cards and thus they received no extra pay, although the employers would tell them they included it in their pay. Workers did have an hour lunch break and worked six days a week (half day on Saturday). The only thing the company was concerned about was cut, make and trim (CMT).[13]

During the interview, Thamae was especially focused on the treatment of women. He said that the conditions in the factory were very dangerous for women. They had no heating or ventilation systems. And when it was cold the women were not allowed to wear blankets and the men were not allowed to wear jerseys. The rationale was that such items would interfere with production. The only time you could get water to drink was when you went to the toilet and you were not allowed to go to the toilet more than three times during the entire day.[14]

At the time of the interview with Thamae in August 2011, he was considering returning to the factory because of financial issues. Although the current owners of the factory (South Africans) have said that better working conditions are in the pipeline, he does not believe them.[15]

As Figure 4.3 indicates, Lesotho has been the largest beneficiary of the AGOA Textile and Apparel Provision. By mid-2004, Lesotho had an estimated fifty garment factories employing 55,000 workers. These included factories that had moved from South Africa to avoid international sanctions as well as many Taiwanese-owned companies. By the end of 2004, six large factories closed as a result of the MFA phase-out and several more closed at the beginning of 2005. In 2006, it was estimated that Lesotho had thirty-nine garment factories, thirty-two of which were owned by Taiwanese companies (De Hann and Stichele 2007: 20). Between 2000 and 2004, as a result of AGOA, the sector grew significantly, with exports to the USA increasing by 223.5 percent. Then, in 2005, on the heels of the ending of the MFA, exports to the USA declined by

17.2 percent (Central Bank 2010). Currently between 32,000 and 36,000 workers are employed by AGOA companies.[16]

Lesotho is the only African country that was able to rebound from the shock of 2004 as a result of the ending of the MFA. This was due to several reasons. The first was the measures taken by the USA and Europe to safeguard their own industries against the onslaught of products coming from China. The suppliers wanted to diversify their supply base. The second factor was that some buyers wanted to be 'socially responsible' and help Africa. In this regard, there was an MFA Forum that had as its goal to promote 'social responsibility and competitiveness in national garment factories that are vulnerable in the new post-MFA trade environment,' and Lesotho was identified as a country of focus (De Hann and Stichete 2007: 21–2).

The third factor was the fact that the US extended the third-country fabric rule and the fourth was the depreciation of the South African rand against the US dollar. A fifth factor was when the South Africa–China agreement put quotas on goods imported from China into South Africa (see Chapter 3); this had a positive effect on both Lesotho and Swaziland since South Africa had to find another place to source needed goods (ibid.: 21). Factor number six was that some of the factories had lost their space in China and Vietnam, so they had to return to Lesotho.[17]

The final factor has its origins in 1967, when Lesotho gained its independence and established the Lesotho National Development Corporation (LNDC) with the objective of promoting industrial development. The LNDC had built and paid for factory shells for potential investors (foreigners can't own land in Lesotho). In addition to modifying the shells to accommodate the specific needs of particular investors, the LNDC would provide the necessary infrastructure (ibid.: 24–5).

When the first AGOA companies closed down in Lesotho in 2004, to entice others to remain, the government amended the incentives, including reducing tariffs to 0 percent for companies outside the SACU region. Taxes for companies within the SACU region were reduced to 10 percent. The country also implemented the Duty Credit Certification Scheme (DCCS), designed to allow exporters to recoup duty they had paid on raw materials. In summary the government provides:

- Tax-related incentives
- Good infrastructure
- Utilities
- One-stop shops to facilitate easier investment and trading. (Ibid.: 23)

The tax-related incentives are further elaborated:

- Preferential Corporate Income Tax rate of 0% for exporters outside SACU; 10% for other manufacturing firms

- 5% depreciation allowance for industrial buildings
- 125% training expense deduction
- No withholding tax on dividends distributed by manufacturing firms to local or foreign shareholders
- Free repatriation of profits derived from manufacturing firms
- VAT [tax] deferment facility for imports for manufacturing exporters
- Upfront VAT refund scheme for local purchases by textile and garment exporters
- Duty free imports of raw materials and capital goods for manufacturing exporters. (Ibid.: 23)

The garment industry in Lesotho remains the largest employer in the country. In studies undertaken by the Centre for Research on Multinational Corporations in Amsterdam, the Trade Union Research project, the Lesotho Clothing and Allied Workers Union (LECAWU), and the Lesotho Department of Labor, it was deemed that the working conditions in factories that were exporting under AGOA were terrible. These included long working weeks, often seven days per week; overtime that was often forced and unpaid; violations of health as well as safety standards; dismissals that were illegal; union rights that were repressed; job insecurity with workers often being employed as casual labor for years; and verbal abuse by managers, including beatings (ibid.: 24–5). In addition, it was determined that the salaries were too low (ibid.: 26).

The studies further concluded that with the garment industry concentrated in the capital of Maseru and Maputsoe (in the industrial parks), most women had to travel long distances to work and had to leave their children behind. In this regard, because the salaries were so small, they were not able to pay for transport to see their families, nor were they able to send enough money to take care of them, including for educating their children. These women also lived in urban settings without access to decent housing, clean water, clothing or even medical facilities (ibid.: 26). Although there have allegedly been some improvements in the working conditions, workers are still subjected to harsh conditions and the Lesotho government is concerned about scaring away investors (ibid.: 28). Not only does the government turn a 'blind eye to labour conditions,' it also ignores the environmental impact poor water treatment filters have on the community at large (ibid.).

The unconscionable treatment of workers has been problematic since the beginning of the AGOA regime in 2001. In fact, in 2001 an independent South African contractor investigated Nien Hsing, a factory that produced Gap jeans, and found the following violations of workers:

- Bribes being demanded of new employees by some managers
- Extreme heat and cold in the factory, and no temperature regulation
- Hard, backless chairs for sewing operators

- Workers are physically searched and forced to disrobe before leaving the plant
- Extremely high production quotas that the government of Lesotho has declared unfair
- Evidence of child labor, with children under the age of 15 performing the same work as adults
- Blocked exits
- Workers in the union are discriminated against, and are fired for union activity. (Pdfio.com 2002)

Strikes by workers had started by 2002. In fact, it was on 26 March, during a protest against abusive labor conditions at the Nien Hsing garments factory, that Marashalane Ramalieha, who was a twenty-four-year-old supervisor, was stabbed with a sharp pair of scissors by the factory director and had to be hospitalized (Wales 2002).

During these early years, however, such unconscionable treatment was not just confined to Basoto workers, but was also experienced by Chinese workers. According to B. Shaw Lebakae, deputy general secretary of the Lesotho Clothing and Allied Workers Union (LECAWU), and David Maraisana, also of LECAWU,

> We had a flood of Taiwanese coming in as well as from mainland China. Some were women prisoners from China because they had violated the policy of only one child in China. They had their parole officer with them. We knew this was the case because the officer was with them when they went to the shops. They were not allowed to buy goods themselves. They had to tell their parole officer what they wanted and he would purchase it for them. These Chinese women were very aggressive against pregnant African women in this country ... The government didn't want to believe there was prisoner labor in this country until they saw a Chinese chained to a fence ... When the Labor Department found the Chinese man tied to the fence, the Chinese got rid of all prisoners.[18]

To this day, according to Lebakae, AGOA workers continue to be mistreated. Two major issues are at play. The first relates to the employment status of workers and the second to wages. With respect to the first issue, Lebakae notes that in Lesotho there are three types of official workers' contracts: (1) fixed-term contract; (2) contract with no reference to time (permanent employment with an obligation to pay the person if you tell him or her to go home); and (3) a contract with a special task. The Chinese, however, have illegally introduced two additional types of contracts. The first is casualization (which doesn't exist legally in Lesotho). In this case most people come to work at night and leave early in the morning and they get paid as they are leaving work. Because they are casual laborers, their pay should be higher, but it's not. With casual labor, there is no maternity leave, no paid holidays, no educational leave. The second illegal form of employment is short-term, which is the same as lay-off. If the company doesn't have enough orders, people are told to stay home and they don't get paid. These illegal forms of employment are possible because government officials are bribed by the Chinese not to implement labor laws. Lebakae emphasizes that 'this is a known fact.'[19]

With respect to the issue of wages, the five textile sector unions in the country continue to fight for a living wage for the AGOA workers. With wages still below or at the poverty level, the unions consider a living wage to be R2,020 (Lebakae 2011). In addition to these two issues, workers are still being intimidated if they belong to a union, and most are extremely poor, and continue to be abused.[20] One of the problems with the poverty-level wages is that many of the women have to resort to either taking out loans from their employer or getting involved in prostitution.[21]

In terms of the labor conditions, Lebakae and Maraisane felt that the 'problem with the US is that it says it wants factories that are not sweatshops, but when it comes to Africa they change the goal posts.' This is also the case when it comes to ethical working conditions and child labor. With respect to the latter, they refer to America having double standards for Africa as opposed to places like Vietnam and Cambodia.[22] It is the case that most Americans believe that AGOA is making a difference to the lives of most Africans and helping to bring them out of poverty, as the statement below by US Senator Coons indicates.

> One of the best things we can do to strengthen America's long-term economic security is to invest in the fastest-growing economies in the world, the majority of which are in sub-Saharan Africa ... AGOA and its Third Country Fabric Provision are helping to build a strong middle class in Africa, lessening dependency on U.S. foreign aid, and opening important new markets to American companies. (Senator Coons, as quoted in AGOA.info, 3 August 2012)

This is a total fallacy, as Jason Hickel, in an article entitled 'Africa: trading with the enemy' (2012), so succinctly puts it: 'The vast majority of beneficiaries under AGOA are not impoverished Africans, but wealthy foreign corporations.'

In this regard, Mzimkhula Sithelo of the Economic Justice Network of Lesotho is concerned that the country is not in control of its textile industry and therefore 'AGOA has not benefited Lesotho. There were supposed to be 6,400 product lines. All we produce under AGOA are T-shirts, caps, and jeans. The government is not even getting taxes from workers' wages and the companies don't pay anything; we have tax evasion ... we don't have ownership in any way.' In addition, Sithelo is concerned that there is no transfer of skills and no foreign direct investment (FDI). 'Because of the situation set up with factory shells already in place, there's nothing the companies leave behind and they endanger our human species and cause serious environmental degradation' (see Lesotho Environmental Justice and Advocacy Center 2008). 'We have blue rivers as a result of the pollution of our rivers.'[23]

Another problem stemming from AGOA has been serious consequences in the changing dynamics of male–female relations. Lebakae calls it a paradigm shift in that women are now working and men are not. With tens of thousands of men having been laid off from working in the mines in South Africa, the majority of people working in formal employment are women in the textile industry. 'One of the consequences is that women as young as eighteen have men living with them that they don't even know. This is one of the major reasons HIV is spreading among women. These women, some of them are just small girls, when they are not working get drunk and forget who they are. They are not aware of what's happening to them,' Lebakae argues. Some of them have three to four children and they send them back to the rural areas to be taken care of. 'People are really dying here like flies. Again, women have become men.'[24]

In the final analysis, the AGOA Textile and Apparel Provision may have been implemented with good intentions on the part of the US Congress, but the unintended consequences have been devastating for Lesotho, and the US government has turned a blind eye to this reality.

Swaziland The stories coming out of Swaziland stemming from the development of the garment sector as a result of AGOA are just as alarming as those from Lesotho. The 400 workers at Sheung Lee were unexpectedly confronted with the reality of the closure of the company and were not paid their terminal benefits when the owner fled the country and disappeared without trace. When the workers at Suntay Lon had not been paid for two weeks, they were instructed to return to work to get their pay. Upon returning they were not paid and the management had disappeared, not only stripping the factory, but also leaving the Chinese supervisors behind without pay or a ticket home. The Taiwanese embassy in Lesotho gave them money for food and arranged for San Tay Lon to buy plane tickets so they could return home. The following other companies closed down after 2004: Brand Knitting (800 employees); Diamond Textile (300 employees); Say Light (120 employees); Kasimi (600 employees); A&L Garments (800 employees); First Garments (800 employees); Nantex (650 employees); New Biella (150 employees); and Welcome (1,200 employees) (De Hann and Stichele 2007: 35). According to Esther de Haan and Myriam Vander Stichele, these departing companies did not leave anything behind, including the keys, and they did not pay the workers. To make matters worse, there was fundamentally nothing the government could do (ibid.: 35).

Ms M. had been working at a Chinese-owned AOGA plant for three years in Swaziland. Based in the packing department, she had been hired on a permanent basis, earning R372 every two weeks. She worked from 7 a.m. to

5 p.m., with a thirty-minute break at 12.30. She paid into a pension scheme from her salary but was not able to access the money when the factory closed. She could not find her employer to enquire about her pension. Ms M. says that while working at the company – San Tay Lon – the treatment experienced by workers was appalling. In addition to being shouted at, employees who were perceived as working too slowly would be beaten by Chinese supervisors. On one occasion an employee responded by attacking the supervisor and she was fired. Since the closure of San Tay Lon, Ms M. has had to resort to being a domestic worker, earning 400 rand less than she had while working for San Tay Lon. Along with her three children, she had no alternative but to live with her mother (ibid.: 38).

As in Lesotho, the working conditions in most of the garment factories in Swaziland were/are harsh. There are health and safety issues, the refusal of the companies to recognize labor unions, casual employment as well as contract work. The wages are low, with the minimum being about 200 rand weekly in 2006, which is not enough to take care of an average family of five to ten people. There is compulsory overtime work. Legally mandated sick and maternity leave are often not paid and workers are not confident that they will ever receive a pension (ibid.: 38). In addition, there was no transfer of skills (ibid.: 31).

The garment industry in Swaziland did not take off until the country became eligible for the Textile and Apparel Provision on 26 July 2001. Following this, foreigners invested in more than thirty factories between 2001 and mid-2004. When the sector was at its peak, it employed approximately thirty thousand workers, with most of the plants being located in the main industry center of Matsapha (ibid.: 31).

Swaziland experienced a phenomenal increase in its garment exports to the USA from 2001 to 2004. While in 2001 the figure was only $8.2 million, by 2004 this had increased to $176 million. However, with the ending of the MFA, exports had dropped to $134 million by 2006. By July 2007, there were only seventeen to eighteen garment companies remaining in Swaziland, which were all owned by foreigners (ibid.: 31–2). 'The government has spent a great deal of money attracting the industry, and although there is definitely frustration with the returns on the investment, there is a strong will to keep the industry going. This makes the government vulnerable to pressure from buyers and manufacturers wanting even better deals' (ibid.: 39).

The government of Swaziland, like that of Lesotho, made a serious commitment to creating an environment that would attract foreign investors. This included:

• Signatory to several economic and trade agreements, giving exports from Swaziland preferential access to overseas markets.

- Providing and constantly reviewing incentives for investors.
- A review of general business regulations that create bureaucratic obstacles to investment, in order to remove controls on trade.
- The development of infrastructure, including road and rail links.
- The supply of readily available commodities, support services and professionals (including attorneys, accountants, engineers and architects). (Ibid.: 32–3)

Again, like Lesotho, they built factory shells and paid for the infrastructure development for foreign investors. Other financial incentives included:

- 10% corporate tax rate and exemption from withholding tax on dividends for ten years for qualifying investments in the manufacturing, tourism, mining and international services sectors;
- Duty-free importation of capital goods, new machinery and equipment for use in manufacturing enterprises;
- Duty-free importation of raw materials for exports outside the Southern African Customs Union;
- Depreciation allowances for capital goods and buildings;
- An Export Credit Guarantee Scheme granted through Commercial Banks and supported by the Central Bank of Swaziland for export-oriented enterprises;
- Double taxation agreements with the Republic of South Africa, Mauritius, the United Kingdom and China (Taiwan);
- A Human Resources training rebate of 150% cost written against tax;
- Repatriation of profits and dividends in full. Repatriation is also allowed for salaries of expatriate employees and for capital repayments. (Ibid.: 33)

When the MFA phase-out occurred, many of the companies, especially those from Taiwan, intensified their lobbying of the government. They wanted less stringent labor regulations, including lower minimum wages and more incentives to increase their presence in the country. One company, for example, indicated it was willing to develop a textile mill, but in return for less stringent labor and environmental laws and the prices of electricity and water being decreased by half. In addition, the company wanted the government to subsidize workers' wages (ibid.: 34).

The government responded to these and other requests by noting they had already spent too much money on building factory shells and the grace period for tax holidays for foreign companies was five to seven years, which meant that the government received no income during this period. As someone from the Ministry of Enterprise and Employment stated in January 2006, it was from desperation that they had built the factory shells (ibid.: 36). Obviously out of frustration, Mr Vilane, who at the time was with the Swaziland Investment Promotion Agency (SIPA), said, 'We have spent billions, but it has not cost the

US government anything, nor the companies that are buying here, all have only profited. It has cost us and they have profited' (ibid.: 37).

In July 2012 a representative of the Swaziland Textile Export Association noted several reasons why the industry had shed over two-thirds of the 30,000 jobs since 2004. They included the potential expiration of the third-country AGOA fabric provision, the problematic US economy, unfavorable exchange rates, high Swazi wages compared to those of Asian workers, and a lack of local investment (GantDaily.com 2012).

In April 2012, Cynthia Lushaba lost her textile factory job, along with 1,999 other workers, allegedly through business being bad. Lushaba commented that her salary was so low that the only thing she could do was provide two meals a day for her two children and pay the rent (ibid.).

Uganda

> Apparel Tri-Star has been roaming Africa, closing down in one country without paying the benefits or wages, and setting up shop in other countries for just a few years, after which they leave behind the same situation. (De Hann and Stichele 2007: 41)

Tri-Star in Kampala, Uganda, opened in response to AGOA in January 2003, with 1,200 employees. It immediately started producing textiles for the US market. 'President Museveni saw Tri-Star as offering thousands of jobs to people who had never dreamed of having a regular income.' On 21 October 2003, following the 'disciplinary' beating of a female worker, the 'AGOA girls' (they were never referred to as women) went on strike (ibid.: 44), and were dismissed. Before she was dismissed, Ms Doreen, who was twenty-one, had to leave the dormitory for the factory before 7 a.m. and didn't return to the dormitory until after 6 p.m. She had no protective gear in a factory that was filled with fumes and particles from woolen materials. Because she was feeling a pain in her chest, Ms Doreen asked the company managers whether an X-ray could be taken. The response was no, and when she requested to be moved to a different area of the company they refused again, so she decided to quit. Only then was she transferred to a different area of the factory. Although the premises were unsafe to work in, the managers refused to open the doors to allow ventilation because they were concerned that materials would be stolen. In addition, the Tri-Star 'girls' were denied drinking water while they worked. They were not allowed to bring any into the warehouse and the managers refused to provide it for them. In addition, they could not leave the premises to get a drink of water. In order to get any water, they had to fill out a request form, which went through several bosses. It could take up to half an hour just to get permission to leave the premises to get a drink of water. Ms Becky, another 'girl' who was dismissed because of the strike, had to sew seventy-five pairs of trouser pockets daily. If she didn't, she risked being dismissed from her job. The 'girls' were constantly shouted at and exposed to abusive language and harassment (Mulumba 2003). Some were even sexually abused, and the company refused to recognize workers' unions (De Hann and Stichele 2007: 44). Eventually the strike was broken and Tri-Star fired approximately 293 workers without giving them their severance pay (ibid.). President Museveni announced to the press that, 'I sacked those girls because of indiscipline, as their action would have scared off investors who had plans to set up business here ...' (ibid.: 45). The strike was broken when anti-riot police led by the inspector general of the Ugandan police, Major General Katumba Wamala, were sent into the dormitories. A water cannon truck was used, along with police in plain clothes to invade the dormitory. The boss of Tri-Star, Vellupillai Kananathan, commended the operation, saying the objective was to 'clean up the saboteurs' (Wall Street Week 2003).

Four months before the strike, the working conditions at the factory were discussed in the Ugandan parliament, with reports of workers not being able to use the toilet during working hours and overall mistreatment. During the strike, over two hundred AGOA 'girls' spent the night in the Ugandan parliament building demanding that the government intervene in the dispute. Panic was caused by the situation in government circles, especially since government policy is to encourage investment in the country. During an investigation by journalists, it was determined that Tri-Star was receiving US$200,000 a week from its export of textiles to the USA, but was not paying any taxes on the income. In addition, it did not have to pay taxes on any machinery or equipment when it started operating (ibid.). As a result of the strike and the resultant concerns of government ministers, the Ugandan cabinet asked Tri-Star to at least respect the terms of the Ugandan Employment Act, which meant that if the women were not going to be reinstated they should at least be given three months' salary and transportation costs back home (ibid.).

When Ruth Apio began working for Tri-Star Uganda in late 2003, the working conditions had not changed and so she quit a year later. 'I left because I could not see my children. I had not seen them for one year.'[25] Because the majority of AGOA 'girls' migrated to Kampala from rural areas to work for Tri-Star Uganda, they lived in dormitories supplied by the company. Although this meant they were fed three meals a day by the company, in the end their salaries were the equivalent of US 20 cents an hour (ibid.). Also, they were required to stay in the dormitories year round, which meant they could not take leave to visit their families. In fact, only on Sundays could they leave the premises to go to prayers and to shop, but if they did not return the same day, they were sacked. There were from fifteen to 150 women in each dormitory room, depending on the size.[26]

Apio had no identity in the factory; she was known only as number 5041.

Her job was to put seams on pockets and seams on the center-back of trousers. She worked a double needle machine. 'You continued until you made the target of 750 pieces per day. Fifty-three women had to make 750 items per day, so you would sometimes have to work until midnight.' The management shouted, embarrassed and teased people. 'They would chase you if you spoiled the garment and then you were fired.'[27]

She further explained that she couldn't send any money to her children because her salary was so low, only 80,000 shillings (US$40) per month. So her children were taken care of back in her home of Tororo in eastern Uganda by her mother and brother.

Hygiene in the dormitories was horrible, according to Apio. There were only two women cleaning toilets. There were four bathrooms for the seven thousand or so workers, most of whom were women, each with only four toilets. Each bathroom had one shower and one tub. The bathrooms were outside, about thirty meters from the dormitories. If they were nearer, Apio said, you would die from the smell. People got sick from the bad hygiene and some died. There were medical facilities, 'but you were only given painkillers. There were so few men working that they used the staff bathrooms for men.'[28]

In terms of working conditions, the management was extremely harsh.

You had to wake up at 5 a.m. Breakfast was served at 6 a.m. which consisted of dry tea (without milk) and two slices of bread. Sometimes you got one piece of banana or one egg. At lunchtime you had to run back to the dormitory to get your plate and cup, which was stored under your bed. You had meat for lunch on Thursday, Saturday and Sunday, and beans for dinner on Sunday and a cup of dry tea. When you worked on the electrical machines you needed to take drinks. There was never enough water to drink and there were no breaks until you finished work. You had to keep your empty bottle of water, but often the water was not clean. Apio made men's and children's trousers; tour shorts with six pockets each; and one kind of shirt. Most of the managers were from Sri Lanka and you were told that Americans were paying your salaries, but you only saw Sri Lankans. All the labels on the clothes said 'made in the US.'[29]

The factory was divided into several rooms. There was a cutting room, a room for sewing, one for washing and drying and one for ironing. 'One day I just decided to take my last paycheck and leave. Besides not being able to see my children, the working conditions in the factory were so bad!'[30]

The Ugandan government had invested heavily in Tri-Star Uganda in order to export textiles under AGOA. In addition to incentives already mentioned, including generous tax breaks, President Museveni welcomed Tri-Star to Uganda by giving the company a loan of US$5 million from the Uganda Development Bank. The Tri-Star premises were provided free of charge and the training of the workers was subsidized by the government. A warehouse was converted into the factory, along with dormitories. Power lines and three standby generators were also provided by the government. In total, the Ugandan government invested approximately US$3.8 million in Tri-Star to get it up and running (De Haan and Stichele 2007: 45). Eventually Tri-Star closed and the government failed to recoup its investment. However, around 2007 the company was taken over by LAP Textiles Ltd (Libya African Investment Portfolio), which was a new company 'established in Uganda as a joint venture between LAP Mauritius and the Government of Uganda. Its main objective is to manufacture quality readymade garments for export markets. LAP textiles operates under the African Growth and Opportunity Act (AGOA),' and according to a company document, it is 'committed to all aspects of AGOA' (LAP Textiles n.d.).

The above account of Tri-Star, a company established in Sri Lanka in 1979 (De Hann and Stichele 2007: 41), is a reflection of the havoc the company wreaked on several countries in Africa in the name of AGOA. In Botswana during 2001, the government welcomed the company and encouraged its 500 employees to work hard. During the middle of 2003, the factory closed, leaving its existing 641 employees without paychecks, although there was an industrial court order against the company to pay the wages (ibid.). In Kenya, Tri-Star closed in 2004, giving the workers one month's notice. In the interim, workers were harassed, forced to meet unrealistic work targets, were not paid for overtime, not given annual leave, and some were dismissed so the company would not have to provide terminal benefits. Once the company closed, 'workers were not paid their full benefits and were told they would get the difference after the machines had been sold. These machines were exported and sold abroad ...' (ibid.: 42).

Tri-Star Tanzania was opened in 2003 in the presence of the US ambassador to Tanzania and US Senator McDermott. By April 2005 the company had been placed in receivership and the following month it was closed (ibid.: 43). According to one worker:

> ... life in the factory was tough ... all pregnant women were ordered to write a resignation letter so the factory could avoid having to meet the legal requirements of maternity leave; working hours were increased by 1½ hours to a total of 9½ hours per day; overtime was compulsory, forcing workers to work from Monday through to Sunday, without rest days. When workers had to work overnight as overtime after a full day's work, the hours were 6 p.m. to 6 a.m. and workers had to report back to work the day after, having had only three hours of rest. Workers were not entitled to any leave; if there was a funeral of a close relative, only a day's leave was given without pay; Indian and Sri Lankan expatriate staff verbally and sexually abused young women workers; trade unions were not allowed at all. Anyone discovered having contacts with a trade union representative was immediately dismissed without pay. (Ibid.: 44)

Namibia Monica Shaiyengauge worked for Ramatex in Namibia from 2003 to 2007. She spent the entire day sewing sides and sleeves to T-shirts or sewing trousers. 'There was a lot of mistreatment; if you made a mistake the Malaysian boss would tear it apart and tell you to go home. You would be sent home at 9 a.m. and couldn't come back until the next day.'[31] There were lots of chemicals in the plant, Shaiyengauge notes, and with no protection there was a great deal of sickness. Even worse, you were fired if you stayed home because you were sick.[32]

In addition to the above, according to Shaiyengauge, the Malaysian boss beat people, and if you wanted a toilet break you had two to three minutes to take care of your business.

> We had to work seven days a week. On Saturday and Sunday the working hours were from 7 a.m. to 7 p.m. You would get overtime pay of N$4 per hour. But you were required to work overtime. If you didn't you were given five warnings and then you were fired. If I worked Monday to Friday I was paid N$500 per month and if I worked overtime I was paid N$900. My rent was N$300; transport N$15 per day; food N$30 per day. I had no money left and I had a child to take care of.[33]

Mukuka N. Emilia's story does not differ much from that of Shaiyengauge. She also worked for Ramatex from 2003 to 2007. Her daily job was to attach cuffs and the necks to T-shirts. She said she had many warnings about being fired. The management always talked aggressively to her. However, they did give her water and she had an hour for lunch. Emilia worked from 7 a.m. to 7 p.m. and made only N$500 per month. She received no benefits (sick leave, pension, vacation), but the government did force Ramatex to pay social security. Because she had a child to take care of, Emilia remained in the job until the factory closed in 2007.[34]

Franciska Geinus' tenure with Ramatex lasted only three months. 'I walked each day to work because with the salary I was getting I couldn't afford to pay for transportation.' As a trainee for three months, she was paid only N$300 per month. The managers were disrespectful, and there was no protection against the environment in the factory. In addition, workers were not given pensions. The official work hours were from 8 a.m. to 5 p.m., but often Geinus had to work until 8 or 9 p.m. inserting zippers in pants all day. 'I just finally quit.'[35]

At its peak of hiring, Ramatex is said to have had 8,000 employees, 5,000 of whom were said to be Asian. The Asians lived in hostels on the premises and were making more money than local employees.[36] Geinus believes there were so many Asians because they were bringing their families over to work.[37] Volker Winterfeldt indicates that no one really knows how many Asians were employed by Ramatex, noting that the company was never transparent about the number of foreign workers of Asian descent it hired. Winterfeldt puts the initial number at 1,900 by mid-2004, but the media reports suggest a higher figure. They estimate a total of 2,260, with 1,000 Chinese (800 from Malaysia and 200 from mainland China), 750 Filipinos, and 510 from Bangladesh (2007: 83). Each nationality at some point during Ramatex's tenure in Namibia went on strike for various reasons, including demands for better wages (ibid.: 83–4). As general policy, Ramatex took their passports upon arrival and they had to agree to contracts of three years. Most of these workers were said to be employed because of their skills, but many ended up being managers over the African workers, which proved to be problematic. The Africans accused the Asians of being arrogant while the Asians accused the Africans of having low performance levels and a lack of work discipline (ibid.: 83).

Workers' strikes began shortly after the mega-complex that housed the company was completed in 2002. According to a member of the Namibian governing party, the South West Africa People's Organization (SWAPO), the workers began to strike for better wages and working conditions, including protection against harmful chemicals; for transportation money; for pay (allegedly sometimes they didn't get salaries or their overtime pay for two months); and against tremendous environmental pollution from chemicals being used for production.[38] A site visit by the author to the now closed Ramatex factory put the level of environmental degradation in perspective, with green water sitting in what was one of the ponds serving as an outlet for the chemicals used in the processing of the AGOA textiles and apparel; this five years after the factory had closed. An environmental study released in 2004 determined that Ramatex had not built (nor did it ever build) the promised and required water waste treatment plant (an agreement to this end had been established between Ramatex and Namibia's capital city of Windhoek). As a result, Ramatex was temporarily storing the water 'in large evaporation/oxidation ponds' that were filled beyond their capacity. The ponds began to overflow and dump pollutants 'into the groundwater as well as into the Goreangab Dam, one of Windhoek's major water reservoirs' (Winterfeldt 2007: 88–9). Residents in the area began to get sick and complained of the stench emanating from the waste water. Finally, the city of Windhoek had to build the recycling plant for Ramatex (ibid.).

How can the unlikely alliance between the Namibian government and Ramatex be explained? Prior to Ramatex, Namibia did not have a textile industry, but the government was so anxious to attract foreign investment that it gave Ramatex incentives to invest in its export processing zone (EPZ) which were very enticing to the company. The story of how Ramatex ended up in Namibia is an intriguing one.

What became known as Ramatex Namibia was part of the Ramatex Group or Ramatex Berhad Company. The latter was established in 1982 as a small textile manufacturing entity under the name of Gimmill Industrial (M) Sdn, in Batu Pahat, Malaysia (LaRRI 2007: 31–2). Today known as the Ramatex Group, it 'expanded vertically from dyeing and knitting mills into yarn manufacturing in 1989 and continued its growth into finishing fabrics and printing in 1992' (LaRRI 2003: 8). As Malaysia's only and largest vertically integrated manufacturing enterprise, it exports most of its textiles and apparel to countries in the North. Since 1996, the Ramatex Group has been registered on the Kuala Lumpur stock exchange (Winterfeldt 2007: 71). Fifty-nine percent of the company shares are owned by the Ma family and there are branches in China, Cambodia, Singapore, and Mauritius (ibid.: 72). Of course, there was also a branch in Namibia until 2007, and in South Africa until 2003. At the time that the Namibian government was able to convince Ramatex to open operations in Windhoek's Otjomuise district, it had three factories in South Africa: in Dimbaza, King Williams' Town, in the Eastern Cape Province (ibid.).

Ramatex South Africa's original plan was to extend its operations in the Eastern Cape, leading to the employment of an additional 18,000 workers. The negotiations between Buffalo City and Ramatex South Africa came to a stalemate when the South African cabinet felt it had exhausted all the privileges it could offer the company. Not satisfied, 'Ramatex South Africa began to look for another place to invest that would allow it more privileges' (ibid.: 72) and still allow it to take advantage of the AGOA provisions. So the Namibian government stepped up to the plate and made the Ramatex Company an offer it couldn't refuse.

The massive size of the Ramatex investment was a dream come true for the Namibian government, which, with a view to attracting foreign investment, had created an EPZ in hopes of creating more jobs and boosting the country's manufacturing capacity (LaRRI 2003: 5). The EPZ Act would allow:

- Corporate tax holidays (no taxes on profits of EPZ companies)
- Exemption from import duties on imported intermediate and capital goods
- Exemption from sales tax, stamp and transfer duties on goods and services required for EPZ activities
- Reduction in foreign exchange controls
- Guarantee of free repatriation of capital and profits
- Permission for EPZ investors to hold foreign currency accounts locally
- Access to a streamlined regulatory service ('one-stop shop')
- Provision of factory facilities for rent at economical rates
- Financial support for staff training. (Ibid.: 5)

When the EPZ Act was passed in 1995, the government did not want the Labour Act to apply. However, the major trade union in the country, the National Union of Namibian Workers (NUNW), were opposed to this provision, arguing that it was a violation of Namibia's constitution and International Labour Organization (ILO) conventions. Rather than go to court to settle the issue, it was agreed that the Labour Act would be applied in the EPZ, but that for five years strikes and lock-outs would not be allowed (ibid.: 5–6).

The incentive package put together for Ramatex by the Namibian government included water and electricity that would be subsidized; and a ninety-nine-year lease on 43 hectares of pristine land in an industrial park in Otjomuise district. While the leasehold was valued at N$16.9 million, Ramatex only had to pay a fee of N$1 monthly. Then, upon the request of the company, the leased land was increased to 160 hectares. The city of Windhoek paid for the grading of the hilly and rocky area and also built an access road to the factory at a cost of N$1.5 million. Electricity, water and sewage infrastructure were provided free of charge to the factory site. The parastatal company in charge of Namibia's deep-sea harbor at Walvis Bay – NamPort – provided wharfage free of charge, and a new container terminal was included in the incentive package to transport thirty containers a day between Windhoek and Walvis Bay. The city of Windhoek paid a total of N$106.12 million. Added to this was the N$17 million for the new TransNamib's Windhoek terminal (Winterfeldt 2007: 70). Finally, because of the EPZ rules, Ramatex was entitled to receive 75 percent of the cost involved in training Namibians to work for the company (Flatters and Elago 2008: 8).

After all this, Ramatex violated the law proscribing the building of living quarters in the EPZ and constructed housing for its Asian employees. Although the city of Windhoek protested about this, the government ignored their complaints. Also, during its first two years, the company ignored many other policies of the government (see Winterfeldt 2007: 74).

Most disconcerting of all was the treatment of the workers. The salaries were so low that most of the women had to walk long distances to work, including through an area that was extremely dangerous. When Ramatex was questioned about the alleged requirement for women to take a pregnancy test and pay for it themselves, Ramatex initially denied that this was the case. Later on they did acknowledge this was the case and that women who were pregnant were denied employment. This was against the labor laws of the country.

Also against the labor laws was the fact that initially unions were forbidden from entering the premises of the plant, thus preventing the workers from exercising their right to collective bargaining. There was so much conflict at the plant and unfair practices that five 'wildcat' strikes brought the company to a halt. Two of the strikes were by Namibians and three by the Asian workers (ibid.: 77).

Ramatex finally closed its doors in 2007. 'When the people came to work the company was locked down. They came the next day and the same thing happened. The workers were not given any warning.'[39]

My site visit to the huge Ramatex complex in March 2012 found equipment being removed and people buying the remaining Ramatex cloth and clothing. I am in possession of summer shorts for children meant for 'The Children's Place' in the USA. The price tag says $6.50 each or three for $15. The inside label says 'Made in Namibia.'

AGOA's future

Prior to the phase-out of the MFA, it was predicted that SSA countries would be among the greatest losers. However, De Hann and Stichele argue that the changes, especially for Lesotho and Swaziland, have not been as devastating as predicted (2007: 13). Nonetheless, there is no denying that Figure 4.3 indicates a significant decline in both countries' exports to the USA under AGOA. There are those who believe that the African garment market will survive the current crisis and others who don't believe it will be possible. Perhaps one of the most important reality checks comes from Mark S. Bennett of the Tanzania Cotton Board. He argues that 'Some US members of Congress want to remove duty-free access to the US market in textiles for Cambodia and Bangladesh. If this occurs, Africa is finished! These two countries export 7½ times more textiles to the USA than all of Africa. And the duties they pay on their exports are more than [those for] all goods exported to the USA by African countries.'[40]

The AGOA legislation will be up for renewal in 2015. While there is talk among members of Congress of extending AGOA until 2019 and beyond, as Bennett notes above, it is the case that consideration is being given to extending AGOA preferences to countries such as Bangladesh, Cambodia, and Sri Lanka. This will be in addition to likely finally removing the third-country fabric provision for less developed countries. Even more alarming is the fact that the proposed legislation 'also considers a new UN definition for "least developed countries",' which could see a number of current beneficiaries losing their AGOA beneficiary status (Naumann 2012: 5).

Niall Condon and Matthew Stern are of the opinion that if the US government liberalized African products that are labor intensive and imported into the country under tariff rate quotas with rules of origin that are non-restrictive, then the impact of AGOA would be improved (2011: 6). This, of course, would mean competition with mainly US agricultural producers, which is not likely to happen.

A symbiotic relationship between globalization from above and globalization from below and an unimaginable tragedy

Allegedly under the watchful eye of the US government, a tragedy has transpired in AGOA apparel and textile factories. The collision between globalization from above and globalization from below allows us to deconstruct this tragedy. Many issues are raised growing out of the stories that have been presented. They include the violation of labor laws by employers; whether or not AGOA workers have been able to find opportunities to build prosperity; the abuse of AGOA provisions by investors; civil society protest; and the alliances established between civil society and the government of Namibia in an effort to put a stop to serious environmental degradation by an AGOA company.

Building prosperity for AGOA workers and violation of labor laws The data collected for this chapter raises an important question about international labor laws and whether or not AGOA workers have been able 'to find opportunities to build prosperity,' which is a major objective of the Act. At face value, the reading of the case studies in this chapter would indicate a resounding no. If this is the case, then what are the major constraints to the realization of this objective? In January 2011 an Obama administration official noted that '... while the scheme has delivered benefits, these had not been "as great as we would have wished"' (AGOA News 2011). Further to the point, Nicolas van de Walle argues that reforms need to be made to AGOA with a view to enhancing its ability to better promote economic poverty alleviation and economic growth, as well as democracy and good governance (2009: 19).

In a scathing critique of US AGOA policy, Hickel notes that, according to the AGOA Act, beneficiary countries are supposed to protect workers' rights, 'including the right to organize and bargain collectively'; not allow compulsory or forced labor; enforce a minimum age for children to be employed; and provide 'acceptable conditions of work with respect to minimum wages, hours of work, and occupational safety and health' (Hickel 2012). According to Hickel:

> In practice, however, none of this actually applies. Countries renowned for corruption, human rights abuses, and labour law violations are routinely approved for AGOA eligibility. Indeed, the countries with the most flagrant abuses are those that trade the most under AGOA, giving a blatant lie to the claim that good governance is a necessary precondition for successful US investment in Africa. Cameroon, for example, enjoys AGOA eligibility even though the government there rules an undemocratic, one-party state, regularly obstructs political meetings, harasses journalists, tortures human rights activists, and turns a blind eye to child labour. But it has a lot of oil. (Ibid.)

With respect specifically to the AGOA Textile and Apparel Provision, Steve Ouma Akoth argues that there are 'taboo subjects' around this industry. The first he identifies as 'precarious and poverty jobs.' One of the major consequences of AGOA and similar trade arrangements 'is that for the first time after the industrial revolution, such huge numbers of unorganised labourers, especially women, are coming under the productive sway of large-scale capital' (Akoth 2009). While such women who are employed by companies in export processing zones (EPZs) are able to make more money than in the informal sector, it has been taboo to discuss exactly what these women are actually doing and what type of job security they have (ibid.).

Specifically, in 2009 Akoth observed that for the last nine years, since AGOA was implemented, women had been employed only for their manual dexterity and thus jobs that didn't impart skills, but merely required repetition and didn't result in forward or backward linkages with any other sector of the company. These were therefore what he calls 'precarious poverty jobs.' Even though the EPZs boast of creating in some areas up to thirty thousand jobs, the women who work in the garment factories don't feel that their jobs are helping them or their families work out of poverty. In addition to the low wages, short-term contracts (in some cases no contracts), and unhealthy working conditions, they have to work a great deal of overtime just to meet their minimum basic needs. As a result, in 2009, there were 2,635 employees with cases pending again EPZs in Kenya for various reasons (ibid.).

The second taboo subject identified by Akoth is the impact the EPZs have on a country's labor laws and practices. Although, according to Akoth, 'AGOA is crafted under the rhetoric of rule of law,' the reality is completely different. He posits that the corporations work with bureaucrats in the Ministry of Labor in Kenya who have been 'captured' by the corporations, and seek to 'wiggle' out of such laws. In addition, he argues that the International Monetary Fund (IMF) and the World Bank have put pressure on the Kenyan government 'to adjust their labor laws to meet the sourcing companies' demands.' The message being that market forces instead of government should define labor standards (ibid.).

The third taboo concerns US government trade policies. In Kenya, by 2012, the garment industry reportedly produced all of its own cotton, which is in keeping with the phase-out of the AGOA provision that allows the less developed countries to source their fabric from a third party. In essence, in order for Kenya to continue to export under AGOA's Textile and Apparel Provision, all the cotton must be domestically produced. But Akoth argues that it is taboo to talk about the billions of dollars in trade-distorting subsidies given to US and EU cotton farmers annually. Therefore, US officials double-speak about AGOA, while US corporations and major stores and brands (e.g. Target, Wal-Mart, Hagar, Sears) exploit workers ('make it flexible and make it cheap') and make huge profits from the goods they make (ibid.).

As export-led growth becomes the *sine qua non* of developing countries such as Kenya,

> the pool of potential suppliers has increased massively, with thousands of producers on every continent vying for a place in their chains ... In maintenance of harmony in these factories, the EPZ employers with tacit support from the US sourcing companies have put in place strategies to minimize resistance and 'de-teeth' local trade unions. The companies' toolkit included hiring more vulnerable workers who are less likely to organize – women, often immigrants into the urban centres – and intimidate or sack those who try to create trade unions and stand up for their rights. (Ibid.)

In the final analysis, Akoth argues that those who are in the business of selling their labor have inalienable rights, premised on the basic understanding that people have the right to a dignified life. This is made clear by the International Labor Organization Convention (ibid.), respect for which is a requirement in order for SSA countries to be eligible for AGOA. It appears, however, that market forces and corporations have become more important to the USA than ensuring that ILO provisions are guaranteed to workers. So while workers' oppression might foster economic growth, it will not promote human development. 'Such production for trade provides "growth opportunity" not to Africans, but to foreign owners' (Thompson 2010: 469).

Reinforcing the above, the US government, as the hegemonic power operating from the level of globalization from above, has sanctioned the horrific abuses in the global sweatshops created under AGOA in Lesotho, Swaziland, Botswana, Uganda, and Namibia.

AGOA-affiliated corporations who are agents in the hegemonic world have created these global sweatshops under the pretense of making life better for the non-hegemonic world in specific African countries. In this regard, global capital, again under the watch of the US government, abused the MFA principle vis-à-vis creating temporary companies in these countries, then abandoning the workers without any recourse from the USA. This is neoliberal globalization at its nadir.

Africa's trade regimes Since AGOA was first signed into law in 2000, concerns have been raised about the implications of the Act if it were not made permanent. While there are many inherent contradictions in what the Act says and what in practice has happened to the AGOA workers, the reality is that, as it currently exists, AGOA is promoting suffering in Africa. If the current trajectory remains the status quo in the AGOA factories and AGOA is not made permanent two outcomes are likely. The first will result in those who have at least been able to get jobs in garment factories losing them. The second is that Africa will never be able to become self-sufficient and internationally competitive in the garment industry. Seemingly the United States, like most developed countries, gives gifts to Africa with one hand, and takes them away with the other. To date, AGOA's Textile and Apparel Provision has had limited impact on Africa's trade regimes and the lives of people working in AGOA factories. Thus, the ability of AGOA's Textile and Apparel Provision to enhance Africa's integration into the world economy has been very limited.

Conclusion

When John Maynard Keynes from the United Kingdom and Harry Dexter White from the United States were at the helm of creating a post-World War II new international economic order in 1944, the prospective new rules for international trade positioned the great powers of the hegemonic Western world as the guardians of the system. Among the factors that gave rise to the perceived need to create a new system was the collapse of the international economic order stemming from World War II and the Great Depression. The conference to establish a new international economic order had as one of its major objectives the creation of a system that would guarantee that nations would never, owing to a financial crisis, resort to withdrawing from international trade. International trade was the *sine qua non* of a healthy and vibrant international economic order, which was one of the lessons learned from World War II and the Great Depression.

The conference to create a new international economic order was held in Bretton Woods, New Hampshire, in 1944, under the leadership of Keynes and White. The forty-four nations represented created the IMF, the World Bank, and the General Agreement on Tariffs and Trade (GATT). With respect to the latter, trade was to be controlled at the hegemonic level, and through a series of trade negotiation rounds, tariff and non-tariff barriers to trade would gradually be removed with a view to creating a world of freer trade. Needless to say, the majority of the countries that were expected to be included in this system in the future were still under colonial rule, thus their voices were silenced at Bretton Woods.

Throughout the decades since, the hegemonic international economic system marginalized the majority of the world's population trying to make a living wage through the informal economy and through illegal activities. This reality eventually gave rise to the non-hegemonic world or globalization from below, the subject of this volume.

Trade at the level of globalization from below is predicted to grow exponentially. Consequently, academics, trade officials, and policymakers can no longer afford to ignore trade regimes at the non-hegemonic level. This trade is difficult to monitor, financial transactions are elusive, and the networks are complicated. With the continued marginalization of the global South and South-East within organizations such as the WTO, the IMF, and the World Bank, those on the ground involved in trade at the level of globalization from below will continue to operate under the radar of governments and security structures. To their credit the poor of the world have found a way to survive in this challenging global environment in the wake of the refusal by the Western powers to compromise and create a world in which, among other things, fair trade becomes the norm. As will be discussed in the companion volume, provisionally entitled *Africa's International Trade Regimes: Globalization from Above*, the post-World War II international economic order put in place to facilitate trade among the most powerful countries in the world is dysfunctional owing partially to the failure of the North to concede any of the major demands of the South. Globalization from below is one response to this intransigence. The greatest losers of the failed post-World War II international economic order, unfortunately, are the governments of the South and South-East, which are not able to collect much-needed revenue as a result of the elusive nature of the transactions in the non-hegemonic world. The formalization of these transactions would enhance potential development in the South provided leaders actually used such revenue for economic development.

This volume has attempted to answer the question: How have Africa's trade regimes affected the lives of Africans in this study who are operating at the level of globalization from below? This is where the majority of the people in the world exist, with Africa hosting the largest number of people in the informal economy. Some individuals live a precarious life, never knowing whether their legal or illegal activities will compromise their existence. Most people at this level are self-employed and they do not pay taxes on their income to their respective governments, unlike their counterparts in the world of globalization from above.

In an attempt to begin to deconstruct Africa's trade regime at the level of globalization from below, we examined the plight of African traders in Guangzhou, China; trade relations between African and Chinese traders and their clients in several African countries; and the Textile and Apparel Provision of the US African Growth and Opportunity Act (AGOA).

As noted in this book, even those who mostly operate at the level of globalization from above often appreciate the world of globalization from below, thus carrying out many of their own transactions below the radar of governments. Globalization from below is not only here to stay, but will increase its visibility as an integral part of what is being developed into a new international global order in the twenty-first century. And the symbiotic relationship that exists between globalization from below and globalization from above will deepen.

The theoretical constructs of globalization from above and globalization from below are discussed in this book. Efforts to separate the seemingly separate worlds – the hegemonic world of globalization from above and the non-hegemonic world of globalization from below – are impossible. Though operating at two different levels, again they are part of one world economy.

Globalization from above and globalization from below provide one of the most dynamic frameworks for analysis used by political economists to describe, explain, and predict the future of global trade.

Nonetheless, there is a missing link; namely, where in this study do African leaders fit? Such leaders are at the forefront of promoting neoliberal global-ization, thus preventing Africa from realizing its development potential. For this study we have adopted the theory of 'Afro-neoliberal capitalism and the elite consensus' which has resulted in African leaders supporting the liberal orthodoxy to guarantee the continuation of neoliberal capital accumulation that is fundamentally anti-developmental.

With respect to the latter, this study has pointed to the reality that there is minimal correlation between Africa's trade regimes and development. At best we see the improvement in the lives of some agents in this study and at worst we see the hegemonic world of globalization from above ensuring that those working for hegemonic companies remain in abject poverty, most evidenced by our discussion of AGOA.

Our investigation of Chocolate City (Guangzhou) in China is a case study of African traders in Guangzhou, China, who have migrated to the area in hopes of realizing their entrepreneurial objectives. Through ethnographic interviews it has been determined not only that many have been successful, but also that some have become wealthy. Others have not been so lucky. Many traders, however, manage to at least make a living through shipping thousands of containers of Chinese goods to Africa. These goods have become the mainstay of those living at the level of globalization from below. African traders are making a dif-ference in the lives of millions of Africans who heretofore have not had access to such goods, despite them usually being fake, counterfeit, or of low quality. Unfortunately, as previously noted, economic development remains elusive.

Finally, we learned a great deal about what it is like to be an African entre-preneur in China. This includes those who settle in the country and thus are caught up in the everyday world of entrepreneurial life, and also those who come only for short periods to buy merchandise for their shops back home. The oppressive environment that the less successful African traders find them-selves in means their lives are not necessarily changed for the better by their trade activities in China, with many in search of ways to leave the country. With an estimated 95 percent of African traders living in Guangzhou, China (the world's factory), illegally since they have overstayed their visa and need significant financial resources to secure a required exit visa, it appears that large numbers might be stuck in China for some time to come. And many such individuals remain in China in poverty, often isolated from their fellow traders.[1] Other African traders, upon hearing the plight of their counterparts, are opting to avoid China and to seek their entrepreneurial aspirations in places like Turkey, Vietnam, and Bangladesh.

Chapter 3 took us to Africa, where we explored globalization from below and the growing tension between agents in this world – Africans and Chinese. Our major questions to be answered are: (1) is it possible for these two agents (African and Chinese traders) to survive and thrive together at the level of globalization from below; and (2) what are the potential consequences of the growing tensions, at times violent, between these two agents? In terms of African traders in the markets, several in this study have clearly become millionaires (by African standards) as a result of buying and selling Chinese goods. Chinese traders have been able to infiltrate the informal sector in Africa (appropriately referred to as globalization from below), which is the sector that has allowed Africans to survive. As most of the African traders in this chapter acknowledge, they cannot compete with the cheaper products the Chinese bring into the continent. Nonetheless, there are those who feel that the influx of Chinese goods into their countries is positive for the economy.

What has become obvious is that very often with African traders the issue is not so much that there is an influx of Chinese goods into these countries, but that the Chinese are able to buy directly from the factories in China and thus get goods at a cheaper price than Africans who import the goods into the continent after buying from shops and/or suppliers in China. They are both selling the same items, although many African traders who go to China to source their goods argue that they buy more upscale items than those the Chinese bring into their countries. In the end, however, very often both the Chinese and Africans are selling counterfeit goods from China. Here there are winners and losers. In the case of African traders, the winners are those who are able to make tremendous profits from selling Chinese goods and the losers are those who are not. In the case of the Chinese, the winners are traders such as those in Oshikango, Namibia, who are making tremendous profits from Angolans who cross the border daily to buy goods using US dollars. The losers, of course, are those who are not able to compete successfully against their African or Chinese counterparts.

In any case, there are two overarching issues around the infiltration of Chinese into the non-hegemonic world of African markets. The first is that African governments are constantly being accused of being 'in bed' with the Chinese and thus allowing this infiltration to occur without any constraints. These same critics say this is because of the rents leaders are receiving in the form of money, infrastructure development, the construction of major governmental buildings, etc. The second issue is that in many African countries civil society is fighting back against the Chinese invasion at the level of globalization from below and hence some of these same leaders who have bought into neoliberal globalization are being forced to take a stand against the Chinese in order to contain civil society unrest.

The case of the South African textile industry and China does point to the reality that the powerhouse of the continent cannot compete with Chinese textiles, and indeed textiles from other countries as well. Even after an agreement was reached between South Africa and China to place quotas on some Chinese textiles entering the country for two years, the South Africans ended up importing textiles from other countries to replace those from China.

The case study of the steel industry in Ghana and the competition that exists from cheaper steel that is of poorer quality being imported into Ghana speaks to a larger problem in trade relations between Africa and China; namely that such imports would not be possible if African governments were committed to protecting their internationally competitive industries. Here we discover a serious clash among the elites in the country who are not concerned about the potential job losses, especially for those living in the non-hegemonic world.

The Chinese trading post in Oshikango, Namibia, is a reflection of the corruption inherent in non-hegemonic China–Africa trade relations. The Chinese who come to Africa looking for places to do business are clearly at an advantage and have more money than local Africans. So in the case of Oshikango, instead of prime land on the Namibian side of the border being resold to local Namibians, it was sold to Chinese. At the heart of so much of what is transpiring at the level of non-hegemonic China–Africa trade relations is greed. The issue of greed permeates Africa's post-colonial history. Very few African leaders since independence have been concerned about development. So it is that the Chinese were not only able to buy the prime land from the Namibians who owned it, but also have been allowed to get away with mistreating local Namibians who work for them. Again, many throughout this study have made reference to African governments being 'in bed' with the Chinese. Thus in my haste to find out the truth about the level of corruption in Oshikango, I barely escaped being arrested by immigration officials. Here we clearly see Chinese operating at the level of globalization from below benefiting from leaders who buy into the thinking of Afro-neoliberal capitalism.

We next looked at the Chinese who have entered Ghana illegally and have been actively engaged in illegal mining. While the Ghanaian government had to be aware of the estimated 20,000–50,000 illegal Chinese in the country, they took action to deport the Chinese only once civil society rebelled against them. The tragedy of this situation is that most of the Chinese who traveled to Ghana hailed from an extremely poor part of the country and were thus competing with the poor of Ghana. The clashes that ensued were inevitable and inform us about the growing danger of the poor competing against each other at this level of the global economy.

Finally we were introduced to the trafficking of women as prostitutes by unscrupulous Chinese. This is certainly a grave injustice. On the other hand, we are also introduced to the notion of the trade in prostitution as a commodity in Cameroon. Specifically, there exists competition between local prostitutes in

Doula and their Chinese counterparts. Here we have competition for contested terrain. Perhaps it should not be a surprise that this issue has entered the debate on China–Africa trade since it is the oldest profession in the world. This is certainly an integral part of the underworld of globalization from below.

We continued to see Africa's marginalized position within the global economy in Chapter 4. Though designed to provide most African countries with greater access to the US market, with the exception of a few countries (mostly producers of oil), SSA has gained very little from being involved with AGOA. From a focus on the textile and apparel factories, it is obvious that African workers have not been able to obtain a living wage nor working conditions that comply with the standards of the International Labour Organization (ILO), a major stipulation of the Act when it was implemented in May 2000. With primarily Asian countries investing in AGOA factories, it has been under the watchful eye of the US government that the workers have been exposed to working conditions that resemble those of global sweatshops. Although US government officials continue to proclaim that AGOA has lifted large numbers of Africans out of poverty, this in fact is not the case. In an effort to humanize AGOA workers through personal interviews and other sources of primary data, we saw that in many cases they have been left worse off than prior to working in such factories. This does not bode well for a government that prides itself on promoting human rights and good governance. Here one also has to ponder how African governments have allowed and continue to allow their workers to be treated in these factories as if they are not human beings. To date the trade unions in Lesotho have not been successful in getting the Asian (mostly Chinese) owners of AGOA factories to provide a living wage to their workers, along with proper gear to protect them against unhealthy and unsanitary working conditions. What is obvious is that there is a clash between globalization from above and globalization from below. Finally, one cannot but notice that the trade between Africa and the Asian agents who own the AGOA factories has left African traders marginalized.

Africa's trade regimes

A great deal of rich data is contained in this volume that allows us to make some tentative conclusions and/or recommendations about the way forward as it relates to Africa's trade regimes. As indicated in the introduction to this volume, any attempt to try to understand Africa's trade regimes is a daunting task.

One of the most fascinating aspects of this research has been discovering the vast African trading networks at the non-hegemonic level. One can only wonder how far these networks date back. We do know that in ancient times Africans traded in gold and elephant tusks (among other things) with traders as far away as China. In this study, the networks begin in Africa, go to the Middle

East, Asia, the USA, the EU, and return to Africa. And within Africa, they are extremely complex and warrant a study of their own. These networks are keeping people alive and thriving. However, the unfortunate reality demonstrated in this volume is that the majority of the goods that are being transshipped throughout the continent are from China. This does not bode well for African economies and the future of the continent. While the undermining of Africa's manufacturing sector through SAPs in the 1980s is partially responsible for this phenomenon, African leaders are also responsible. They have failed to create 'developmental states' that would enhance Africa's industrialization and hence greater incorporation into the capitalist world economy with high-tech commodities instead of primary products. Nonetheless, we can certainly say that Africa's trading networks allow us to have a much better understanding of how Africa is incorporated into the global economy.

Just as the talk in Guangzhou, China, is about African traders beginning to bypass China in search of other trading posts, in the next few years we are likely to hear and read about African traders in such places as Turkey, Bangladesh, and Vietnam. Such networks will remain below the radar of formal governmental institutions and thus will operate at the level of globalization from below. The potential for exporting to Africa different and even better-quality items is great. The downside of this remains the same – namely, that as long as African countries can import luxury items that heretofore have remained elusive there will be further deindustrialization and no incentive to add value to the goods produced on the continent. This means the current structural linkages of dependence and underdevelopment growing out of colonial rule will remain in place. Though countries may for a short time experience economic growth, economic development will continue to remain elusive. So what future will Africa have without economic development?

Africa's markets and globalization from below

The most alarming finding of this research is the extent to which Chinese traders have invaded the non-hegemonic world of African market traders. Sadly, most Chinese who journey to Africa in hopes of fulfilling their economic aspirations come from abject poverty, as do many Africans whose space has been invaded by the Chinese. Although it is impossible to ascertain whether the Chinese invasions have been more widespread than those by earlier invaders of Africa, if the ILO statistics are correct, Africa is the most informalized region in the world, with an estimated 73 percent of individuals who work in the non-agricultural sector working informally, increasing to over 93 percent in West Africa (Meagher and Lindell 2013: 58). These are alarming figures as we watch the Chinese deepening their presence in the informal economy, putting large numbers of Africans out of business.

Even though some human rights advocates feel that the removal of Chinese

143

traders from Africa's informal economy networks is a violation of their rights, the real question is do they fundamentally have a right to be in the markets in the first place? The resounding opinion of the African traders seems to be they do not have a right, and in the case of Ghana and the small mining sector, the law clearly states that only Ghanaian citizens have the right to legally mine gold. Members of civil society are 'speaking with their feet' (staging major protests) in many African countries against these invasions. The situation is likely to implode over the next several years unless governments take action to either remove Chinese traders from the markets and/or find formal sector jobs for those in the informal sector who cannot compete with the Chinese (the latter is most unlikely to happen). Another aspect of the problem that has not been fully examined is the fact that many Africans buy their goods from Chinese wholesalers. So just removing them physically from the market will not necessary solve this growing problem.

What is most interesting about this situation is that in Guangzhou, African migrants contribute tremendously to the economy of the region. Not only do they pay taxes on a regular basis, but they are also forced to hire Chinese workers, including in their factories. In addition, because of the huge amount of goods purchased by Africans for export to Africa and throughout the world, thousands of Chinese who live at the level of globalization from below are gainfully employed. No such benefits are realized by Africans, and in fact among the most serious problems caused by Chinese in the markets is that very often they hire other Chinese workers over local Africans. And the situation African workers find themselves in by virtue of AGOA complicates their ability to thrive under the US trade regime.

The future of Africa's world trade

It has been shown that for the most part the lives of Africans in this study have been changed through African trade regimes operating at the level of globalization from below. The massive trade that is taking place among Africans at this level has perhaps been one of the most positive developments in the area of trade for some time. In the midst of the collapse of the post-Bretton Woods international economic order, Africans have clearly rebelled against the system put in place by the North to control the flow of goods and capital through the GATT and now the WTO. With the overwhelming percentage of Africans marginalized from such hegemonic institutions, they have used their creativity to enhance their living status and the status of those who buy their products. The creative trade networks developed by African traders/entrepreneurs undermine the economic revenue that should be accumulated by their respective governments. However, this will remain the status quo unless such leaders abandon their support for neoliberal globalization and thus reject Afro-neoliberal capitalism and the elite consensus. If this occurs, African economic development instead of African economic growth might become a reality. In this regard, it might be possible for such leaders to contain the potential devastation still to be wreaked on Africa's world trade by external actors, including China and the USA through AGOA.

While we have merely scraped the surface of Africa's trade regimes, the studies in this volume leave us with a great deal to ponder. It has been argued that when we meet and learn about traders at the level of globalization from below, we are challenged to rethink our perceptions about trade and how the majority of the poor in this world survive. And this volume is mostly about the poor – both African and Chinese. These are the people and networks that are usually ignored when governments throughout the world calculate their trade statistics. In most cases the statistics are incorrect because they do not include transactions at the level of globalization from below (see, for example, Mathews et al. 2012). The forthcoming companion volume to this study will continue to enlighten us about Africa's trade regimes, albeit at the hegemonic level. Many of the themes in this volume will resurface and become points for deeper analysis, and new issues will emerge that will allow for a greater understanding of how people in these two worlds – globalization from above and globalization from below – merge their respective worlds into one global economy focused on enhanced world trade.

Appendix

A: Trade Act of 2002

In 2001, Congress amended AGOA for the first time through the Trade Act of 2002 (P.L. 107-210), which included adjustments in the textile and apparel provisions. An important change pertained to the cap that AGOA had set on imports of apparel assembled in an AGOA country from fabric made in an AGOA country ... The Trade Act of 2002 doubled this cap, increasing it to 7% in FY 2008. The act, however, left the cap unchanged at 3.5 under the special rule for lesser-developed countries. The act also allowed Namibia and Botswana to qualify for the special rule for lesser-developed countries, even if their per capita incomes exceeded the limit set under AGOA. In addition, it specifically extended AGOA benefits to knit-to-shape articles and the garments cut in both the United States and an AGOA beneficiary country ('hybrid cutting') and made a correction to extend AGOA benefits to merino wool sweaters knit in AGOA and beneficiary countries. (*Source*: Jones and Williams 2012: 22)

B: AGOA Acceleration Act of 2004

In 2004, Congress further amended AGOA through the AGOA Acceleration Act of 2004 (P.L. 108-274). This legislation extended the deadline for AGOA benefits to 2015, and it also extended the special rule for LDCs from September 2004 to September 2007. It further stipulated that the cap on the volume of allowable U.S. apparel imports under this rule would be decreased starting in the year beginning September 2004, with a major reduction in the year beginning October 2006 (from 2.9% to 1.6%). The rationale behind this change was to encourage fabric production and vertical integration of the apparel industry in Africa. For apparel imports meeting the yarn forward rules of origin, the cap was set to remain at 7% until the expiration of the benefits in 2015 ... The AGOA Acceleration Act also clarified certain apparel rules of origin to reflect the intent of Congress. Apparel articles containing fabric from both the United States and AGOA beneficiary countries were specifically allowed, as were otherwise eligible apparel articles containing cuffs, collars, and other similar components that did not meet the strict rules of origin. There was also clarification that ethnic printed fabric would qualify for duty-free treatment, as long as the fabric met certain standards regarding its size, form, and design characteristics. In addition, apparel articles containing fabrics and yarns recognized in the North American Free Trade Agreement (NAFTA) as being in short supply in the United States were declared as eligible for duty-free treatment, regardless of the source of such fabric and yarns. The legislation also increased the maximum allowable content of non-regional or non-U.S. fibers or yarns in AGOA eligible apparel imports, otherwise known as the *de minimis* rule, from 7% to 10%. (*Source*: Jones and Williams 2012: 22–3)

C: Miscellaneous Trade and Technical Corrections Act of 2004

In December 2004, the Miscellaneous Trade and Technical Corrections Act of 2004 (P.L. 108-429) was passed, which included a technical correction to the AGOA Acceleration Act. The legislation also allowed Mauritius to qualify for the special rule for LDCs for the one year beginning October 1, 2004, with a cap of 5% of total eligible imports under this rule. (*Source*: Jones and Williams 2012: 23)

D: Africa Investment Incentive Act of 2006

Congress passed the Africa Investment Incentive Act of 2006 in December 2006 (Title VI of P.L. 109-432), which extended the textile and apparel benefits of AGOA until 2015. This act also extended until 2012 the special rule for LDCs, which allows textiles and apparel quota- and duty-free access to the U.S. market regardless of the source of materials used, as long as assembly takes place within an AGOA-eligible LDC. The act also increases the cap on square meter equivalents under this rule back to the initial level of 3.5%. It also contains an 'abundant supply' provision stipulating that if a certain fabric is determined by the U.S. International Trade Commission to be available in commercial quantities in AGOA beneficiary countries, then the special rule will no longer apply to apparel and textiles containing that particular fabric. (*Source*: Jones and Williams 2012: 23)

Notes

1 Globalization from above and below

1 Duménil and Lévy argue that neo-liberalism is 'fundamentally a new social order in which the power of the upper fractions of the ruling class – the wealthiest persons – was re-established in the wake of a setback. We denote as "finance" this upper capitalist class and the financial institutions through which its power is enforced' (2005: 9).

2 This section of the chapter was taken from Margaret C. Lee, 'Africa belongs to "us" – the continent's current development paradox', Africa Institute of South Africa Occasional Paper no. 5, Africa Institute of South Africa, Pretoria, 2010, pp. 7–8. It has been modified for this section of the chapter.

2 Chocolate City

1 Interview with Mr Sam, Bole Market, Chocolate City, 23 May 2011 (his name has been changed).

2 Ibid.

3 Interview with an African trader at Bole Market in Chocolate City, 23 May 2011.

4 Qin dynasty, 221–206 BC.

5 The two Opium Wars were fought to get the British to discontinue exporting opium to the Chinese population because of the devastating impact it was having on consumers.

6 It is very difficult to get exact dimensions for Chocolate City. This particular definition grew out of a conversation with Joe Tucker, an infectious disease doctor located in Chocolate City. I asked him to clarify for me what area is considered to constitute Chocolate City and this was the definition provided to him by two African community leaders in Chocolate City. I had this discussion with Dr Tucker in my office at UNC-Chapel Hill on 28 September 2012.

7 For more details about the notion of Guangzhou as an 'ethnic enclave', see Zhang (2008: 383–95).

8 Interview with Mr Kingsley, Bole Market, Chocolate City, 15 May 2012.

9 Ibid.

10 Ibid.

11 Ibid.

12 Interview with Mr Nwoso, Nigerian trader, Huanshi Zhong Road, Guangzhou, 4 June 2013 (his name has been changed).

13 Interview with Mr Baron, Cannon Market, Chocolate City, 11 May 2011.

14 Ibid.

15 Ibid.

16 Interview with Mr Nwoso.

17 Ibid.

18 Ibid.

19 Interview with Mr Bah, 20 May 2011.

20 Interview with Mr Nwoso, 19 May 2011.

21 Ibid.

22 Interview with Mr Nwoso, Guangzhou, 24 May 2013.

23 Interview with Mr Nanga (his name has been changed), Tangqui Market, Chocolate City, 20 May 2011.

24 Ibid.

25 Interview with Amos Muthui, trader from Kenya, Overseas Trading Mall, Guangzhou, 19 May 2001.

26 Interview with Mr Ojukwu Emma, head, Association of the Nigerian Community of Guangzhou, Chocolate City, 11 May 2011.

27 Ibid.

28 Ibid.

29 Interview with Mr Feato Sengabo, Guangzhou, 18 May 2011.

30 Ibid.

31 Ibid.

32 Ibid.

33 Ibid.

34 Ibid.

35 Ibid.

36 This was due to language barriers and the fact that none of the African traders was willing to try to introduce me to any Chinese traders. Many noted that people would be afraid to talk, especially since China does not have an open society and thus they would be suspicious of what I would do with the information collected.

37 Interview with Mr Ali, Guangzhou, 8 June 2013.

38 Interview with Mr Mutesa, Guangzhou, 21 May 2011.

39 Ibid.

40 Interview with Mr Stones, Bole Market, Chocolate City, 17 May 2011.

41 Interview with Mr Bah, Overseas Trading Market, Guangzhou, 20 May 2011.

42 Ibid.

43 Ibid.

44 Interview with Mr Bah, Guangzhou, May/June 2013.

45 Interview with Mr Ali Mwanje, Guangzhou, 23 May 2011.

46 See, for example, Coloma.

47 Interview with Nigerian trader, Guangzhou, 8 June 2013.

48 Interview with Mr Nwosu, Guangzhou, 4 June 2013.

49 Ibid.

50 Interview with Mr Sam, African trader, Bole Market, 23 May 2011.

51 Interview with Mr Nwoso, 4 June 2013.

52 Ibid.

53 Interview with Mr Bah, Guangzhou, 20 May 2011.

54 Interview with Nigerian traders, Bole Market, 22 May 2011.

55 Ibid.

56 Interview with Mr Nwosu, 4 June 2013.

57 Interview with Mr Ojukwu Emma, Guangzhou, 21 May 2013.

58 Interview with Mr Bah, Guangzhou, 20 May 2011.

59 Interview with Yu Qui, Guangzhou, 3 June 2013.

60 Ibid.

61 Ibid.

62 Ibid.

63 Ibid.

64 Ibid.

65 Translation of the Chinese constitution by Yu Qui in email correspondence, 14 July 2013.

66 Interview with Mr Bah, Guangzhou, 4 June 2013.

67 Ibid.

68 Ibid.

69 Interview with Mr Ojukwu Emma, Guangzhou, 21 May 2013.

70 Ibid.

71 Interview with Mr Nwoso, Guangzhou, 3 June 2013.

72 Interview with Mr Sam, Bole Market, 23 May 2011.

73 Ibid.

74 Interview with Mr Nwoso, Guangzhou, 11 May 2011.

75 Ibid.

76 Ibid.

77 Ibid.

78 Ibid.

79 Frank is a Nigerian trader who has a shop in Tangqi Market, Chocolate City.

80 Ibid.

81 Interview with Mr Ali, Ugandan trader, 23 May 2011.

82 This is a direct quote from an interview Bertoncello and Bredeloup conducted with a merchant in Guangzhou who is from Ghana.

83 My research assistant and I never understood why the women would not grant us formal interviews, especially since most were traders buying goods to return home. Since my first visit in 2011, a growing number of African women have migrated to Guangzhou and have opened their own shops. Even in 2013 I found that some would agree to be interviewed and then would not be available in their shops on the day the interview was scheduled. My initial observation is that the women who come to buy are very clear about their goals and objectives and don't want to take time to talk to you. This appears to be the case because many of the women I was able to interview in Africa

travel to China to buy goods. In the case of relatively new shopowners in Guangzhou, I think it might take much longer to build up trust with the women than with the men. A separate study needs to be undertaken of African women traders in Guangzhou.

84 Interview with Mr Nwoso, 24 May 2013.

85 Ibid.

86 Ibid.

3 Africa–China trade

1 Interview with Clement F. A. Nyaaba, Director of Multilateral, Regional and Bilateral Trade, Ministry of Trade and Industry, Accra, Ghana, 22 March 2011.

2 Interview with Aswne Ngom, Quebec Central House, Johannesburg, South Africa, 13 March 2012.

3 Interview with Auntie Emily, Kampala Market, Kampala, Uganda, 13 August 2010.

4 Ibid.

5 Ibid.

6 Ibid.

7 Interview with Auntie M., Kampala trader, Kampala Market, Kampala, Uganda, 12 August 2010.

8 Interview with Nelson and Josephine Matemu, Karikoo Market, Dar es Salaam, Tanzania, 5 August 2010.

9 See for example, Lall (1995); Riddell (1992).

10 Interview with Nelson and Josephine Matemu and others.

11 Interview with Alice Fashion workers, Makola Market, Accra, Ghana, 14 March 2011.

12 Interview with Akua B-Puni, Accra, Ghana, 25 March 2011.

13 Ibid.

14 Ibid.

15 Ibid.

16 Ibid.

17 Interview with Mr Nana Yaw, Makola Market, Accra, Ghana, 14 March 2011.

18 Ibid.

19 Interview with Ms Zuweratu, Accra Market, Accra, Ghana, 14 March 2011.

20 Interview with Mrs LPA, Makola Market, Accra, Ghana, 14 March 2011.

21 Interview with Tanzanian trader in COMESA Market in Lusaka, Zambia, 22 July 2011.

22 Interview with trader in COMESA Market, Lusaka, Zambia, 22 July 2011.

23 Interview with trader in COMESA Market, Lusaka, Zambia, 22 July 2011.

24 Interview with Senegalese trader, Johannesburg, South Africa, 13 March 2012.

25 Interview with Yolande Fariab, Johannesburg, South Africa, 13 March 2012.

26 Ibid.

27 Interview with Ethiopian trader, Johannesburg, South Africa, 13 March 2012.

28 Ibid.

29 Interview with South African trader, Johannesburg, South Africa, 13 March 2012.

30 Interview with South African trader, Johannesburg, South Africa, 13 March 2012.

31 Interview with Malian trader, Johannesburg, South Africa, 13 March 2012.

32 Interview with Mr Ngom, Johannesburg, South Africa, 13 March 2012.

33 Naím refers to black holes as 'regions in the universe where the traditional – Newtonian – laws of physics do not apply' (2005: 261).

34 Résumé of E. Kwasi Okoh.

35 Interview with Kwasi Okoh, Accra, Ghana, 21 March 2011.

36 Interview with Mr Ali, Guangzhou, China, 23 May 2011.

37 Interview with Mr Bah, Overseas Trading Mall, Guangzhou, China, 20 May 2011.

38 Interview with Dr Terry Kahuma, director of Uganda's National Bureau of Standards, Kampala, Uganda, 10 August 2010.

39 Ibid.

40 Ibid.

41 Interview with Mr Mackay Aomu, deputy executive, Uganda Bureau of Standards, Kampala, Uganda, 10 August 2010.

42 Interview with Dr Terry Kahuma.

43 Interview with Ms Jane S. Nalunga,

Country Director, SEATINI, Kampala, Uganda, 13 August 2010.

44 Interview with Dr Terry Kahuma.

45 Ibid.

46 Interview with Chinese trader, Kampala Market, Kampala, Uganda, August 2010.

47 Interview with Dr Terry Kahuma.

48 Ibid.

49 Ibid.

50 Interview with Ugandan official, Kampala, Uganda, 28 March 2012.

51 Interview with Fair Trade Commission of Tanzania, Dar es Salaam, Tanzania, 6 August 2010.

52 Ibid.

53 Ibid.

54 Ibid.

55 Interview with Clement F. A. Nyaaba, Director of Multilateral, Regional and Bilateral Trade, Ministry of Trade and Industry, Accra, Ghana, 22 March 2010.

56 Interview with Chinese trader #5, Oshikango, Namibia, 7 March 2012.

57 Ibid.

58 Interview with Chinese trader #2, Oshikango, Namibia, 5 March 2012.

59 Interview with Chinese trader #6, Oshikango, Namibia, 6 March 2012.

60 Ibid.

61 Interviews with Namibians working in Chinese shops in Oshikango, Namibia, 5–7 March 2012.

62 Ibid.

63 Interviews with Chinese traders #1–6, Oshikango, Namibia, 5–7 March 2012.

64 Interview with government official, Oshikango, Namibia, 7 March 2012.

65 Ibid.

66 Interview with Paulina Haimbodi, Oshikango, Namibia, 5 March 2012.

67 Ibid.

4 Humanizing the AGOA

1 This provision allows for less developed beneficiary countries to source fabric from anywhere in the world.

2 Interview with Lieketseng Lephallo, Maseru, Lesotho, 3 August 2011.

3 Ibid.

4 Ibid.

5 Ibid.

6 Ibid.

7 The Lesotho currency is the loti (pl. maloti). However, through the Common Monetary Area the loti is pegged to the South African rand (R).

8 Interview with Lieketseng Lephallo, Maseru, Lesotho, 3 August 2011.

9 Ibid.

10 Interview with Thabo Thamae, Maseru, Lesotho, 3 August 2011.

11 Ibid.

12 Ibid.

13 Ibid.

14 Ibid.

15 Ibid.

16 Interview with B. Shaw Lebakae, Maseru, Lesotho, 3 August 2011.

17 Interview with B. Shaw Lebakae and David Maraisane, Maseru, Lesotho, 2 August 2011.

18 Ibid.

19 Interview with B. Shaw Lebakae, Maseru, Lesotho, 3 August 2011.

20 Ibid.

21 Interview with B. Shaw Lebakae and David Maraisane, Maseru, Lesotho, 2 August 2011.

22 Ibid.

23 Interview with Mzimkhula Sithelo, Maseru, Lesotho, 4 August 2011.

24 Interview with B. Shaw Lebakae, Maseru, Lesotho, 2 August 2011.

25 Interview with Ruth Apio, Kampala, Uganda, 10 August 2010.

26 Ibid.

27 Ibid.

28 Ibid.

29 Ibid.

30 Ibid.

31 Interview with Monica Shaiyengauge, Windhoek, Namibia, 9 March 2012.

32 Ibid.

33 Ibid.

34 Interview with Mukuka N. Emilia, Windhoek, Namibia, 9 March 2012.

35 Interview with Franciska Geinus, Windhoek, Namibia, 9 March 2012.

36 Interview with a member of the Namibian governing party, the South West Africa People's Organization (SWAPO),

Windhoek, Namibia, 9 March 2012, as well as Ramatex workers Shaiyengauge, Geinus, and Emilia.

37 Interview with Franciska Geinus.

38 Interview with a member of the Namibian governing party, the South West Africa People's Organization (SWAPO), 9 March 2012.

39 Ibid.

40 Interview with Mark S. Bennett, Tanzania Cotton Board, Dar es Salaam, Tanzania, 4 August 2010.

Conclusion

1 Interview with Auntie R., Guangzhou, China, 8 June 2013.

Bibliography

AGOA News (2011) 'U.S. focus on Africa to rise, but AGOA extension may hit resistance,' *AGOA News*, 21 January.

Akoth, S. (2009) 'What they don't tell you about AGOA: tackling taboos around the African Growth and Opportunity Act,' www.pambazuka.org/en/category/features/58271/print.

Alves, P. (2006a) 'It's time to stop blaming China alone over textiles,' *Business Day*, 5 June, www. Saiia.org.za/index.

— (2006b) 'More sour than sweet in SA–China trade relations,' *Sunday Times*, 25 June.

Anas, A. (2009a) 'We quit sex trade: Chinese girls,' *Modern Ghana News*, 19 February.

— (2009b) 'Undercover: Inside the Chinese sex mafia,' *The Crusading Guide*, 17–23 February.

ANC (1994) *The Reconstruction and Development Programme: A Policy Framework*, Johannesburg: ANC.

Andrew, A. (2010) 'Contemporary issues,' in R. Andre LaFleur (ed.), *Asia in Focus: China*, Santa Barbara, CA: ABC-CLIO.

Axelsson, L. (2012) 'Making borders: engaging the threat of Chinese textiles in Ghana,' Doctoral dissertation, Sweden: Stockholm University.

Axelsson, L. and N. Sylvanus (2010) 'Navigating Chinese textile networks: women traders in Accra and Lomé,' in F. Cheru and C. Obi (eds), *The Rise of China and India in Africa*, London and New York: Zed Books.

Baregu, M. (2008) 'The three faces of the dragon: Tanzania–China relations in historical perspective,' in K. Ampiah and S. Naidu (eds), *Crouching Tiger, Hidden Dragon: Africa and China*, Cape Town: University of KwaZulu-Natal Press.

Bax, P. (2012) 'Ghana's gold sparks conflict with illegal Chinese miners,' *The Atlantic*, 8 October.

Bertoncello, B. and S. Bredeloup (2007) 'The emergence of new "African trading posts" in Hong Kong and Guangzhou,' *China Perspectives*, 1(94).

Bodomo, A. (2010) 'The African trading community in Guangzhou: an emerging bridge for Africa–China relations,' *China Quarterly*, 203.

— (2012) *Africans in China: A Sociocultural Study and Its Implications on Africa–China Relations*, Amherst, NY: Cambria Press.

Bodomo, A. and G. Ma (2010) 'Africans in Yiwu: China's largest commodities city,' *Pambazuka News: Pan-African Voices for Freedom and Justice*, 484, 6 March, pambazuka.org/en/category/africa_china/64915.

Bourdieu, P. (1998) 'Utopia of endless exploitation: the essence of neoliberalism,' *Le Monde diplomatique*, English edn, mondediplo.com/1998/12/08/bieu.

Brautigam, D. (2009) *The Dragon's Gift: The Real Story of China in Africa*, Oxford: Oxford University Press.

Brink, G. (2006) 'The Memorandum of Understanding and quotas on clothing and textile imports from China: who Wins,' Working paper, www.tralac.org.

Brooks, A. (2010) 'Spinning and weaving discontent: labour relations and the production of meaning at Zambia-China Mulungushi Textiles,' *Journal of Southern African Studies*, 36(1).

Busigne, J. (2013) 'Government sets conditions for women traveling to China for business,' *Independent*, 9 January, www.independent.co.ug/news/news/7173-government-sets-conditions-for-women.

Business and Financial Times (2011a) 'We

must stop the Chinese onslaught – Aluworks boss,' 8 March.

— (2011b) 'Imports from China killing local Ghanaian industry,' *Business and Financial Times* (Ghana), 4 March.

Buxi (2008) 'Fools's Mountain: Blogging for China,' http://blog.foolsmountain.com/2008/06/14chocolate-city-africans-seek-their-dreams-in-china.

CallimacHi, R. (2012) 'Senegalese slipper makers refuse to sell to Chinese, as country's shadow grows long in Africa,' Associated Press (Senegal), 12 August.

Central Bank (2010) 'Recent developments in the manufacturing subsector in Lesotho: prospects for diversification over products and markets,' *Economic Review*, 114, www.centralbank.org.ls/publication.

Chanda, N. (2002) 'Globalization means reconnecting the human community,' *Yale/Global*, 19, http://yaleglobal.yale.eud/about/essay.jsp.

Cheng, Y. (2011) 'From campus racism to cyber racism: discourse of race and Chinese nationalism,' *China Quarterly*, 207(1).

Chinese Constitution of the People's Republic of China (n.d.) English. peopledaily.com.cn/constitution/constitution.html.

Chironga, M., A. Leke, S. Lund and A. Wamelen (2011) 'Cracking the next growth market: Africa,' *Harvard Business Review*, 89(5).

Citifmonline (2011) 'Chinese women trafficked into Ghana for prostitution,' 14 November.

— (2013a) 'Influx of Chinese prostitutes worries GIS,' www.citifmonline.com/index.php?id=1.658883.

— (2013b) 'Chinese women trafficked into Ghana for prostitution,' www.citifmonline.com/index.php?id=1.287144.1657580.

Colás, A. (2005) 'Neoliberalism, globalisation and international relations,' in A. Saad-Filho and D. Johnston (eds), *Neoliberalism: A Critical Reader*, London: Pluto Press.

Coloma, T. (2010a) 'Where the lion rides the dragon: Africa does business in China',

Le Monde Diplomatique, 2 May, monde diplo.com/2010/05/02africansinchina.

— (2010b) 'In African town, everything to gain,' *Globe and Mail*, 17 May, www.theglobalmail.com/news/opinions/in-africa-town-everything-to-gain/article1.

Condon, N. and M. Stern (2011) *The Effectiveness of African Growth and Opportunity Act (AGOA) in Increasing Trade from Least Developed Countries: A systematic review*, London: EPPI-Centre, Social Science Research Unit, Institute of Education, University of London, March.

Corkin, L. (2009) 'All's fair in loans and war: the development of China–Angola relations,' in K. Ampiah and S. Naidu (eds), *Crouching Tiger, Hidden Dragon: Africa and China*, Cape Town: University of KwaZulu-Natal Press.

— (2012) 'Angolan political elites' management of Chinese credit lines,' in M. Power and A. C. Alves (eds), *China and Angola: A Marriage of Convenience?*, Oxford: Pambazuka Press.

De Hann, E. and M. Stichele (2007) *Footloose Investors: Investing in the Garment Industry in Africa*, Amsterdam: Somo.

De Morais, R. (2011) 'The new imperialism: China in Angola,' *World Affairs Journal*, March/April.

Department of Finance (1996) *Growth, Employment and Distribution: A Macroeconomic Strategy*, South Africa: Department of Finance.

Diamond, J. (2009) 'US–African trade profile,' *U.S. Department of Commerce International Trade Administration Market Access*, Compliance/Office of Africa, July.

Dobler, G. (2008) 'From Scotch whisky to Chinese sneakers: international commodity flows and new trade networks in Oshikango, Namibia,' *Journal of the International Institute*, 78(3).

— (2009) 'Chinese shops and the formation of a Chinese expatriate community in Namibia,' *China Quarterly*, 199(1).

Dong, L. (2013) 'Chinese miners lured by Ghana's gold rush hit rock bottom after crackdown,' *Global Times*, 13 June.

Draper, P. and N. Khumalo (2007) *One Size Doesn't Fit All: Deal-Breaker Issues in the Failed US–SACU Free Trade Negotations*, Johannesburg: South African Institute of International Affairs.

Duménil, G. and D. Lévy (2005) 'The neoliberal (counter-)revolution,' in A. Saad-Filho and D. Johnston (eds), *Neoliberalism: A Critical Reader*, London: Pluto Press.

Dyer, G. (2008) 'Africans in China: the attraction of Guangzhou's Tianxiu Mansions,' *Financial Times*, 23 January.

Economic Review (2010) 'Recent developments in the manufacturing subsector in Lesotho: prospects for diversification over products and markets,' *Economic Review*, 114, January.

Eeden, J. van (2009) 'South African quotas on Chinese clothing and textiles: economic evidence,' *Research Note*, 9.

Elliott, K. (2010) *Reviewing AGOA*, Center for Global Development, 30 September.

Faucon, B., C. Murphy and J. Whalen (2013) 'Africa's malaria battle: fake drug pipeline undercuts progress,' *Africa News*, 29 May.

Fernandez-Stark, K., S. Fredrick and G. Gereffi (2011) *The Apparel Global Value Chain: Economic Upgrading and Workforce Development*, Center of Globalization, Governance and Competiveness, Durham: Duke University.

Flatters, F. and P. Elago (2008) *Ramatex Namibia: Government Policies and the Investment Environment*, Gabarone, Botswana: South African Global Competiveness Hub.

Foreign Teachers Guide to Living and Working in China (n.d.) http://middlekingdomlife.com.

Fowale, T. (2008) 'The long road to the East: African immigrants in China,' *American Chronicle*, 3 January, www.americanchronicle.com/articles/views/47741.

— (2009) 'The worsening plight of Africans in China: effects of the global downturn on African migrants in Chinese cities,' www.suite101.com/content/the_worsening_plight_of _africans_in_china-a150147?temp, 19 September.

GantDaily.com (2012) 'AGOA uncertainty hurts textile workers,' gantdaily.com/2012/07/17agoa-uncertainty-hurts-textile-workers/.

Garrett, V. (2002) *Heaven Is High, the Emperor Far Away: Merchants and Mandarins in Old Canton*, Oxford and New York: Oxford University Press.

George, S. (1999) 'A short history of neo-liberalism: twenty years of elite economic and emerging opportunities for structural change,' Bangkok: Conference on Economic Sovereignty in a Globalising World, www.globalexchange.org/campaigns/ecom.101/neoliberalism.html.pdf.

Grant, C. and G. Chapman (2011) 'South African Customs Union: myths and reality,' www.saii.org.za/feature/southern-african-customs-union-myths-and-reality.html.

Green, A. (2012) 'Africa: U.S. law helps China in Africa,' *This Is Africa*, 14 December, m.allafrica.com/stories/201212141055.html/.

Ha-Joon Chang (2002) *Kicking Away the Ladder: Development Strategy in Historical Perspective*, London: Anthem Press.

Hartzenberg, T., G. Erasmus, C. McCarthy, R. Sandrey, M. Pearson, H. Jensen, J. B. Cronje, T. Fundira, P. Kruger, W. Vijioen and S. Woolfrey (2012) *The Tripartite Free Trade Area: Towards a New African Integration Paradigm*, South Africa: Tralac.

Harvey, D. (2005) *A Brief History of Neoliberalism*, Oxford: Oxford University Press.

Haugen, H. (2012) 'Nigerians in China: a second state of immobility,' *International Migration*, 50(2).

Hayes, S. (2011) Testimony by Stephen Hayes, President and CEO Corporate Council on Africa before the Foreign Relations Subcommittee on African Affairs, 1 November.

He, H. (2013) 'Ghana gold mines suggest larger crisis for China,' *General News of Sunday*, 12 June.

Held, D. and A. McGrew (2001) 'Globalization,' in J. Krieger (ed.), *The Oxford Companion to Politics of the World*, 2nd edn, Oxford: Oxford University Press.

Herman, F. (2011) 'Textile disputes and two-level games: the case of China and South Africa,' *Asian Politics and Policy*, 3(10).

Hickel, J. (2012) 'Africa: trading with the enemy,' *TalkAfrique*, 3 August.

Ikhuoria, E. (2010) 'The impact of Chinese importers on Nigerian traders,' in A. Harneit-Sievers, S. Marks and S. Naidu (eds), *Chinese and African Perspectives of China in Africa*, Cape Town: Pambazuka Press.

Jiang, C. (2013) 'Africa or bust: Chinese gold miners take huge risks,' *World Times*, 4 July.

Jiao, Y. (2013) 'China in Africa: the real story,' Guest blog, www.chinaafricareal-story.com/2013/06/guest-post-chinese-illegal-gold-miners.html, 21 June.

Jones, V. and B. Williams (2012) *U.S. Trade and Investment Relations with sub-Saharan Africa and the African Growth Opportunity Act*, Congressional Research Service, 26 June.

Kaplinsky, R. (2008) 'What does the rise of China do for industrialisation in sub-Saharan Africa,' *Review of African Political Economy*, 35(115).

Labour and Research Institute (2007) *An Assessment of the Africa Growth and Opportunity Act (AGOA) and Its Implications for Namibia*.

Lall, S. (1995) 'Structural adjustment and African industry,' *World Development*, 23(12).

— (2005) 'FDI, AGOA and manufactured exports by a landlocked, least developed African economy: Lesotho,' *Journal of Development Studies*, 41(6).

LAP Textiles (n.d.) 'Libya Africa investment portfolio,' Unpublished document.

LaRRI (2003) *RAMATEX: On the other side of the fence*, Katutura, Windhoek: Labour Resource and Research Institute (LaRRI), October.

— (2007) *An Assessment of the African Growth and Opportunity Act (AGOA) and Its Implications for Namibia*, Katutura, Windhoek: Labour Resource and Research Institute (LaRRI), July.

Le Bail, H. (2009) 'Foreign migration to China's city-markets: the case of African merchants,' *Asie Visions*, 19, Centre Asie Ifri.

Lebakae, S. (2011) 'Minimum wages report to rally,' Unpublished document by five trade unions in Maseru, Lesotho, 11 June.

Lee, M. (2003) *The Political Economy of Regionalism in Southern Africa*, Cape Town: University of Cape Town Press.

— (2004) 'America's trade adventure in Africa: AGOA and the implications of a US–SACU FTA,' Occasional Paper no. 73, South Africa: Africa Institute of South Africa.

— (2010) 'Africa belongs to "us": the continent's current development paradox,' Occasional Paper no. 5, South Africa: Africa Institute of South Africa.

Lee, M., H. Melber, S. Naidu and I. Taylor (2007) *China in Africa*, Current African Issues no. 33, Uppsala: Nordic Africa Institute.

Lesotho Environmental Justice and Advocacy Center (2008) *Industrial Water Pollution in Lesotho: The Case of the Textile Industry: The Symposium Report*, 31 August.

Levin, D. (2013) 'Ghana's crackdown on Chinese gold miners hits one rural area hard,' *New York Times*, 29 June.

Li, Z., L. J. C. Ma and D. Xue (2009) 'An African enclave in China: the making of a new transnational urban space,' *Eurasian Geography and Economics*, 50(6).

Lin, L. (2012) 'Africans' protests highlight tensions in Guangzhou,' *China Realtime Report*, 20 June, blogs.wjs.com/china realtime/2012/06/20/Africans-protests-highlights-tensions-in-guangzhou.

Lindell, I. (2010) 'Introduction: The changing politics of informality – collective organizing, alliances and scales of engagement,' in I. Lindell (ed.), *Africa's Informal Workers: Collective Agency Alliances and Transnational Organizing in Urban Africa*, London and New York: Zed Books.

Lu Aiguo (2000) *China: The Global Economy since 1840*, New York: St Martin's Press.

Luke, F. (n.d.) 'Trade-related capacity

building for enhanced African partici- pation in the global economy,' aaerc africa.org/documents/chapter%204.pdf.

Lyons, M., A. Brown and L. Zhigang (2012a) 'In the dragon's den: African traders in Guangzhou,' *Journal of Ethnic and Migration Studies*, 38(5), dx.doi.org/ 10.1080/1369183X.2012.668030.

— (2012b) 'Journal of the dragon's den: African traders in Guangzhou,' *Journal of Ethnic and Migration Studies*, 35(5).

Macauhub (2010) 'Oshikango, near Angola, is example in Chinese investment in Africa,' (Macau, China) www.machau hub.com/.mo/en/print.php?pageurl=/ en/news.php?ID=9125, 22 March.

Malawi News Agency (2012) 'Malawi bans Chinese retailers to trade in rural areas,' 5 July.

Marks, S. (2007) *African Perspectives on China in Africa*, Fahamu: Networks for Social Justice.

Mataboge, M. (2009) 'China's quota betrayal,' (Johannesburg, South Africa) mg.co.za/printformat/single/2009- 04-04-chinas-quota-betrayal, 4 April.

Mathews, G. (2012) 'Neoliberalism and globalization from below in Chungking Mansions, Hong Kong,' in G. Mathews, G. Lins Ribeiro and C. Alba Vega (eds), *Globalization from Below: The World's Other Economy*, London and New York: Routledge.

Mathews, G. and C. Alba Vega (2012) 'Intro- duction: What is globalization from below?', in G. Mathews, G. Lins Ribeiro and C. Alba Vega (eds), *Globalization from Below: The World's Other Economy*, London and New York: Routledge.

Mathews, G. and Y. Yang (2012) 'How people pursue low-end globalization in Hong Kong and mainland China,' *Journal of Current Chinese Affairs*, 21(2).

Mathews, G., G. Lins Ribeiro and C. Alba Vega (eds) (2012) *Globalization from Below: The World's Other Economy*, Lon- don and New York: Routledge.

Meagher, K. (2013) 'Celebration of Nigeria's recovery sits awkwardly with the realities of catastrophic poverty and unemployment in both the north and south of the country,' *Current History*, May.

Meagher, K. and I. Lindell (2013) 'ASR Forum: Engaging with African informal economies: social inclusion or adverse incorporation?', *African Studies Review*, 56(3).

Michel, S. and M. Beuret (2009) *China Safari: On the Trail of Beijing Expansion in Africa*, New York: Nation Books.

Milios, J. (2005) 'European integration as a vehicle or neoliberal hegemony,' in A. Saad-Filho and D. Johnston (eds), *Neoliberalism: A Critical Reader*, London: Pluto Press.

Modern China News (2013) 'Chinese traffickers in tears over jail sentence,' *Modern China News*, 26 June.

Mulumba, B. (2003) 'Uganda: a glimpse inside Apparels Tri-Star,' *The Monitor*, 30 October, allafrica.com/stories/ printable/200310300039.html.

Naidu, S. (2008) 'India's engagements in Africa: self-interest of mutual partner- ship?', in R. Southall and H. Melber (eds), *A New Scramble for Africa*, Cape Town: University of KwaZulu-Natal Press.

— (2010) 'China in Africa: a maturing of the engagement,' in A. Harneit-Sievers, S. Marks and S. Naidu (eds), *Chinese and African Perspectives of China in Africa*, Cape Town: Pambazuka Press.

Naím, M. (2005) *Illicit: How Smugglers, Traf- fickers, and Copycats are Hijacking the Global Economy*, New York: Doubleday.

Naumann, E. (2008) 'The Multifibre Agree- ment – WTO agreement on textiles and clothing,' Tralac Working Paper 4.

— (2010) 'AGOA at 10: Reflections on US–Africa trade with a focus on SACU countries,' Working paper, Tralac.

— (2012) 'Overview of AGOA's apparel provisions in the context of US–Africa trade', *tralac*, www.tralac.org.

Ndjio, B. (2009) '"Shanghai beauties" and African desires: migration, trade and Chinese prostitution in Cameroon,' *European Journal of Development and Research*, 21(4): 606–21, www.palgrave- journals.com/ejdr/.

Ngozo, C. (2012) 'Malawi's new law targeting the Chinese traders in rural areas draws criticism,' *Guardian*, 9 August, www.guardian.co.uk/global-development 2012/aug/09/new-law-targets-chinese-traders.

Nkwanta, F. K. (2013) 'Illegal mining gets Chinese rich and locals mad,' *Ghana Herald*, 31 July.

Nossiter, A. and Y. Sun (20130 'Chasing a golden dream, Chinese miners are on the run in Ghana,' http://sankofaonline. com/chasing-a-golden-dream-chinese-miners-are-on-the-run-in-ghana/.

Ogunsanwo, A. (2008) 'A tale of two giants: Nigeria and China,' in K. Ampiah and S. Naidu (eds), *Crouching Tiger, Hidden Dragon: Africa and China*, Cape Town: University of KwaZulu-Natal Press.

Okoh, E. (2011) 'Imports from China killing local business,' *Business and Financial Times*, 4 March.

Orvis, S. (2001) 'Civil society in Africa or African civil society,' *Journal of Asian & African Studies*, 36(1).

Osnos, E. (2009) 'The Promised Land: Guangzhou's Canaan Market,' *New Yorker*, 9 February, find.galgroup.com. libproxy.lib.unc.edu/gtx/printdoc.do.

Pdfio.com (2002) 'Factory director stabs worker: the truth behind Nien Hsing,' www.pdfio.com/k-798261.html.

Peet, R. (2010) *Unholy Trinity: The IMF, World Bank and WTO*, 2nd edn, London and New York: Zed Books.

People's Republic of China. Title 30 (1986) Regulations on Administration Penalties for Public Security.

Pilger, J. (2001) 'The real story behind America's war,' *New Statesman*, 130: 4568.

Pomfret, J. (2009) 'Out of Africa and into China, émigrés struggle', www.reuters.com/assests/print? aid=USTRE57K00K20090821.

Rabossi, F. (2012) 'Ciudad del Este and Brazilian circuits of commercial distribution,' in G. Mathews, G. Lins Robeiro and C. Alba Vega (eds), *Globalization from Below: The World's Other Economy*, London and New York: Routledge.

Ramonet, I. (2008) 'Africa says no – and it means it,' *Le Monde Diplomatique*, January.

Rennie, N. (2010) 'Africans in China: sweet and sour in Guangzhou,' www. theafricareport.com/archives2/ frontlines/3286473-africans-in-china-sweet-and-sour, 1 February.

Ribeiro, G. L. (2009) 'Non-hegemonic globalizations: alter-native trans-national processes and agents,' *Anthro-pological Theory*, 9(3).

— (2012) 'Conclusion: Globalization from below and the non-hegemonic world-system,' in G. Matthews, G. Lins Ribeiro and C. Alba Vega (eds), *Globalization from Below: The World's Other Economy*, London and New York: Routledge.

Riddell, B. (1992) 'Things fall apart again: structural adjustment programmes in sub-Saharan Africa,' *Journal of Modern African Studies*, 30(1).

Robson, S. (2010) 'Culture,' in R. Andre LaFleur (ed.), *Asia in Focus: China*, Santa Barbara, CA: ABC-CLIO.

Rotunno, L., P. L. Vézina and Z. Wang (2012) 'The rise and fall of (Chinese) African apparel exports,' Working Paper WPS/2012-12, www.cesa.ox.ac.

Saad-Filho, A. and D. Johnston (eds) (2005a) *Neoliberalism: A Critical Reader*, London: Pluto Press.

— (2005b) 'Introduction,' in A. Saad-Filho and D. Johnston (eds), *Neoliberalism: A Critical Reader*, London: Pluto Press.

Satgar, C. (2009) 'Global capitalism and the neo-liberalisation of Africa,' in R. Southall and H. Melber (eds), *A New Scramble for Africa? Imperialism, Invest-ment and Development*, Cape Town: University of KwaZulu-Natal Press.

Schikonye, L. (2008) 'Crouching tiger, hidden agenda?: Zimbabwe–China rela-tions,' in K. Ampiah and S. Naidu (eds), *Crouching Tiger, Hidden Dragon: Africa and China*, Cape Town: University of KwaZulu-Natal Press.

Schiller, B. (2009) 'Big trouble in China's Chocolate City,' www.thestar.com/ printarticle/6749696.

Schneidman, W. and Z. Lewis (2012) *The African Growth and Opportunity Act:*

Looking Back, Looking Forward, Africa Growth Initiative, Brookings Institution.

Shiviji, I. (2009) 'Mwalimu Nyerere's non-alignment still needed today,' *PambazukaNews*, www.pambuzuka.org/rn/category/features/59998/ptint.

South China Morning Post (2013) 'Easy riches draw illegal Chinese miners to Ghana,' *South China Morning Post*, 13 June.

Stanford Encyclopedia of Philosophy (2002) 'Globalization,' plato.stanford.edu/entries/globalization/.

Thompson, C. (2010) 'US trade with Africa: African growth and opportunity?', *Review of African Political Economy*, 31(101).

Tralac (2012a) 'Senators Coons, Isakson praise Senate's reauthorization of key provision of Africa trade law,' *AGOA Info*, 3, August, www.agoa.info/index.php?view=.&story=news&subtext=1678.

— (2012b) 'Africa: The perfect storm for an enhanced AGOA,' *Manchester Trade* (Washington, DC), 11 December, www.agoa.info/index.php.

UNDCP (1998) *Economic and Social Consequences of Drug Abuse and Illicit Trafficking*, 7, www.unodc.org/pdf/technical_series_1998-01-01_1.pdf.

University of Pennsylvania (n.d.) *A Quick Guide to the World History of Globalization*, www.sas.upenn.edu/~dludden/global l.htm.

US Congress (2000) H.R. 434, 106d.

— (2011) *China's Growing Role in Africa: Implications for U.S. Policy: Hearing Held by Senate Committee on Foreign Relations Subcommittee on African Affairs. Remarks by David H. Shinn*, Senate Committee on Foreign Relations Subcommittee of African Affairs.

Van de Walle, N. (2009) 'US policy towards Africa: the Bush legacy and the Obama administration,' *African Affairs*, 109(434).

Van Dyke, P. C. (2005) *The Canton Trade: Life and Enterprise on the China Coast, 1700–1845*, Hong Kong: Hong Kong University Press.

Wales, Z. (2002) 'Growing pains in Lesotho's textile biz,' *Business News*, 12 April, www.upi.co,/Business_News/2002/04/12/Growing-pains-in-Lesotho-textile-biz/up.

Wall Street Week (2003) 'Ugandan government intervenes in AGOA dispute,' www.wsw.org/articles/2003.

Wang, D. (2007) 'Guangzhou', in *Encyclopedia of Western Colonialism since 1450*, vol. 2, New York: Macmillian Reference.

Wang, F. (2013) 'Ghana's gold-mine arrest, China's latest headache in Africa,' *The Atlantic*, June.

Whitby, P. (2010) 'Copycats go for the kill,' *BBC Focus on Africa*, January–March.

Wild, H. (2009) 'South Africa's textile and clothing industry: reflecting on two years of quotas on textile clothing imports,' *Centre for Chinese Studies*, 37.

Williamson, J. G. (2002) 'Winners and losers over two centuries of globalization,' National Bureau of Economic Research, Working Paper 9161, Cambridge, MA: NBER.

Winterfeldt, V. (2007) 'Liberated economy? The case of Ramatex Textiles Namibia,' in H. Melber (ed.), *Transitions in Namibia: Which Changes for Whom?*, Uppsala: Nordic African Institute.

Xinhua (2010) 'China "saves" prostitutes from Congo,' 7 December.

Yan, Z. (2011) 'Chinese women rescued from Angolan den of vice,' *China Daily*, 17 November.

Yang, Y. (2012) 'African traders in Guangzhou: routes, reasons, profits, dreams,' in G. Mathews, G. Lins Ribeiro and C. Alba Vega (eds), *Globalization from Below: The World's Other Economy*, London and New York: Routledge.

YouTube (n.d.) 'Traders protest Chinese running "kiosks",' www.youtube.com/watch?v=BLtrVV3JGOU.

Zhang, L. (2008) 'Ethnic congregation in a globalizing city: the case of Guangzhou, China,' *Cities*, 25.

Zoellick, R. (2001) 'Countering terror with trade,' *Washington Post*, 20 September.

Index

Tri-Star Tanzania, closure of, 128
Tri-Star Uganda, 125; government
  investment in, 128
Tripartite Free Trade Area (TFTA), 2
triple illegality of immigrants, 27, 39–45,
  54, 55, 57
Turkey, 50, 59, 108, 139, 143
TW Garments company, 116

Uganda, 51, 62–4, 125–8, 136; Chinese
  migrants in, 88–9; immigration into, 106
Uganda National Board of Standards
  (UNBS), 89
Ugandans, in Guangzhou, 38
unemployment, 50, 105, 106; in China, 51;
  in Ghana, 87 see also job losses
United Kingdom (UK), relations with
  China, 21
United Nations International Drug Control
  Programme (UNDCP), 48
United States of America (USA), 136, 142;
  difficulties for African traders to access
  markets of, 109; quota-free access to
  markets of, 111; relations with African
  governments, 1; trade policies of, 135
US–Africa relations, overview of, 107–8
unreported transactions, 35
using different names to enter countries,
  42, 47

Vianney, Nzamwita M., 35–6, 35
Vietnam, 50, 59, 139, 143
Vilane, Mr, from Swaziland, 124–5
visas, 28; corruption in industry of, 44;
  fake, 42, 43; in China, 34, 36, 41, 43, 96,
  99 (exit visas, 50, 55, 57; restrictions
  of, 57; rules regarding, 29); obtained
  through agents, 43; of Nigerians, 49;
  overstaying of, 6, 40, 42, 43, 49, 55, 139
  (charging for, 44)

Volcker, Paul, 10

wages, 5, 85, 97, 100, 119, 122–3, 142;
  minimum, 109, 124; of AGOA workers, 121
Wamala, Katumba, 126
Washington Consensus, 65
water, drinking, in workplaces, 115–16, 117,
  125
Welcome company, 122
welfare state: elimination of, 9; Keynesian, 9
White, Harry Dexter, 137
Windhoek, problem of recycling plant, 130
women: African, in China, 57; African men
  overly direct with, 37; Chinese, beat
  men, 46; employed in export processing
  zones, 134; travel distances to work,
  119; walking to work, 132; working
  conditions of, 117
women prisoners from China, in Lesotho,
  120
work permits: in China, 96, 99; in Namibia,
  for Chinese traders, 95
workers' contracts, in Lesotho, 120
workers' rights, 109
working conditions, 109, 117, 123, 125, 126,
  129, 134, 135, 142
World Bank, 109, 135, 137
World Trade Organization (WTO), 3, 12,
  77, 78, 80, 108, 113, 137, 144; China's
  accession to, 23

Xiaobei, African traders in, 24

Yaw, Nana, 68
Yeboah, Adu, 100
Yu Qui, 45–6

Zambia, 69–70; Chinese migrants in, 69
Zifran, James Sam Shan, 102
Zuweratu, Ms, 68–9